THE
BOROUGH
MARKET
COOKBOOK

THE BOROUGH MARKET COOKBOOK

BOROUGH MARKET

WITH ED SMITH

HODDER &
STOUGHTON

First published in Great Britain in 2018 by Hodder & Stoughton
An Hachette UK company

1

Copyright © Borough Market Business Limited 2018
Photography by Issy Croker © Hodder & Stoughton 2018
Borough Market map illustration © James Oses 2018 on pages 10–11
Additional photography by Stephanie McLeod © Hodder & Stoughton 2018 on pages 200, 224– 227

The images on the following pages are from Borough Market's archive, held by London Metropolitan Archives,
City of London: 154 (archive ref. ACC/2058/04/05/004); 155/Associated Press London
(archive ref. ACC/2058/03/282); 156 (archive ref. ACC/2058/07/07/012); 157/Kent Messenger Group
(archive ref. ACC/2058/03/282)

A CIP catalogue record for this title is available from the British Library.

Hardback ISBN: 978 1 473 67868 2
eBook ISBN: 978 1 473 67869 9

Colour origination by Altaimage
Printed and bound by Firmengruppe APPL, aprinta druck, Wemding, Germany

Hodder & Stoughton policy is to use papers that are natural, renewable and recyclable products and made from
wood grown in sustainable forests. The logging and manufacturing processes are expected to conform to the
environmental regulations of the country of origin.

With thanks to the performers on pages 66–69 and 216–219:
Castellers of London (castellersoflondon.org.uk), Folk Dance Remixed (folkdanceremixed.com)
and the Lions part (thelionspart.co.uk)

Senior Commissioning Editor: Tamsin English
Publisher: Liz Gough
Project Editor: Laura Herring
Design: Alice Laurent
Photography: Issy Crokcr
Food and Props Stylist: Emily Ezekiel
Senior Production Controller: Susan Spratt

The Borough Market team:
Director of Development and Communications: Kate Howell
Head of Commissioning: Claire Ford

Hodder & Stoughton Ltd
Carmelite House
50 Victoria Embankment
London EC4Y 0DZ

www.hodder.co.uk

CONTENTS

INTRODUCTION

BOROUGH MARKET

Borough Market has many attractions – atmospheric passageways, cookery demonstrations, the buzz of surrounding restaurants, pubs and bars – but the greatest draw is, of course, its food. People come here to buy carrots that were pulled from the soil in Kent just the day before, whose sweetness and vibrancy are a reminder of how carrots should really taste; cheeses whose flavours reflect the environment in which they were made, and which evolve in character from day to day; sweet, firm scallops, plucked by hand from the Dorset seabed; beautifully marbled beef from rare-breed cattle raised on a family farm by one brother and butchered at the Market by the other.

Our purpose, though, extends far beyond the simple pleasure of enjoying food, compelling though that is. Borough Market is run by a charitable trust whose role is to provide a market for the public benefit and ensure the long-term viability of this centuries-old institution. Its trustees have decided that the best way to fulfil these objectives is to construct a culture that favours traditional, low-impact, sustainable production methods, one in which traders are chosen as much for their values as for their obvious expertise. While global food systems become ever more opaque and mechanised, with their complex supply chains and heavily processed foods, Borough has moved in the opposite direction, choosing instead to offer a clear and confident alternative.

The result is an environment that brings customers into closer contact with food. The traders don't hide the fact that meat comes from animals, that proper bread goes stale in a few days, that your favourite ingredients might only be available for two months of the year. Yes, you'll have to scrub mud from your vegetables and wash sand from your shellfish, and you may well need advice about how best to prepare, cook or store your purchases, but your relationship with the food you eat and the people who create it will be much more real, much more personal.

While elsewhere food shopping has become increasingly depersonalised, here you have no choice but to interact. This may go no further than a 'thank you' and a smile, but it can also extend into something far more meaningful. The traders you buy from might well have nurtured, made or caught the goods you hold in your hand, and all will offer genuine insight into the food and the manner of its production. Through these daily interactions, as well the Market's cookery demonstrations, events and website articles, customers are encouraged to eat with the seasons, consider the social and environmental impact of their purchases, buy only what's needed and eat every bit of it.

These ideas are given substance by this book. Ed Smith, whose connections to Borough – as a shopper, trader, writer and chef – run deep, has created a set of beautiful recipes that should bring some of the spirit of this remarkable place into your kitchen and, we hope, encourage you to truly appreciate the produce sold here. That vibrant and sweet carrot or pungent, washed-rind cheese may taste good – better than almost any other you could find – but in their own small way they're also doing good. Borough Market's aim is to show that delicious food and deeply held convictions can go hand in hand; this book is part of that mission.

A YEAR AT THE MARKET

ED SMITH

The aim of this cookbook is to capture the essence of Borough Market, while also inspiring home cooks to bring seasonal market produce back into their kitchens.

You will see that the following pages focus on shopping and eating through spring, summer, autumn and winter, with each season offering a set of recipes based on market ingredients at their peak at that time. In addition, at the end of each seasonal section there are recipes highlighting key categories of traders, which should help provide inspiration should you find yourself with an urge for a particular type of ingredient.

Some of the recipes are simple and humble, others require a bit of effort and are celebratory in nature. Some are of a classical style of cooking, others more contemporary. Some recipes feature 'hero' Borough Market products, yet they could still be cooked even if you can't make it to London Bridge. And all are united by the fact that they celebrate and benefit from the kind of ingredients that Borough's stalls specialise in: the seasonal, sustainable, slow and sustaining.

Interspersed through the book are trader profiles, key events and scenes from a year at the Market. In addition, there are essays that touch on Borough Market's history and core values, by celebrated writers and experts in their fields who are friends of the Market. It's just a snapshot, but these pieces give a sense of place and atmosphere, and, along with all the images taken over the course of a year, will help bring the Market to life in all its diversity and abundance. Primarily though, this is a cookbook that promotes inquisitive shopping and cooking from scratch; one that encourages us to take full advantage of the amazing things on offer at markets specialising in fresh, quality and artisanal ingredients.

Borough Market is an inspiring cornucopia of world-class ingredients. More than that, it's a vibrant and energising community, a real mish-mash of personalities, cultures and influences, yet distinct and defined values. If you're not a regular already, come for a visit, or head to your nearest produce market, find out where your food comes from, buy something you've not seen before, then cook and enjoy eating it.

Ed Smith, London 2018

USING THIS BOOK

MARKET SHOPPING

The shopping experience at a produce market is very different to time spent in modern supermarkets (and indeed the online alternatives). At any given visit you're bound to find something different. Markets invariably help us to discover and experience new and old traditions, the rare, the wholesome, the best and most flavourful food there is to be had. It's invigorating and sensorial: look, smell, touch and try – and take the opportunity to interact with traders, as all are experts in their products, and many will have been directly involved with the farming or production.

Though some (but really not all) ingredients can cost more than mass-produced food, the difference in taste between unique and sometimes imperfect looking products, and the modern and monotonous alternatives, is often so great as to be near incomparable. You get much more for your money with produce that tastes as it should. It's also worth remembering that by buying from farmers and producers, not only are you more directly connected with the ingredients you cook with, you're helping to ensure their craft, knowledge and expertise continue.

Crucially, with great ingredients there's less need for fancy technique. Quality makes cooking simple. This doesn't just apply to the food you might buy for a special occasion: market produce is often modest, and we should use it for our every-week meals too.

SEASONAL EATING

The book is presented in four seasonal sections. However, in reality, life, shopping and eating cannot be so neatly divided: seasonal market produce changes on a weekly, not quarterly basis, and though some dates are official (as with the British asparagus season, and the dates furred and feathered game can be shot) the timetable for the availability of most fruit, vegetables, meats and fish is not absolutely set. So it's worth reading across the four sections of the book to see what might be around next time you're at a produce market, then return for more specific instruction once back home with full shopping bags. As Sybil Kapoor eloquently points out later on in these pages: shop and eat what is in front of you; eating seasonally is about your appetite and desires, as well as the ingredients you use.

RECIPE ORDER

Each seasonal section begins with ideas for breakfast, then moves through sides, snacks, starters and light touch assemblies, before offering low-effort lunches and suppers, family-style 'one-pot' dishes, more involved feasting ideas, then baking, desserts and drinks. These seasonally inspired ideas are followed by recipes that feature particular types of produce. Head to The Cheesemongers section in Spring, for example, if you have an urge to cook with and eat the amazing dairy ingredients available at the Market.

KEY INGREDIENTS

A number of the recipe introductions reference where you can find key ingredients at Borough Market. Often, there will also be other traders who stock relevant produce – use the trader directory on page 317, or www.boroughmarket.org.uk to find out more about the traders and the produce they sell. In every instance it will be possible to purchase suitable alternatives elsewhere.

TACKLING WASTE AT HOME

One subject close to Borough Market's heart is the issue of avoiding waste. There's more on this later, as well as suggestions for making the most of your shopping scattered through the recipes. Ultimately, though, when cooking do pause and look again at 'waste' items, and consider whether they might actually be the starting point for the next thing you cook. Moreover, feel free to be pragmatic: for example swap créme fraîche for cream rather than opening two different pots of similar ingredients, and treat instructions with a pinch of flexibility – if the quantities suggested leave you with a fraction of an ingredient, then add that too rather than let it go unused.

KITCHEN NOTES

For best results:

Butter – should be salted unless otherwise stated
Eggs – are mostly large and always free-range
Milk, créme fraîche and yoghurt – should always be full fat
Salt – should be flaked sea salt, not fine, unless otherwise stated
Herbs – are fresh unless otherwise stated, and if in doubt about quantities it's always best to be generous
Cooking fat – can be sunflower, vegetable, light olive oil, butter or whatever medium you prefer to use, unless specifically stated
Cooking vessels – are recommended within the recipes, but few dishes will fail if the tin, tray or dish you use is not exactly the same dimension
Fan oven – convection oven temperatures are provided, but the fan oven setting will be most reliable and effective
Pastry – should be well-chilled, as this ensures it's easier to work with and avoids shrinkage when cooked. The stages set out in the recipes help to achieve best results. If you are in a rush, shop-bought pastry may save time
Before you begin cooking – find a moment to read the recipe in full; a number of the recipes have multiple stages, and can (or should) be started well before eating.

MAP
10

MAP OF BOROUGH MARKET

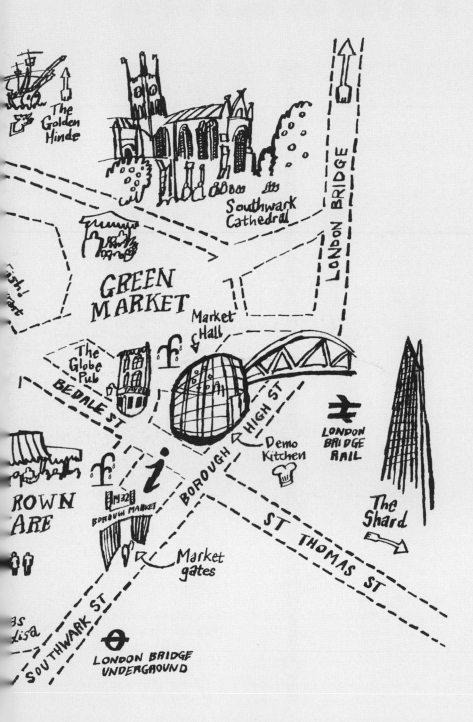

MAP
11

The Golden Hinde

Southwark Cathedral

LONDON BRIDGE

GREEN MARKET

Market Hall

The Globe Pub

BEDALE ST

HIGH ST

Demo Kitchen

LONDON BRIDGE RAIL

The Shard

ROWN ARE

BOROUGH MARKET

BOROUGH

ST THOMAS ST

Market gates

SOUTHWARK ST

LONDON BRIDGE UNDERGROUND

TIMELINE

The earliest date we have – found in a Norse chronicle – for when a market started trading at the foot of London Bridge, the only crossing into the city

1014

With their revenues threatened, **London authorities forbid their citizens** from buying food from the Market

1270ˢ

The City of London starts to take control of the Market, a controversial process that will continue for over a century

1406

Edward VI completes the sale of Southwark to the City and **agrees to extend the Market from two to four days per week**

1550

As the Market grows in size along the high street, strict rules are published for the traders in **an effort to rein in the chaos**

1624

A devastating fire sweeps through the area, destroying the market house – the Market's administrative centre

1676

Parliament moves to shut down the Market in order to ease the suffocating congestion on the high street

1754

Funded by parishioners, **the Market reopens in a new spot** 'for the convenience and accommodation of the public'

1756

A railway viaduct is constructed through the heart of Borough Market, completely changing its character

1862

A German bombing raid causes serious damage to the Market's roof and its main office building

1917

Charlie Chaplin's offer of sponsorship turns the traders' annual sports day into a major national news story

1930

The wholesale operation reaches its peak. The buildings on Three Crown Square are demolished to create a large trading space, and new Art Deco gates are installed

1930ˢ

Pioneering retailers such as Brindisa Ltd and Neal's Yard Dairy move into warehouses left vacant by the decline of the wholesalers

1990ˢ

Emboldened by the success of the Food Lovers' Fair, Borough begins to reinvent itself as a **retail market**

1998

Three Crown Square reopens after the construction of a new viaduct, and the ribbon is cut on the new Market Hall

2013

The installation of **public water fountains** helps fuel a growing national debate about plastic waste and environmental responsibility

2017

A new public space is created in Jubilee Place, and facilities are provided for a new generation of wholesalers with an emphasis on skills and crafts

2018

SPR

SPRING

When spring arrives, a new palette presents itself along with a burst of energy and optimism. The bright green shoots of spring vegetables account for much of that change. Over this period we see the likes of Italian artichokes, wild garlic, asparagus, young leeks and eventually the arrival of eager courgettes, peas and beans.

There's colour and vitality beyond the grocers, too, with early lamb being touted (though hogget and mutton are best right now) and wood pigeon. Food lightens up a little, with smoked fish, fresh fish and shellfish seeming particularly appropriate to eat right now – razor clams, sea trout, hake and more. Similarly, the sharpness of tropical fruits and sweet tang of fresh goat's cheese and feta, green herbs and bunny rabbits appeal (in fur to some, and in chocolate form to most).

Another reason for cheer is the raft of annual events that this time of year heralds. Borough Market gets dressed up for St George's Day with the feast day of the patron saint of England providing ample opportunity for flag waving, medieval knight costumes and the pushing of patriotic produce. Lent and Easter fall within the period, marking a time to clear out and use up store cupboard items, to abstain from one or two treats, and prepare for the feasts that follow. Shrove Tuesday sees traders run and flip for a pancake race, and because the traders are an international bunch, there are home comforts from further afield too, such as Scandinavian cream buns.

You'll see traders shedding one or two of their thermal layers and eventually their gloves, and those manning the coffee carts (always the earliest to set up) are grateful their days begin again in sunlight. On the subject of waking up, now is the time that Britain's growing season grinds into gear and buds begin to bloom –

with the Market florists Chez Michèle and The Gated Garden providing further proof of this, if more were needed.

· *SEASONAL HIGHLIGHTS*

Asparagus
Broad beans
Cauliflower
Field rhubarb
Jersey royals
Leeks
Lettuces
Monk's beard
Peas
Purple sprouting broccoli
Radishes
Samphire and sea beet
Sorrel
Spinach
Spring onions
Watercress
Wild garlic

Guinea fowl
Hogget
Mutton
Rabbit
Wood pigeon

Clams
Crab
Gurnard
Haddock
Hake
Lemon sole
Native oysters (until April)
Plaice
Scallops
Sea trout
Skate

WILD GARLIC GREEN EGGS

Wild garlic's long and broad green leaves are heavily scented and unmistakable when stumbled upon in wet, shady spots. While there are a few urban areas in which it can be found, a more reliable place to 'forage' is at the Market.

Though harsh if eaten raw, when wilted the taste is rounded and pleasingly garlicky, and it works particularly well in a brunch-style dish. Eggs in this shakshuka-esque format are often labelled as baked, but the most reliable way to keep the yolks runny is to keep the cooking on the stove, using a lid to help the steam cook the whites at the last minute.

If you feel the urge to eat this outside wild garlic season, simply add 2 crushed garlic cloves to the cooked leeks 2 minutes before adding the spinach.

SERVES *2–4*, DEPENDING ON
EGG APPETITE

350–400g large leaf spinach
about 15 wild garlic leaves
50g butter
250g leeks, trimmed, washed and sliced
    into 2–3mm-thick discs
⅕ nutmeg
4 large eggs
100g Greek yoghurt
juice of ¼ lemon
1 teaspoon Aleppo chilli pepper flakes (pul biber)
fresh bread, to serve

Wash the spinach thoroughly. Cut the leaves from the stems then cut the stems into roughly 1cm lengths. Refresh the wild garlic in a bowl of cold water.

Put a heavy-based sauté pan (for which you have a lid) over a medium-high heat – a 20–22cm-diameter works best. Add 20g of the butter and allow it to melt, then add the leeks, chopped spinach stems and a pinch of flaky sea salt. Stir, reduce the heat a touch and cook for 8–10 minutes, stirring occasionally, until the greens are much reduced, meltingly soft and sweet. Place the washed spinach leaves and wild garlic on top and leave to steam, folding them into the leeks as they wilt. After 5–6 minutes the spinach should be soft, and water will be leaching out.

Grate the nutmeg onto the spinach and add a good few grinds of black pepper, plus another pinch of salt. Mix well. Increase the heat to medium-high, create 4 holes in the greens and crack an egg into each hole. Place a lid on top and cook for just under 3 minutes, until the whites appear set but the yolks are still runny.

Meanwhile, season the yoghurt with a pinch of salt, plenty of pepper and the lemon juice. Heat the remaining butter in a small saucepan with the Aleppo pepper, until it melts and begins to foam.

Take the green eggs off the heat, add 8 dollops of yoghurt over the greens and spoon the foaming butter on top. Serve immediately, with fresh bread for scooping and mopping up the juices.

BUTCHER'S BACON AND FARMHOUSE CHEDDAR SLICES

There's no contest in flavour or texture between dry-cured bacon bought from the butcher and commercial alternatives. One significant explanation for this is the type of pig the bacon derives from: most good butchers favour high welfare heritage breeds, which grow slowly and ultimately taste better than the alternative. These slices are an excellent vessel for good-quality bacon and can be prepared in advance – keep unbaked slices in the fridge overnight and a fresh bacon-filled pastry will be only a brief blast in the oven away the next morning.

Smoked back bacon has the edge here, but if you prefer it 'green' or streaky, then use that. You must, though, use one of **Heritage Cheese**'s punchy mature farmhouse cheddars or cheese of similar strength to stand up to the meat.

MAKES 4

plain flour, for dusting
320–375g block all-butter puff pastry
8 slices of dry-cured back bacon
70g mature farmhouse cheddar, grated
1 large tomato, cut into 8 slices
whole milk, to brush pastry
3–4 tablespoons maple syrup

Preheat the oven to 220C fan/240C/460F/ gas mark 9 and line a large baking sheet with baking parchment.

Dust a clean surface with flour. Roll out the pastry to make a square approximately twice the length of one rasher of bacon and 2–3mm thick. Cut the pastry into four equal squares, keeping things neat by using a sharp knife and your rolling pin as a guide.

Transfer the pastry squares to the lined baking sheet. Imagine the squares are diamonds and place two pieces of bacon across each piece of pastry, orienting them from tip to tip. The bacon should 'top and tail', so there's a thin and wide end of a rasher at each end. Sprinkle the grated cheese evenly over the bacon rashers and place a tomato slice 2cm in from the ends of each rasher of bacon.

You now have two untouched corners of pastry on each square. Fold one into the middle without stretching it – it should reach just over and beyond the filling. Brush the top of that folded pastry with a little milk, then fold the remaining corner over and onto the top of it. Repeat with the other three squares. Ensure there are a few centimetres of space between each slice, then brush all the exposed pastry with more milk. Bake towards the top of the oven for 16–18 minutes, until the pastry is puffed and golden, and any exposed bacon crisp. (If you are making them in advance, leave the milk wash until just prior to baking.)

Remove the slices from the oven and brush all the surfaces with maple syrup (pastry, bacon, tomatoes… everything). Leave to cool for 5–10 minutes before serving.

HOT RADISH PICKLES

Market shopping provides plenty of opportunity to pick up things like proper hot-water-crust pork or game pies, Scotch eggs and mighty sausage rolls.

Such porcine treats need an acidic and spiky condiment to go with them, though. A little mustard is good. Also, pickled hot radish such as the extraordinary watermelon, honeydew and Japanese black radish varieties, which greengrocers like **Turnips** often stock. Each of their spherical outsides appear plain and unpromising, but when cut open look remarkable and are peppery enough to make your nose hairs stand on end.

SERVES 6–8

300g spherical, hot radishes (honeydew,
*   watermelon or black)*
2 sprigs of dill
120ml white wine vinegar
2 teaspoons caster sugar
2 teaspoons flaky sea salt
1 teaspoon black peppercorns
1 teaspoon coriander seeds, gently tapped
2 teaspoons yellow mustard seeds
120ml water
1 garlic clove, crushed

Peel the radishes with a vegetable peeler, then cut them into 1–2mm-thick slices using a mandoline (watch your fingers) or, if you prefer to use a knife, cut into 1–2cm dice. Put the radishes and dill sprigs in a Tupperware container, jar or bowl in which they fit snuggly.

Put the remaining ingredients, except the garlic, in a small saucepan with 120ml water and bring to the boil. Remove from the heat, add the garlic, stir, then pour the hot mixture over the radishes. Leave to cool to room temperature then refrigerate for at least 6 hours, or up to 2 days.

WHIPPED HOT-SMOKED SALMON WITH SPRING CRUDITÉS

A number of the Market's fishmongers stock thick wedges of hot-smoked salmon, which sit proudly like rose gold bullion – like those of **Oak & Smoke**, from a century-old smokehouse in Arbroath, Scotland. Though ready and willing to be flaked into a salad or sandwich, the salty, smoky edge is particularly good when whipped up with dairy to something akin to a taramasalata, and served with fresh and crunchy vegetables or thin crackers. As such, this dish makes an excellent canapé or informal start to group feasting.

SERVES *6–12* AS A DIP

200g hot-smoked salmon
200g full-fat crème fraîche
2–3 tablespoons full-fat Greek yoghurt
finely grated zest and juice of ½ lemon
⅓ nutmeg

TO SERVE

selection of seasonal crudités, such as chicory
*   leaves, radishes and their leaves, 1–2cm-thick*
*   slices of fennel, cucumber, young carrots or*
*   other bright and crunchy fresh vegetables*
cracker bread

Peel the skin from the salmon and discard. Flake the flesh into a food processor and add the crème fraîche, 2 tablespoons of the yoghurt, the lemon zest and juice. Blitz for 30 seconds or more until light and smooth. Taste, then season with freshly grated nutmeg, black pepper and flaky sea salt (take care with the latter). Blitz again, taste and season for a second time, adding the remaining yoghurt if you think it could be a touch looser.

Serve with a selection of seasonal crudités and cracker bread.

CHILLED ASPARAGUS SOUP

British asparagus season officially begins on 23 April and lasts for eight weeks; asparagus is a genuinely seasonal ingredient, and so much better at this time than an out-of-season or imported alternative. Make the most of it from the first to the last moment it reaches your local market.

For much of that time just blanching the spears, rubbing them with butter and seasoning them liberally is enough. Perhaps the occasional grating of parmesan will be welcome too, but as a general rule it rarely pays to go too far beyond a simple approach. That said, if towards the end of the asparagus season you're keen to mix things up a little, a chilled soup could well be the way to go.

SERVES 4 AS A STARTER

30g butter
2 banana shallots, finely sliced
400–450g bunch of asparagus
2 garlic cloves, crushed
500ml hot vegetable stock
150g baby spinach
100g Greek yoghurt
juice of ½ lemon
extra-virgin olive oil
12 king prawns, shelled (optional)

Put a medium, heavy-based saucepan over a medium-high heat. Add the butter, then the shallots and a pinch of flaky sea salt. Sweat and soften without letting them brown for 3–4 minutes, stirring occasionally.

Cut the tips from the asparagus spears and set them to one side. Chop the remaining spears into 4cm batons, stopping once the spear becomes discouragingly woody (discard those ends).

Add the garlic to the shallots and cook gently for 1 minute then add the asparagus batons (not the tips) and cook for 1 minute more, stirring frequently. Add the hot vegetable stock and simmer for 4 minutes until the asparagus is tender. Remove from the heat and put the spinach in the pan. Leave it to wilt and the soup to cool for 15 minutes, then transfer to a blender and blitz to a loose purée. Add 80g of the yoghurt (saving the remainder to add a dollop when you serve) and blitz again until silky smooth, then season with salt, pepper and lemon juice to taste. You will need to taste it for seasoning again just before serving, as once chilled the flavours will be muted a little.

Refrigerate for at least 1 hour before serving.

Garnish the soup with a dollop of yoghurt, the raw asparagus tips cut in half on the diagonal and dressed with olive oil, lemon juice, salt and black pepper, and, if you wish, fresh prawns, seasoned with lots of salt and fried in a little oil.

GLOBE ARTICHOKES WITH LEMON AND HERB BUTTER

Some vegetables that take centre stage in a greengrocer's display can look, to many, more like decorations than something to eat. It would be understandable, for example, to query where, how or why you might cook an artichoke.

Well, one of the easiest and best ways is to cook and consume the whole thing – simmer the artichoke until tender, then pluck the woody petals, dip into a vinaigrette or melted butter, and suck them as you make your way to the tender heart in the middle. Two dips are suggested below.

SERVES 2–4

2 large globe artichokes, woody stalks removed
2 tablespoons white wine vinegar
2 teaspoons flaky sea salt
2 tablespoons olive oil
2 bay leaves

FOR THE DIJON VINAIGRETTE

1 tablespoon Dijon mustard
1 teaspoon golden caster sugar
1 small garlic clove, crushed
2 teaspoons red wine vinegar
60–75ml extra-virgin olive oil
1 teaspoon tepid water

FOR THE LEMON AND HERB BUTTER

200g butter, cubed
1 small garlic clove, crushed
finely grated zest and juice of ½ lemon
2 tablespoons tepid water
50g finely grated parmesan
1 tablespoon finely chopped herbs (parsley,
tarragon or thyme leaves)

Find a large, non-aluminium saucepan in which the artichokes will fit, then fill it two-thirds full with water, adding the vinegar, salt, olive oil and bay leaves. Cover and bring to the boil, then add the artichokes and top up with more water if necessary to ensure the artichokes are fully immersed. Reduce to a simmer and cook for 30 minutes with the lid ajar (in part to keep the artichokes submerged). They are cooked once you can fairly easily pull away a petal. Drain the artichokes and serve them on large plates, with the dip in the middle of the table, bowls in which to discard sucked petals, and teaspoons at the ready to scoop out the tender hearts once they are reached.

To make the Dijon vinaigrette, whisk together the mustard, sugar, garlic and vinegar. Add quarter of the oil plus the tepid water and whisk again, then add the remaining oil (you may not need it all) in a steady stream, whisking continuously. It should be fairly thick and completely emulsified. Season the vinaigrette with salt and black pepper.

Alternatively, to make the lemon and herb butter, melt the butter in a heavy-based pan over a low heat. Add the garlic, lemon zest and tepid water, shake the pan and let that warm and mellow for a few minutes, without letting the butter foam or brown. Add the parmesan and let it melt in, again shaking the pan to bring the sauce together. Carefully re-heat just before serving, stirring in the lemon juice and chopped herbs at the last minute and seasoning with black pepper.

RAZOR CLAMS, MARINDA TOMATOES AND MONK'S BEARD

Razor clams are harvested from beaches all round Britain, at slightly different times of the year depending on the specific coastline. As a general rule, they rarely poke out of the sand when it's very cold (or more to the point fewer people wish to harvest them in inclement weather), and it's not good practice to eat them in the summer months, as this is spawning season; so spring and autumn are good times to look out for them at **Shellseekers Fish & Game Ltd**, for example. They're easy to cook – similar to other molluscs, they just need to be steamed from their shells. Here, the thick-skinned, sharp Marinda tomatoes, which you will find at **Turnips**, are an ideal partner, not least because they are sharp, sweet and flavourful in late winter and spring, months before summer varieties are ready.

SERVES 4 AS A STARTER

12 razor clams (live and frisky)
70ml water
2 Marinda tomatoes
small handful of monk's beard (or samphire)
5 tablespoons extra-virgin olive oil
1 small shallot, finely diced
2 garlic cloves, finely sliced
1 teaspoon caster sugar
1 tablespoon sherry vinegar
leaves picked from 4 sprigs of parsley,
*   finely chopped*

Plunge the clams into a bowl of cold water to clean them, removing them after 10 minutes. Discard any that do not shrink or move if tapped.

Put a large saucepan for which you have a lid over a medium-high heat and add 70ml water. Place the lid on top and, when it reaches the boil, add the clams and swiftly close the lid again. Cook for 2 minutes, shaking the pan, until all the shells have opened. Remove the clams and leave to cool for 2–3 minutes, then remove the meat from the open shells. Use a sharp knife to cut out any the dark stomach and intestinal tract, retaining the clean, sweet meat. Slice that diagonally into 2cm pieces, set to one side and keep the shells warm.

Cut each tomato into 8 segments then each of those in half. Trim the muddy, woody ends from the monk's beard and refresh in cold water (or pick the samphire into 3–4cm fronds).

Put a heavy-based frying pan over a low-medium heat and add 2 tablespoons of the olive oil. Add the shallot and garlic and heat them in the oil for 2–3 minutes, without frying. Add the tomatoes, sliced clam meat and monk's beard or samphire and stir them in the oil for 2 minutes, gently warming them through, again without frying.

Line the clam shells on a platter or divide between plates. Divide the contents of the pan between them, then add the rest of the oil to the pan, along with the sugar, vinegar and parsley. Stir together with a spatula, then spoon this dressing over the clams.

QUINOA, MANGO AND SUGAR SNAP SALAD

Mangoes are available all year round, though there's a particular peak in late spring when a handful of India's myriad varieties (which are often quite different but always perfumed, sweet and memorable) make their way to these shores. At the same time, the Market tends to be warming up and sunlight hours begin stretching. Now feels like the time to bring the summer months closer, with the help of fresh and aromatic food. For that reason, you can't really overdo the fresh herbs in this salad, which are an excellent foil for oily and white fish, or with the embellishment of feta or cured meats, the basis of a cheering salad.

SERVES 2 AS A MAIN, 4 AS A SIDE DISH

250g quinoa
4cm piece of fresh ginger, peeled and finely grated
finely grated zest and juice of 1 lime
2 tablespoons extra-virgin olive oil
2 teaspoons golden caster sugar
1 firm but ripe mango (350–400g)
1 cucumber, peeled and halved lengthways
leaves picked from 20g mint, roughly chopped
leaves picked from 20g basil, coriander and/or
*   parsley, roughly chopped*
150–200g sugar snap peas, washed
1–2 spring onions, trimmed and thinly sliced
*   (optional)*

Put the quinoa in a saucepan and add 4 times its volume in cold water. Bring to the boil then simmer over a low-medium heat for 20 minutes until the little white tails spring out. Drain and rinse under cold running water until cool.

In the meantime, make a dressing by whisking together the grated ginger, lime juice and zest, olive oil, sugar and a heavy pinch of both flaky sea salt and freshly grated black pepper in a large mixing bowl.

Cut the mango flesh away from its stone and skin, then cut into 1cm dice, transferring all the flesh and any juice to the dressing bowl once done. Use a teaspoon to scrape out the watery seeds from the cucumber, cut it into 3–4 strips lengthways then into 1cm dice and add it to the mango. Add the chopped herbs, sugar snaps and spring onions, if using.

Combine the quinoa with the rest of the ingredients and mix well, adding more salt and black pepper to taste. This can be made 3–4 hours in advance if necessary.

JERSEY ROYALS, CRAB AND ASPARAGUS SALAD

Maincrop Jersey royals are harvested from the end of March through to July, which means they tend to appear on greengrocers' stalls at Borough Market and across the country at broadly the same time as asparagus (see page 27). This salad combines those two world-class vegetables with a brown-crab-meat-enriched dressing, and flakes of white crab meat on top. A bed of pea shoots seems appropriate for late spring, though lamb's lettuce, land cress or baby gem lettuce also work well.

SERVES 2 AS A MAIN, 4 AS A STARTER

400g baby Jersey royals
400–450g bunch of asparagus
1 large or 2 small dressed crabs
100g pea shoots, lamb's lettuce, land cress
*   or baby gem lettuce*
½ lemon

FOR THE BROWN CRAB DRESSING

1 large egg yolk
1 teaspoon Dijon mustard
2 teaspoons white wine vinegar
3 tablespoons olive oil

Ideally the potatoes will be only 3–4cm long – cut any larger ones in half across the middle. Put the potatoes in a saucepan of well-salted cold water and bring to the boil over a high heat. Simmer for 15–20 minutes until the tip of a knife or prongs of a fork slide easily in. Drain and cool under cold running water.

One by one, hold the asparagus spears at either end and bend until the woody base snaps off. Discard that end, then cut the rest into 4–5cm batons. Bring a saucepan of salted water to a rolling boil, add the asparagus and blanch for 2 minutes. Drain and refresh under cold running water.

While the potatoes and asparagus are cooking, use a fork to decant the white crab meat from the crab shell, leaving the brown meat and roe within.

Make the dressing by whisking the egg yolk, mustard and white wine vinegar in a medium mixing bowl until light in colour and increased in volume – this could easily require a minute's worth of elbow grease. Place the bowl on a tea towel to hold it steady and, while continuously whisking with one hand, gradually add the oil, little by little, whisking until it's incorporated and the dressing has a thickness similar to double cream when it's at ribbon stage.

Add the brown crab meat (you should have 150–200g) to the dressing, stir and season with flaky sea salt and black pepper. Ensure the asparagus and potatoes are cool and well drained, then add them to the crab mixture and mix well.

Divide the pea shoots, lamb's lettuce, land cress or baby gem lettuce between plates or salad bowls. Season with salt, black pepper and a good squeeze of lemon juice. Spoon the potato and asparagus mix on top, then top with flecks of the white crab meat.

STEAMED SEA TROUT AND CHARRED LETTUCE

Wild sea trout appears at the fishmongers' counters from April through to October. Stock and size peak in late summer, but this is something worth enjoying for the full course of its season if you can. Though technically the same species as brown river trout, these trout have travelled to sea and returned larger, pinker of flesh and with a silvery sheen akin to salmon.

Lettuce, charred and slightly wilted in browning butter, is a really strong side to the clean-tasting steamed fish. If you can't get hold of sea trout, the lettuce is worth trying alongside steamed salmon.

SERVES 2

2 x 140g sea trout fillets (or salmon)
40g butter
2 baby gem lettuces, halved lengthways
leaves picked from 2 sprigs of mint,
*   finely shredded*
peppery extra-virgin olive oil, for brushing
*   and drizzling*
2 lemon wedges, to serve

Cut a square of greaseproof paper or foil to fit inside a steaming basket with a little space round the edges (to allow steam to filter through). Lay the paper or foil in the basket and brush with a little oil. Season the sea trout flesh with flaky sea salt and black pepper and set both fillets on top of the paper, skin facing up. Bring a suitably-sized saucepan of water to the boil and place the basket on top. Cover with a lid and steam for 4–5 minutes, until the flakes of the fish separate if gently pushed. Remove the steaming basket as soon as the fish is ready, peel the skin from the fillets and carefully transfer the sea trout to two plates.

At the point the steamer basket is placed over the boiling water, put a medium heavy-based saucepan over a high heat. Add the butter and once it has melted and started to foam lay the lettuce halves cut side down in the browning butter and cook for 3 minutes, until golden and a little wilted. Turn the heat off and flip the lettuce halves over so the other sides warm in the residual heat for a minute. Season the lettuce with plenty of salt and black pepper and sprinkle with the shredded mint.

Place two halves of lettuce cut side up next to each piece of sea trout. Drizzle peppery extra-virgin olive oil over the fish and serve with wedges of lemon.

RABBIT AND MONKFISH ARROZ

This is not an authentic paella, but the combination of rabbit, monkfish and silky saffron-infused rice feels an appropriate dish for mid-spring: warming and comforting, but with hints of holidays abroad. Something to cook on St George's Day, perhaps, as a tip of the hat towards the Spanish who celebrate the same feast day as the English.

You will be able to find wild rabbit and monkfish at a number of different Market stalls or your local butcher and fishmonger. If you don't feel up to jointing the rabbit yourself, ask the butcher to do it for you.

This is excellent on its own, but you could also serve it with a crisp green salad, crusty bread and maybe a pile of sharply dressed shaved fennel alongside.

SERVES 4

4 tablespoons olive oil
1 onion, finely diced
1 green bell pepper, deseeded and finely diced
3 garlic cloves, crushed
1 rabbit, jointed into 7 pieces
150ml fino sherry or dry white wine
600ml chicken or vegetable stock
300g calasparra rice (or other short-grain
    paella rice)
200–400ml just-boiled water
10 saffron threads
1 heaped teaspoon sweet smoked paprika
    (Pimentón de la Vera)
200–250g monkfish fillet, cut into 2cm chunks
extra-virgin olive oil, for drizzling
leaves picked from 4 sprigs of parsley
4 lemon wedges, to serve

You will need a 26–30cm paella pan (or a large, wide and deep frying pan) to cook this dish.

Put a small frying pan over a low-medium heat and add 2 tablespoons of the olive oil, then the onion, green pepper and a pinch of flaky sea salt. Cook gently for 15 minutes, so that the vegetables soften and sweeten, stirring occasionally to ensure they do not colour. Add the garlic and cook for a further 3 minutes.

At the same time, put the paella pan over a medium heat and add the remaining olive oil. Thoroughly brown the rabbit pieces in the oil, putting the thigh and leg pieces in first then, after 7–8 minutes, the loin segments. After 12–15 minutes, pour in the fino or wine and let this bubble and reduce by half, before adding the stock and the onion, pepper and garlic mix. Simmer for 20 minutes, then add the rice, 200ml just-boiled water, the saffron and paprika. Stir, then arrange the rabbit pieces evenly around the pan, bring to a gentle simmer and cook over a low heat for 15 minutes until the stock has almost disappeared below the rice (don't stir).

Once most of the stock has been absorbed, check the rice is plump and nearly tender. If not, add another 100–200ml just-boiled water to continue the cooking process. If it's ready, dot the monkfish pieces around the rabbit, pushing them halfway into the rice, then allow to cook for 5 minutes. Remove from the heat, cover the pan with foil and leave to rest for 5 minutes.

Remove the foil and drizzle with extra-virgin olive oil. Sprinkle a few flakes of salt over the top along with the parsley leaves before serving with a wedge of lemon per person.

WOOD PIGEON AND ROAST SHALLOT FLATBREADS

Wood pigeons may get overlooked from late summer through winter, when feathered game like grouse and pheasant are available on butchers' counters. In spring, however, they come to the fore (unlike other birds, pigeons can be shot throughout the year). Happily, the lean and intensely flavoured meat works well with the flavours of the season – ingredients like wild garlic, sweet onions, radishes, early peas, beans and berries. They're a versatile ingredient, suited to a wide variety of cuisines, and this recipe is a particularly fine way to enjoy them: the flatbreads are almost instant to make, and provide a pillow-soft cushion for pink meat, sweet roast shallots, plus a sharp cucumber and spice garnish. Eat with your fingers (with napkins at the ready).

SERVES 4

cooking oil, for frying
6 banana shallots, halved lengthways (skin on)
8 garlic cloves, flattened (skin on)
knob of butter
2 plump wood pigeons, wishbones removed
8 sprigs of thyme
50g Greek yoghurt

FOR THE FLATBREADS

200g self-raising flour, plus extra for dusting
½ teaspoon baking powder
¼ teaspoon flaky sea salt
leaves picked from 8 sprigs of thyme
200g Greek yoghurt

FOR THE CUCUMBER AND SPICE GARNISH

½ cucumber, peeled, deseeded and finely diced
3 tablespoons extra-virgin olive oil
1 tablespoon moscatel vinegar (or other white wine vinegar)
½ teaspoon sumac
½ teaspoon Aleppo chilli pepper flakes (pul biber)

Preheat the oven to 220C fan/240C/460F/gas mark 9.

Begin by making the bread, organising the rest of the meal between the resting and rolling stages. Alternatively, you could cook the bread in advance, reheating in a low oven for 5 minutes when required.

Sift the flour into a mixing bowl and stir in the baking powder, salt and thyme. Spoon in the yoghurt and combine, eventually using a lightly floured hand to push dry and wet together. Knead for about a minute, then shape the dough into a ball. Leave it to rest in the bowl for 15 minutes, covered with a clean cloth (the dough will expand a little).

Divide the dough into 4 and roll each piece out on a lightly floured surface, to about the same size as a side plate. Aim for something akin to a naan bread in shape.

To cook the flatbreads, wipe a griddle or heavy-based frying pan with a little oil and place over a very high heat. When very hot, cook each flatbread (one at a time if necessary) for 2–3 minutes on each side, until lightly charred and puffed.

While the dough is resting, you can get on with the rest of the meal. Put 2 tablespoons of cooking oil in a small roasting tray or baking tin, sprinkle liberally with salt and roll the shallot halves and garlic in it. Arrange the shallots cut side down and place the tray or tin in the centre of the oven for 20 minutes.

Mix together the ingredients for the cucumber and spice garnish in a bowl and set aside.

Put a small frying pan over a high heat and add the knob of butter. Season the pigeons with salt and black pepper inside and out and brown each breast for 90 seconds in the pan. Stuff 4 sprigs of thyme in each bird, add to the tray of shallots and garlic and roast for

8 minutes. Remove and leave the birds to rest upside-down on a warm plate for 5–10 minutes while the shallots finish cooking.

Cut the pigeon breasts from the carcasses, then slice the breasts diagonally into 4–5 pieces, seasoning with salt and black pepper. Spread a tablespoon of yoghurt onto each warm flatbread. Peel away the skin from the shallots and lay three halves on top of each flatbread. Squeeze the roasted garlic flesh out over the shallots and add the meat from one breast

of pigeon. Repeat with the remaining three servings. Spoon over the cucumber and its dressing, plus any juices from the roasting tray and serve.

LAMB MEATBALLS IN PEA AND HERB BROTH

These minted lamb meatballs in a light broth, studded with sweet sugar snap and mangetout peas, feels exactly like the kind of thing we ought to be eating at this time of year.

It's best to make these with the kind of lamb mince you find at a good butcher's shop, with a decent streak of fat running through it, rather than the lean strands found in pre-sealed packets on the supermarket shelf.

Serve the meatball broth with something savoury and nutty like quinoa, or wholemeal grains such as pearl barley or bulgur wheat. Light pasta such as orzo or linguine work very well, too.

SERVES 4

FOR THE MEATBALLS

500g lamb mince
100g ricotta
50g dry breadcrumbs
1 garlic clove, crushed
finely grated zest of 1 lemon
1 large egg
leaves picked from 30–40g mint, finely shredded
½ teaspoon flaky sea salt
½ teaspoon black pepper

FOR THE BROTH

600ml vegetable stock
3 bay leaves
1 garlic bulb, cut in two through the middle
350g mixture of sugar snap peas, mangetout
    and freshly podded peas
leaves stripped from 15g chervil, roughly chopped

TO SERVE

a cooked grain, seed or pasta of your choice
yoghurt

Mix together all the meatball ingredients in a bowl, keeping a quarter of the shredded mint to one side, then get your hands dirty and roll the mixture into balls about the size of a walnut: 20–25g each if you're into measuring. Arrange the meatballs on a baking tray and, if you have time, refrigerate for 1 hour or more.

Around 30 minutes before you plan to serve, heat the oven to 150C fan/170C/325F/gas mark 3. Once the oven's hot, bake the meatballs for 10 minutes.

At the same time, bring the vegetable stock, bay leaves and garlic to the boil in a wide saucepan, then reduce the temperature and simmer for 5 minutes. Transfer the baked meatballs to the stock and poach for 5 minutes before adding the sugar snaps, mangetout and fresh peas. Simmer for a further 2 minutes, then remove the pan from the heat and leave the greens to warm through and the broth to cool a little.

Stir the chervil and remaining mint through the broth and meatballs, then serve with a grain, seed or pasta of your choice, and a dollop or two of yoghurt to stir through the broth.

HAKE AND GREEN BEAN BAKE

When left whole, hake are one of the more impressive components of a fishmongers' 'flash', winding their way between other parts of the display, their teeth-filled mouths gaping, as is often the case on Paul Day's **Sussex Fish** counter. Fearsome to look at, yes, but actually a fairly tame, easy and rewarding fish to cook and eat, particularly when cut through the bone into thick steaks. This one(ish)-dish meal demonstrates the point very nicely indeed.

It's worthwhile using stone-in black olives here, such as the rich and salty Gemlik duble from **The Turkish Deli**. They have more flavour, and none of the soapiness associated with the pitted black olives found in long-life jars and pouches.

SERVES 4

350g fine green beans, woody ends removed
80g black olives (with stones)
400g cherry tomatoes
1 onion, finely sliced
50g salted anchovies in oil, roughly chopped
    (oil reserved)
5 tablespoons olive oil
2 garlic cloves, finely sliced
4 hake steaks, cut through the bone
    (about 150g each)
grated zest and juice of 1 lemon
leaves picked from 8 sprigs of parsley,
    roughly chopped
sourdough or boiled new potatoes, to serve

Preheat the oven to 200C fan/220C/425F/gas mark 7.

Bring a saucepan of salted water to the boil and blanch the beans for 4–5 minutes until tender and just beginning to flop. Drain and refresh under cold running water.

Use the cooking time to de-stone the olives – if you don't have a gadget, place them on a chopping board, tap with the base of a mug to split the flesh and pull the stone out. It doesn't take long.

In a mixing bowl, toss together the cooled beans, tomatoes, onion, olives, anchovies and their oil and 4 additional tablespoons of olive oil. Tip this out onto a large baking sheet with a 2cm-high rim or a shallow roasting tray. Add a few grinds of pepper and cook for 15 minutes near the top of the oven, then remove the tray from the oven and reduce the oven temperature to 180C fan/200C/400F/gas mark 6. Sprinkle the garlic slices over the beans and tomatoes and gently mix to swap those vegetables at the base of the tray with those at the top. Place the hake steaks on top and return the tray to the oven for 10 minutes, after which the vegetables should be sinking a little, yielding and juicy, and the fish just cooked.

Drizzle the lemon juice and remaining tablespoon of olive oil over the fish and the vegetables, and sprinkle the zest and parsley over the top. Serve immediately with some sourdough or boiled new potatoes to mop up the juices.

RACK OF HOGGET, MINTED BUTTER SAUCE AND CRUNCHY CRUSHED POTATOES

Spring is heralded as a time to eat lamb because this is the time of year that we see new lambs bounding around the countryside.

However, if you put two and two together, you will realise that it's far too soon in the year for these to be eaten; much better to hold out until they've matured on a diet of luscious late spring and early summer grass. When browsing at the butchers, like **Rhug Estate**, look for hogget instead, which is 12–24-month-old sheep, intensely flavoured and a much more satisfying thing to eat (though this method will work well with lamb too). The warm minted butter sauce cuts through the rich, blushing pink meat, and the crushed potatoes are a true crowd pleaser.

SERVES 2–3, DEPENDING ON APPETITE

750g baby salad potatoes
5 tablespoons cold-pressed rapeseed oil
1 x 7-bone rack of hogget (about 600g)

FOR THE MINTED BUTTER SAUCE

40g butter
1 garlic clove, crushed
3 tablespoons water
½ teaspoon red wine vinegar
½ teaspoon Dijon mustard
leaves picked from 15 sprigs of mint,
*   finely chopped*
1 tablespoon brined capers, drained and
*   roughly chopped*

Put the potatoes in a large saucepan of well-salted cold water and bring to the boil over a high heat. Reduce the heat and simmer for 15–20 minutes, until the tip of a knife or prongs of a fork slide easily in.

Preheat the oven to 200C fan/220C/425F/gas mark 7.

Drain the cooked potatoes and leave them to steam for 5 minutes before laying them out on a large baking tray or roasting tin. Use a potato masher or palette knife to gently but firmly flatten the potatoes, without breaking them apart. Slosh them with the rapeseed oil and roast near the top of the oven for 15 minutes, then reduce the oven temperature to 180C fan/200C/400F/gas mark 6 and roast for a further 20–25 minutes.

Once the oven temperature has been reduced, remove the hogget from the fridge and place it skin side down in a heavy-based frying pan or skillet. Cook over a medium heat for 6 minutes, during which time the fat will steadily render into the pan. Brown the ends and sides of the meat for 30 seconds at a time, then roast in the oven (ideally in the same pan if it is ovenproof), skin side up, for 8–10 minutes (depending how pink you like your lamb). Remove and leave the meat to rest for 5 minutes.

While the hogget is resting, make the minted butter sauce. Gently melt the butter in a small saucepan (do not let it brown). Add the garlic and 3 tablespoons water and shake the pan so that the water emulsifies with the butter. Add the vinegar and mustard and shake the pan again so that they emulsify with the sauce, then keep the pan warm until needed.

Cut each chop from the hogget rack using the bones as a guide. Stir the mint and capers into the butter sauce at the last minute and spoon it liberally over the chops, with the crushed potatoes alongside.

POT-ROAST CHICKEN WITH CARROT-TOP PESTO

The chickens Borough Market's butchers sell are high welfare, free-range and slow-growing breeds – and are incomparable in taste and texture to the commercial alternatives. One obvious way to enjoy them is roast on a Sunday (or indeed any day of the week). But it's of little value to prescribe a method for that here because everyone will have their own tried-and-tested way, so there are a couple of recipes in this book which offer alternative ways to use a whole chicken (see pages 115 and 256). In this recipe, the chicken is part wine-poached and steamed, part roast, and then the juices are enhanced by a pesto made from carrot tops. It's an excellent, one-pot meal for springtime, which you could serve with boiled baby potatoes or a green salad, if extra washing up is of no concern.

SERVES 4–6

1 tablespoon cooking oil
200g lardons
4 banana shallots, halved
1 garlic bulb, cut in two through the middle
4 celery sticks, cut into 3
4 sprigs of rosemary
600–800g bunch of young carrots with tops,
*   washed and tops reserved for pesto (below)*
1 chicken (around 1.8kg)
½ lemon
1 x 750ml bottle of riesling

FOR THE PESTO

50g toasted, skinless hazelnuts
40–50g feathery carrot tops
25g basil
juice of ½ lemon
1 small garlic clove
140ml extra-virgin olive oil
30g grated parmesan

A large oval flameproof casserole dish is ideal here, though if you don't have one a high-sided round ovenproof pan will do.

Preheat the oven to 180C fan/200C/400F/gas mark 6.

Put the casserole dish or pan over a medium-high heat and add the cooking oil then the lardons and fry, stirring occasionally, until the lardons are golden and plenty of fat has rendered out. Lay the shallots and the halved garlic bulb cut side down among the lardons, allowing them to colour and soften. Add the celery and 2 sprigs of rosemary to the pan and lay the carrots on top. Stuff the cavity of the chicken with the lemon half and the remaining rosemary and season generously with pepper and salt. Sit the bird on top of the carrots, pour yourself a glass of wine, and pour the rest into the pan around the chicken. Bring to the boil, then place a lid on top and cook in the oven for 30 minutes. Remove the lid and return to the oven for another 30 minutes, or until the chicken is golden and the legs pull away easily.

While the chicken is cooking, put all of the pesto ingredients in a food processor or blender and blitz to a purée. Check for seasoning and add salt, pepper and/or more lemon juice and parmesan as preferred.

Place the cooked chicken on a warm plate or carving board. Remove the legs and sit them skin side up on top of the carrots, leaving the crown to rest. Increase the oven temperature to 200C fan/220C/425F/gas mark 7 and return the pan to the oven for a further 10 minutes.

Transfer the vegetables to a large platter. Put the pan back on a hob and boil fiercely for 2–3 minutes. Meanwhile, cut the breasts from the chicken and slice each breast into three or four pieces, split the thighs from the drumsticks, then lay the meat on the vegetables. Stir 4 tablespoons of pesto through the cooking juices and ladle over the platter, with any excess decanted to a gravy jug.

RHUBARB, ALMOND AND ELDERFLOWER LOAF CAKE

Though not as eye-catching as the forced, bright pink version available earlier in the year, field rhubarb is still a real treat – and one of the few native British fruits (well, technically vegetable) available in spring.

This textured and sticky cake makes the most of it, along with another seasonal flavour, elderflower, and is a fine accompaniment to an afternoon tea. Also consider it as an option for pudding, served slightly re-heated, with Greek yoghurt and perhaps an additional spoonful of stewed rhubarb, if you have it.

SERVES 8

250g field rhubarb (3–4 stalks)
160g golden caster sugar
170g salted butter at room temperature,
    plus extra for greasing
60ml elderflower cordial
2 large eggs (room temperature is best)
70g plain flour, plus extra for dusting
1 teaspoon baking powder
½ teaspoon flaky sea salt
100g ground almonds
60g desiccated coconut
50g fine polenta

Preheat the oven to 170C fan/190C/375F/gas mark 5. Grease a 900g/2lb loaf tin with butter and dust it with plain flour.

Cut the rhubarb so you have three pieces that fit the length of the loaf tin. Sprinkle 30g of the sugar into the base of the greased and flour-dusted tin, then lay those three rhubarb pieces in it. Cut the remaining rhubarb (100–150g) into 1cm pieces.

Cream together the butter and remaining sugar in a stand mixer fitted with a paddle attachment, or in a bowl with an electric whisk, until light and fluffy. Continue beating and add the cordial, then the eggs, one at a time, ensuring each liquid is incorporated before adding the next. Combine the flour, baking powder, salt, ground almonds, desiccated coconut and polenta and tip the mixture in a steady stream into the bowl or mixer, stirring or mixing until thoroughly combined. Stop the mixer or whisk and use a spatula to scrape down any batter from the sides of the mixing bowl, then stir in the rhubarb pieces.

Decant the cake mix into the loaf tin, level out the surface and bake for 1 hour, or until a metal skewer inserted into the middle of the cake comes out clean. The timing might seem lengthy, and the cake will have a little crust, but it is necessary. Allow the cake to rest in the tin for 10 minutes then invert it onto a plate or board. Leave to cool completely before slicing, as it's rather delicate when still warm.

COFFEE CHOCOLATE TART

Many shoppers' first stop on arrival at Borough Market will be for a coffee at one of the carts in Green Market, or the iconic **Monmouth Coffee Company** on the corner of Stoney and Park streets; a caffeine break always feels like a good opportunity to change the mindset from travel logistics to food shopping, calibrate lists with friends, and prepare for the imminent sensory experience.

This dessert is a nod to the busy baristas, with a bold treble hit of espresso underscoring a bitter chocolate filling and cocoa-enriched, shortcrust case. Serve in thin slices with crème fraîche.

SERVES 8–10

FOR THE PASTRY BASE

180g plain flour
150g cold unsalted butter, cubed
30g ground almonds
40g unsweetened cocoa powder
40g icing sugar
pinch of flaky sea salt
1 egg, lightly beaten
2 tablespoons chilled water

FOR THE FILLING

200g dark chocolate (85% cocoa solids),
    broken into chunks
300ml double cream
60ml whole milk
triple espresso (60ml)
3 large eggs
150g golden caster sugar
½ teaspoon flaky sea salt

full-fat crème fraîche, to serve

Start by making the pastry base. Rub together the flour and butter until the mix resembles breadcrumbs – you can do this with your fingertips in a bowl, though it is quicker in a food processor. Add the ground almonds, cocoa powder, icing sugar and salt and mix or pulse until thoroughly combined, then add half the beaten egg and the chilled water and bring the pastry together into a ball. Flatten to form a 2–3cm-thick disc, wrap and refrigerate for 1 hour. After chilling, unwrap the pastry and place it between two large sheets of greaseproof paper then roll it out to a thickness of 3mm. Put it back in the fridge for at least 1 more hour then use it to line a deep, 24cm loose-bottomed tart tin. Chill in the fridge or freezer for 15–20 minutes.

Preheat the oven to 180C fan/200C/400F/gas mark 6.

Line the chilled pastry base with greaseproof paper, fill with baking beans or a dried pulse, and bake on the middle shelf of the oven for 10 minutes. Lift the greaseproof paper and its contents from the pastry and bake the pastry for a further 10 minutes. Reduce the oven temperature to 120C fan/140C/275F/gas mark 1. Brush the baked pastry case with the remaining beaten egg and place in the cooling oven for 3 minutes – this will help prevent the base from becoming soggy once filled – then remove from the oven.

You can start to make the filling while the tart case is baking. Place a heatproof bowl over a saucepan of simmering water, making sure the base of the bowl isn't touching the water. Add the chocolate to the bowl and leave it to melt without stirring. Remove the pan from the heat once melted and set aside (leaving the bowl over the warm water). Put the cream, milk and coffee in a saucepan and bring to the boil then turn off the heat.

Whisk the eggs and the sugar together in a large mixing bowl until light and fluffy. Pour a splash of the hot cream mixture onto the eggs. Beat, then gradually pour the remaining hot cream over the eggs to make a custard. Scrape in the melted chocolate and add the salt. Beat until the custard is smooth and silky (it may seem grainy to begin with but will come together). Set aside until the tart shell is blind baked, covered with a piece of baking parchment to prevent a skin forming.

Once the oven is at the right temperature, place the pastry case on a baking sheet, pour in the custard and bake for 25–35 minutes until it most of the filling is set, with a slight wobble in the very centre. Remove from the oven and leave to cool to room temperature before cutting into portions and serving with crème fraîche.

MANGO AND PASSION FRUIT POSSET

This posset provides another way to enjoy the remarkable Indian mangoes that arrive at Borough Market's greengrocers and elsewhere in late spring (see page 33).

It's one of those easy-to-do puddings, that can (and should) be made in advance, and that will have your fellow diners cooing. The mellow and honeyed sweet flavour pairs particularly well with the sharpness of passion fruit, and the flavours of both fruits are even more enjoyable if served with a buttery biscuit (such as the ginger butter biscuits on page 195) or tuile.

SERVES 6

juice of 1 lemon
6 passion fruit
600ml double cream
150g caster sugar, plus 1 tablespoon
1 fresh ripe mango (350–450g)
juice of ½ lime

Put the lemon juice and seeds, flesh and juice from 5 of the passion fruit in a pan and heat gently for 2 minutes, then strain through a sieve into a bowl, pushing all the flavour through with the back of a spoon. Set the juice aside and discard the seeds.

Combine the cream and 150g sugar in a high-sided heavy-based saucepan. Place over a low-medium heat, stirring to dissolve the sugar, then increase the heat a little, gradually bringing the cream to a boil. Let it boil for 2 minutes (the cream will rise significantly, so watch to check it does not spill over), then remove from the heat. Add the lemon and passion fruit juice, stir and leave to cool to room temperature.

Cut the mango flesh away from its stone and skin. Put the flesh in a blender or food processor with the tablespoon of sugar and the lime juice, then blitz to a purée.

Put a teaspoon of mango purée into the bottom of 6 small ramekins or coffee cups (you should have some purée left over). Pour the cream into the cups, slowly so as not to disturb the purée too much. Cover and refrigerate for 3 hours or more to allow it to set. Top each of the possets with the remaining mango purée and the flesh and seeds of the remaining passion fruit divided between each of the possets, and serve.

BASIL VODKA SMASH

This is pretty much what it says on the tin – smashed basil and vodka – though there's also lime and sugar syrup to sweeten and sharpen things just a little. It feels refreshing and sophisticated, and its herbal nature seems to suit the season.

The cocktail works whether for one or in bulk so two methods are provided.

FOR THE SUGAR SYRUP *(8–10 SERVINGS)*
40g caster sugar
60ml water

Combine the sugar and water in a pan and heat gently, stirring until the sugar has completely dissolved. Remove from the heat, leave to cool, then store in the fridge in an airtight container.

1 SERVING
8 large basil leaves, plus extra to serve
½ lime
15ml sugar syrup
50ml vodka

ice cubes
soda water, to serve

Put the basil and lime in a cocktail shaker and use a wooden stick to prod and bash the lime and basil, squeezing the juice from the lime and releasing the basil's oils.

Add the sugar syrup and vodka and fill the shaker with 4 or 5 ice cubes. Place the lid on top, and shake for 30 seconds.

Strain through a fine sieve into a low ball glass. Add 3 ice cubes and a basil leaf and top with a dash of soda water.

10 SERVINGS
50g bunch of basil, including stems,
*   plus extra to serve*
juice of 5 limes
500ml vodka
80ml sugar syrup

1kg ice cubes
soda water, to serve

Put all the ingredients, except for the ice cubes and soda water, in a blender. Pulse for 1–2 seconds 3 or 4 times, then add 15 ice cubes. Pulse 2 more times, then strain the cocktail through a fine sieve into a serving jug (if necessary, repeat the straining so the liquid is clear).

Store in the fridge for up to 2 hours, then serve by dividing between low ball glasses already loaded with ice and another basil leaf or 2. Top each glass with a dash of soda water.

TACKLING WASTE

As Britain's highest-profile food market, Borough Market has a platform to promote alternatives to mainstream methods of food production and consumption. There's a real drive to ensure that 'no waste' and 'sustainable' are practical approaches to everyday life, not just buzz words.

The Market participates in a scheme run by the charity Plan Zheroes, where every Saturday and Wednesday, volunteers collect surplus produce and redistribute it to charities across London. All remaining food waste is sent to an anaerobic digestion plant where it's turned into power, fertiliser and water. Every single piece of packaging provided by our traders aims to be bio-degradable and compostable: bags, plates, cups, straws and every piece of cutlery.

Borough Market's concern goes beyond what happens with waste. Sustainability is a concept that touches every stage of the food cycle, from field to fork. A key driver for the tasting panel who help in the selection process for traders at Borough Market is the provenance and sustainability of the product they sell. It's no coincidence that the largest number of Slow Food-accredited traders in one location in Europe can be found under the railway arches here, while the likes of Gourmet Goat go out of their way to look at waste in a new light,

preferring to see opportunity for their hot food offer where others see surplus; whether that's through championing high welfare kid goat and rose veal, or purchasing excess vegetables from other Market traders.

What can we do at home? Produce markets provide an opportunity to shop and cook more sustainably. We can pick and choose ingredients in a way that is just not possible in the supermarkets: by asking specific questions about provenance and production methods, and buying only what we need and want, rather than what has already been packed and portioned. On which note, market shopping massively reduces the amount of plastic, polystyrene and cardboard in your recycling bin.

• Look out for resourceful practices within this book's recipes:

| Bread – use old loaves as croutons in salads and tray bakes; soak in custard for bread puddings; or turn into crumbs to add crunch.

| Vegetables – roast or fry root-vegetable peelings for snacks, chips and croutons; make the most of the stems and outer leaves of vegetables like cauliflower and broccoli; pickle and preserve whether you've a glut, or a small surplus; use pickling liquor in dressings.

| Herbs – use stems in broths and stocks; mix and match where small quantities are required, rather than buying new bunches; infuse oils with excess stems.

| Fruit – pickle and preserve; turn cooking juices into cordials and syrups.

| Eggs – if a main course requires yolks, make a dessert or drink with the whites (and vice versa).

| Dairy – use ends of cheese for extra flavour in soups and pastas; cream, yoghurt and crème fraîche are often interchangeable when small amounts are required.

| Fish – use bones to make stock; keep up to date with sustainability issues affecting fisheries.

| Meat – value provenance; enjoy all of an animal, not just the prime cuts; turn bones into stock; use leftovers as the basis for your next meal.

Through the introductions and methods in this book, you'll find numerous tips encouraging resourceful cooking – whether that's using unusual cuts or all of an animal, or ensuring absolutely everything you've bought is used up. When food has been produced and then cooked with love, why would you waste it?

AT HOME

• Buy only what you need, avoiding plastic where possible.

• Don't feel restricted by the precise detail of recipes. Experiment, adapt and swap ingredients to suit what you have.

• Make the most of leftovers and surplus ingredients. Don't view them as potential waste; instead make them the inspiration for your next meal.

THE CHEESEMONGERS

*There are more than twenty cheesemongers
and dairies based at Borough Market,
presenting an unparalleled selection of
dairy products. A number of the traders
gather milk and make the cheese that they
sell: Hook & Son, Alsop & Walker, The
Bath Soft Cheese Co., Trethowan's Dairy
and Blackwoods Cheese Company. Others
specialise in importing exceptional cheeses:
Borough Cheese Company, The Parma Ham
and Mozzarella Stand, L'Ubriaco Drunk
Cheese, Bianca Mora and the Ham & Cheese
Company, for example. Others, like Jumi
Cheese and Neal's Yard Dairy, represent a
variety of farmhouse cheeses from producers
they work with closely. Jon Thrupp's Mons
Cheesemongers is similar, representing
lesser-known producers and cheeses from
Switzerland and France.*

JON THRUPP, MONS CHEESEMONGERS

Having worked at and managed the Neal's Yard
Dairy shop between 2001 and 2005, I decided
to use 2006 to conceive of my own business.
I worked in the production of St James cheese
with Martin Gott in Cumbria and travelled
to the Loire in France, to spend time with the
affineur Hervé Mons. Hervé's father founded
this inspiring cheese company in the 1960s,
when he began sourcing artisanal varieties
from his native region of the Auvergne,
maturing them in tunnels and selling them at
local markets and to restaurants. I wondered
whether I could set up a British arm of Mons,
importing some of that cheese, and applied to
Borough Market for a stall. We started trading
in December that year.

We specialise in traditionally made French
and Swiss cheeses, ripened in cellars and
tunnels in St Haon-le-Châtel on the Côte
Roannaise. There are twenty-five to thirty-five
cheeses on the Borough stall at any one time,
depending on the time of year, and we offer
another fifty or so cheeses to our wholesale
customers. Some of the cheeses we sell at the
Market are the big names that people recognise
– blockbusters like Comté, Roquefort and
Vacherin Mont d'Or. To my mind we offer the
very best example of those varieties in their
peak condition. But I'm particularly interested
in representing producers of the cheeses that
are lesser-known in Britain – things like the
tommes, Cantal, Laguiole, St Nectaire and
Salers. I like presenting a diversity of flavour.
Some cheeses have a subtle, complex profile
that doesn't hit the customer immediately;
it's our job to help people discover and
appreciate them.

The moment you get into any form of food
that has been semi-processed before you sell
it, and that is of a perishable nature, then
it's a whole new gamut of retail. It's not like

to react to all of this every time they make cheese, responding with differing amounts of rennet, starter cultures and so on. It's not straightforward. All that impacts on how cheeses ultimately taste, whether that's in a week or so for the fresh cheeses, or eighteen months later for the aged ones. Cheeses made in late springtime will have benefited from all those emerging wild flowers and the luscious grass, so may well reap the benefit when they mature. Some farmhouse cheeses have a particular season, too, with something like the Bûchette de Manon goat cheese only being available March to October.

In Britain everyone goes mad for cheese at Christmas. I suppose vacherin is our stilton, in that people flock to it then more than ever, and that we have to say to people is for life, not just the festivities. Personally, I think we should make some changes to align our cheese-eating habits with the French and Italians, to think of it as a legitimate and delicious source of protein, rather than a treat. And buy large pieces that keep well and eat them over a few days, rather than thin pieces that won't survive more than a night; it's a real shame to discard oxidised cheeses. Try to revolve meals and dishes around what you find, that sort of thing.

Still, I'm grateful that our customers are adventurous. We've plenty of regulars who get excited when there are new things on the table. And it all comes back to the fact that we're here to represent the less obvious cheeses and regions. That's true of many of the cheesemongers at Borough. Neal's Yard Dairy in particular were instrumental in developing a structure that encourages the customer to taste and experience the flavour and value of a product, and allow them an opportunity to pause and choose whether to invest in this, the most affordable of luxuries. I think Borough kicked off a whole wave of food markets around London and all over the country, promoted a different kind of shopping, and is an example that people's buying and eating habits can change.

watching people try jumpers on and re-folding the ones that don't sell. We import, ripen, mature and explain. We gauge and check whether things are on track in terms of the taste profile that we and the producers want by the time it gets to the customer. Logistics are complicated, and the fresh cheeses are particularly tricky – something fresh like Cathare needs to go out within a week of receiving it. We need to make sure that our cheeses taste as they should, rather than the kind of thing that puts hairs on your chest.

Artisanal cheeses change all the time. That's part of their appeal. Cows, sheep and goats feed on different grass depending on the time of year, particularly in the Alps when they're moved to higher and higher altitudes as the snow melts; different milk is produced depending on the age of the young; external temperatures change, and a cheesemaker has

COMTÉ SOUFFLÉ

Comté is one of the more prominent cheeses at the Market, due to the presence of both the **Borough Cheese Company**, who have been importing this French mountain cheese as a key feature of their range since 2003, choosing specific wheels on the basis of their layered, nutty flavour profiles, and **The French Comté**, whose characterful, sweet Comté of various stages of maturity sit alongside other artisanal products from the Jura region.

Undoubtedly, Comté should be enjoyed unadulterated, perhaps with a glass of distinctive Jura vin jaune. It can, however, also be considered as an ingredient for dishes such as a classic cheese soufflé.

Soufflés have the stigma of being difficult and cheffy. They're not really. And in any event, when in sharing format, a soufflé seems less pressured and showy, and instead is the basis of a rustic and convivial lunch or supper. It's perhaps helpful to consider the preparation of a soufflé as two stages: the béchamel base and the whisked egg whites. You can make the béchamel in advance if you wish, whisking and adding the whites shortly before you plan to eat.

Serve with crusty bread and green salad.

SERVES 4

380ml whole milk
80g butter
65g plain flour
1 heaped teaspoon Dijon mustard
150g aged Comté, grated
¼ nutmeg
5 large eggs, separated

TO SERVE

crusty bread
well-dressed green salad

Ideally, you will have a straight sided, deep soufflé dish, 17cm in diameter (though the recipe will still work if your dish is a centimetre or two either way).

Gently heat the milk in a small saucepan to warm it through.

Melt 15g of the butter and use it to coat the insides of the soufflé dish. Rumour has it that if you use a brush and apply the butter in vertical stripes, the rise will be regimented.

Melt the remaining butter in a heavy-based saucepan over a medium heat. Add the flour and cook for 3 minutes, stirring continuously. Add the warm milk a ladle at a time, stirring continuously until the liquid is fully incorporated before adding another ladleful. Simmer for a few minutes until the sauce is quite thick and you can't taste raw flour. Add the mustard, cheese, a good dusting of freshly grated nutmeg and plenty of grinds of the pepper mill. Mix well, then remove from the heat and leave to cool for 10 minutes before stirring in the egg yolks. (If you're making this soufflé base in advance and chilling it, it will need to be gently reheated to loosen it a little before the next stage.)

Preheat the oven to 170C fan/190C/375F/gas mark 5.

Whisk the egg whites until they just reach stiff peak stage. Stir in one third of the whites to the cheese base then fold in the rest of the whites in slow but deliberate and confident swoops with a metal spoon, so the mixture retains as much air as possible. Decant this into the soufflé dish and run a thumb around the edge to leave a gap of about 1cm between the soufflé mixture and the dish. Place in the middle of the oven and bake for 40–45 minutes, removing the soufflé when it has puffed up and is golden with a slight wobble in the middle.

Serve immediately and don't worry if it sinks – the taste remains the same.

BLUE CHEESE AND SWEET POTATO GNOCCHI

Though it might seem implausible to some, occasionally the end of a hard-ish blue cheese, like a Bath Blue from **The Bath Soft Cheese Co.**, Torino from **Bianca Mora** or Fourme d'Ambert from **Une Normande à Londres** is lost to the back of the fridge. Perhaps guests have cut the nose off the rest of it, or you put yourself on a cheese moratorium after over-indulging. This can be galling, not least because you took the time and effort to taste and pick that exact cheese from a taxing range of options (it's a hard task, but someone has to do it). The blue-veined nugget can still be used though, for example as the spark for something like gnocchi.

SERVES 4

700g sweet potatoes
30g finely grated parmesan, plus extra to serve
1 large egg yolk
200g '00' flour, plus extra for dusting
about 70g blue cheese, crumbled (stilton,
    Torino, Fourme d'Ambert, Bath Blue)
semolina, for dusting (optional)
60g butter
200g spinach, trimmed
1 garlic clove, finely sliced
⅕ nutmeg, finely grated
40g toasted hazelnuts, roughly chopped

Heat the oven to 180C fan/200C/400F/gas mark 6 and bake the sweet potatoes for 1 hour. Remove the potatoes from the oven and leave them to cool for 10 minutes. Slice open and scrape the flesh into a large mixing bowl – you should have 400–500g (you will need to add a little more flour if there is more). Whip it to a smooth paste with a wooden spoon then leave to cool. (For a snack, drizzle the leftover potato skins with a little olive oil and return them to the oven on a baking tray for 10–15 minutes. Serve warm, seasoned with flaky sea salt.)

Stir the parmesan and egg yolk into the mash, then add two thirds of the flour. Add more flour until it's quite smooth, dry and comes away from the bowl easily. Stir the blue cheese in, so it's evenly distributed. Turn the dough out onto a lightly floured surface and divide it into 6 pieces. Taking one piece, use the base of your hand to knead it a little then pat it into a cylinder, before rolling it out into a long log about the thickness of your thumb. Cut the log into 3cm lengths and lightly press on each with the prongs of a fork, then squidge the gnocchi back into their original size and place on a tray dusted with flour or semolina. Cover with a clean tea towel and refrigerate until required. Repeat with the remaining dough.

Bring a large saucepan of salted water to the boil and cook the gnocchi in the boiling water for 2–3 minutes (in batches if necessary). If prodded, they will float to the surface when cooked. Drain well.

Meanwhile, melt 20g of the butter in a wide saucepan, add the spinach and garlic and cook until wilted. Season generously with nutmeg, salt and black pepper, then divide between warm bowls or plates. Return the pan to the hob, turn the heat up and add the remaining butter. When the foaming butter calms and smells nutty, add the hazelnuts and turn the heat off. Tip the well-drained gnocchi into the pan, roll to coat in the butter and allow to colour a little. Divide between the plates, pouring any butter from the pan over the top. Serve with more parmesan and black pepper.

BUTTERMILK AND PORTER SODA BREAD

Buttermilk is the liquid left over after churning butter from cultured or fermented cream. It's acidic, due to lactic acid increasing through the process, and this acidity makes it useful when it comes to cooking. For example, it reacts with bicarbonate of soda to create bubbles of carbon dioxide, thus helping soda bread to rise. You can buy buttermilk from **Hook & Son, Kappacasein Dairy** and other dairy stalls at the Market.

Results will be best if you can use a small casserole dish or Dutch oven to bake the bread. And if Borough Market's annual brew using hops grown in the Market Hall is a dark porter, use this to ensure a rich, chocolatey taste. It's ideal served with soups (pages 27, 209 and 227), smoked fish (24 and 244), cured meats and more.

SERVES 8

330ml bottle of porter beer (or a stout)
450g light malthouse flour, plus extra for dusting
1 heaped teaspoon flaky sea salt
1 heaped teaspoon bicarbonate of soda
50g dark muscovado sugar
250ml buttermilk

Preheat the oven to 200C fan/220C/425F/gas mark 7.

Put a small (16–18cm) cast-iron casserole dish with its lid in the hot oven for at least 10 minutes.

Pour 130ml of the beer into a chilled glass and enjoy it at your leisure.

Put the dry ingredients in a large bowl and mix well. Make a well in the middle and pour the beer and buttermilk into the well. Stir to create a wet dough, than scrape the dough out onto a lightly floured surface. Knead the dough for just a minute, then shape it into a compact round loaf to fit inside your casserole dish.

Remove the hot casserole dish from the oven and take the lid off. Quickly dust the inside with flour, then carefully drop in the dough. Place the lid on top and bake in the oven for 50 minutes, by which time the top should be crisp and brown and bottom hollow sounding if you tap it. Remove from the oven and let the bread sit in the casserole dish for 5 minutes, before turning it out onto a wire rack and leaving it to cool for at least 30 minutes.

Soda bread is best eaten on the day you make it, ideally served warm. If making it in advance, reheat it at around 140C fan/160C/325F/gas mark 3 for up to 15 minutes before slicing.

BLUEBERRY AND YOGHURT ICED LOLLIES

It's a late spring and early summer treat to lock the goodness of quality yoghurt from the likes of **Mons Cheesemongers** and **Hook & Son** into virtually no-hassle iced lollies.

If that yoghurt is flavoured and rippled with blueberries and mellowed by good honey, they will certainly be welcomed in April and May, when balmy days are surprisingly common. You could continue making them through summer too, swapping blueberries for blackcurrants, blackberries, raspberries, loganberries, strawberries, or whatever berries are on offer at your local market.

MAKES **6–8**

250g fresh blueberries
juice of ½ lime
300g thick yoghurt
2 tablespoons runny honey

You will need 6–8 ice lolly moulds and sticks.

Put 200g of the blueberries, the lime juice, yoghurt and honey in a blender or food processor and blitz until completely smooth. Taste and consider adding a little more honey or lime if you think it needs sweetening or sharpening, then scatter the whole blueberries through the mix.

Carefully transfer the blueberry mixture into your iced lolly holders – you may find a funnel helps. Add the sticks and freeze for at least 8 hours.

GOAT'S CHEESECAKE, REDCURRANTS AND PISTACHIO CRUMB

Goat's milk and goat's cheese are well represented at Borough Market, with fresh and hard cheeses from all over Europe and Britain, and many flavours of ice cream courtesy of **Greedy Goat**.

This dessert is akin to a build-your-own cheesecake, where sharp and tangy fresh goat's cheese is sweetened and rounded by floral honey, and joined by tart redcurrants and a calming, green pistachio crumb.

SERVES 6

100g shelled unsalted pistachios
40g plain flour
25g caster sugar
50g salted butter, melted
30g icing sugar
200g soft, fresh goat's cheese (chèvre)
230ml double cream
60g runny honey (something floral)
seeds from 1 vanilla pod
1 punnet of fresh redcurrants

Start by making the pistachio crumb. Preheat the oven to 120C fan/140C/275F/gas mark 1. Put 80g of the pistachios, all the flour and caster sugar into a food processor and pulse until the mixture resembles breadcrumbs. Combine with the melted butter, then use a fork to spread the crumbs out in the baking tray – they should be about 50 per cent loose, 50 per cent packed into tight clusters. Bake for 45 minutes–1 hour until dry and firm. Remove from the oven and leave to cool, then mix the crumb with the remaining whole pistachios and store in an airtight container until required (these will keep well for a few days at least).

Put the icing sugar and goat's cheese in a bowl and use a spatula to beat until smooth. Add half the cream and whip this into the mix, then the second half, together with 30g of the honey and the vanilla seeds. Beat until well combined and thick. Refrigerate for at least 30 minutes.

Encourage everyone to build their own cheesecake, beginning with a heavy spoon or two of the cream-cheese mix, then drizzling with honey and scattering with redcurrants and a few spoons each of pistachio crumb.

MARKET EVENTS

ST GEORGE'S DAY
AT BOROUGH MARKET

Though 23 April is marked as the national day of England's patron saint, St George, there are seemingly no established customs, beyond the occasional wave of a flag or rose. Over recent years Borough Market has taken it upon itself to change that, with the Sunday closest to the saintly feast now reserved as a festival of English meat: of sustainable farming, responsible husbandry, skilled butchery and savvy cooking. In the Market Hall, chefs promote nose-to-tail cooking – an ethos that urges we respect and enjoy all of an animal – and the Market's butchers and cured-meat specialists show off dry-aged heritage meats, locally made salamis and whole air-dried muscles that stand shoulder-to-shoulder with the best in the world.

Yet St George stands for much more than carnivorous ventures, and for more than England, too – numerous other countries and regions claim patronage of the man, from his

birthplace of Palestine, through Aragon and Catalonia in Spain, to Malta, Ethiopia and beyond.

Being global in its outlook and indeed its make-up of traders and produce, it comes as little surprise that Borough uses the occasion to embrace St George's multinational fame. The Market's twin, La Boqueria in Barcelona, embraces the same saint, and many of their customs and traditions are staged on the day. In addition to those events shared with Barcelona, Borough welcomes local theatre company, the Lions part, and its St George and the Dragon play. Traditional Morris dancers compare their routines with contemporary group Folk Dance Remixed and their modern interpretation of the maypole dance; the high point of the day comes when the Castellers of London build knee-knocking human towers four or five layers tall.

It's a typical Borough Market event: fun, bustling, irreverent but also educational. There's face painting, medieval costumes, celebratory bakes and plenty of fresh produce for shoppers. It's an awakening of the senses, convivial, and full of theatre and food.

St George of Lydda was a Roman soldier who was executed in AD 303 for refusing to renounce his Christian faith; an event which saw him honoured as a martyr. He was canonised in the fifth century and became venerated in the west during the Middle Ages, with 23 April, the date of his death, recognised as a feast day. The English took a particular shine to the saint, regarding him a special protector, and wearing and waving the flag of St George in battle. Henry V famously invoked his spirit in a stirring speech at Agincourt, and over time George was affirmed as England's sole patron saint. However, his feast day is observed by numerous other Christian cultures, and he is celebrated as a patron saint of many other countries and regions, including Portugal, Georgia, Malta, Lithuania, Palestine, Aragon, and Catalonia, not to mention the Scouts, butchers, shepherds, farmers, saddle makers and soldiers. It has been suggested that his slaying of a princess-stealing dragon with a penchant for lamb is something of a myth.

THE CHARCUTIERS

During a visit to Borough Market, those with a craving for charcuterie can curate platters of world-class, air-dried sausages and sliced meats from right across Europe.

There is French saucisson sec, ventrèche and Jésus du Pays Basque courtesy of Une Normande à Londres, The French Comté and The Ham & Cheese Company; the finest Spanish jamón at Brindisa Ltd; and incredible Italian salumi thanks to Bianca Mora, De Calabria, The Parma Ham and Mozzarella Stand, Alpine Deli and Gastronomica.

Other territories perhaps less well-known for their curing traditions are represented too, including chorizo-style meats from Taste Croatia, and a wide variety of small salamis and sliced meats from the burgeoning British cured meat industry, which is represented at the Market by Cannon & Cannon.

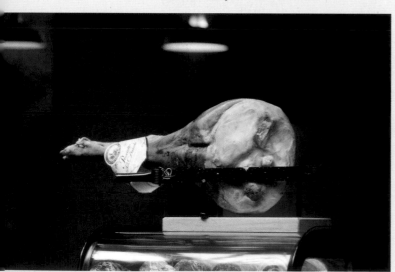

SEAN CANNON, CANNON & CANNON

Charcuterie has always been my favourite thing to eat – since I was a child holidaying in Spain, really – so to find it being produced here in the UK was exciting. My brother and I had been rounding up produce from north Norfolk and taking it to local farmers' markets in that part of the world, when we stumbled across Ian and Sue Whitehead, who were making salami from their own pigs in Suffolk. I was really taken with their passion for the product, but also the husbandry behind it – well-treated, slow-growing animals, small scale, sustainable and so on – and lightbulbs started going off. We found there were fifteen, maybe twenty commercial producers of air-dried, British cured meat, but people didn't really know about them, or indeed that anyone was doing this sort of thing. I thought there might be an opportunity to promote these artisans and their new industry, and to take the products to market. Literally.

Borough seemed the obvious place for us to try and start doing this. It's the hub and beating heart of the British food scene, a place where British and international traders mingle with enthusiastic foodies. Acting on the advice of the Market's tasting panel, we managed to source a selection of produce – probably about eight sausages – and we just went from there. It's been six years now, and things have just grown and grown: the number of products we sell at the stall is about thirty-five (though not all at the same time) and we've a wide-ranging wholesale business which distributes amazing British cured meats across the country. Maybe more interestingly, the British cured-meat scene just keeps growing and growing. There are over 100 producers now, and people don't seem so surprised any more when we tell them that, say, this air-dried beef is from Wales, that fennel salami is from Kent, the coppa is from

Cornwall, the lardo is made locally in Hackney and that venison chorizo up in Scotland!

Maybe curing is not ingrained in our culture like it is in France, Spain, Germany and so on. But then that allows our producers to try unusual combinations, and they also create things that are truly British. I believe our biggest advantage is that the best producers, the ones we represent, use only amazing heritage breeds, farmed ethically, sustainably, slowly. The British Isles farms the best meat in the world.

That said, I still love and adore charcuterie from elsewhere and it's so good that if you come to Borough, within a few metres of each other there's the world's finest prosciutto being sliced to order, rare Basque charcuterie and country ham made from Noir de Bigorre pigs, Tyrolian speck, Jamón Ibérico de Bellota, and then fully cured sausages and air-dried muscles cured in London! It's fantastic. The variety ensures that what we do is up to standard, too.

Curing arose from a need to make fresh meat last and provide protein in the inclement months. Technology and breeding seasons are different now, but there's still an element of seasonality to this type of food; some things like our game salamis only get made in the autumn to late winter. Also, animals do taste different depending on what they've been eating, which might change through the year, and the product we receive varies as a result. I like that. I honestly think I once tasted a bit of dandelion in a piece of air-dried mutton – though I had had a couple of glasses of wine, so might be wrong. You have different cravings in different months too. So in late spring, when we start to creep towards summer again, I like things such as lighter pork loin instead of air-dried beef, or something fresh-tasting like our veal, lemon and thyme salami from Monmouthshire.

It's really important that places like Borough Market provide a window onto the whole of the food cycle. People – kids – can come here and walk around the Market, see pheasants and rabbits in their feather and fur, animal carcasses, whole fish, raw milk, vegetables and fruits that aren't in plastic, as well as the resulting cured meats, cheeses, condiments and bread made from scratch that morning. People can be hands-on, too: in the demo kitchens, at Bread Ahead Bakery & School, or on courses run by other traders. I'm really pleased we can do that. Borough Market works very hard to ensure that it's reminding people where food comes from and how seriously we are in danger of losing our connection back to farm and field.

HAM AND HONEY BUTTER WITH RADISHES

As with cheese, the concept of 'leftover' air-dried meat seems an unlikely one, but it does occasionally happen, apparently (see page 60).

One way to use surplus slices of meat, which have perhaps been left uncovered on a board for longer than is optimal, is to blitz them up in a food processor with butter and a little honey. Spread this on toast, or arguably better still, serve it as something in which to dip colourful heritage or peppery breakfast radishes.

Many types of charcuterie would work in this scenario, provided they're intensely flavoured. Spanish jamón ibérico, serrano and presa, Italian coppa and prosciutto, and Tyrolean speck are all pork-based and ideal. Consider beefy varieties like bresaola and cecina, too.

SERVES 4–6

20–30g air-dried ham, roughly chopped
150g butter at room temperature
1 tablespoon runny honey
bunch of heritage colour radishes or French
*   breakfast radishes*

Put the ham in a food processor (this will not require much capacity, so if you have a mini processor or mini processor attachment, use that). Pulse a couple of times to help break down the ham, then add the butter and honey and pulse until smooth. Transfer to a small bowl and chill until required, though serve at room temperature.

Wash the radishes thoroughly. Plunge the radishes and their leaves into a bowl of cold water then lift the radishes out, drain and refill the bowl with cold water. Repeat until no sand or grit remains. Drain the radishes and spread them out on kitchen paper (or a clean towel or cloth) to dry for 20 minutes (but not for too long as the leaves will become limp).

Encourage everyone to take a decent smear of ham butter with each radish, and to enjoy the peppery leaves too.

COPPA, ROCKET AND DEEP-FRIED CAPERS

Coppa stands next to jamón and the best prosciutto as one of the finest types of cured meat. Made using the crimson-coloured, hard-working muscle from the base of a pig's neck, the end result is always intensely flavoured and marbled with moreish creamy fat.

This simple salad to share as a starter doesn't do much more than show the meat off, though there is a pleasingly crisp, salty twist thanks to the deep-fried capers.

MAKES A PLATTER FOR 4–6

60g brined capers
100g coppa, thinly sliced
2 tablespoons extra-virgin olive oil
2 teaspoons balsamic vinegar
100g rocket
400ml vegetable oil

Drain the capers, rinse, then drain again. Lay them out in one layer on a sheet of kitchen paper to dry for at least 1 hour.

Arrange the coppa on a large platter. Pinch the slices as you lay them on the plate, to create a bit of texture and to make them easier to scoop up.

Make a dressing in a large bowl by mixing the oil, vinegar and lots of freshly ground black pepper (there's no need for salt as the meat and capers provide plenty of that). Have the rocket to hand, but don't toss it in the dressing until the capers are ready.

Shortly before eating, put the vegetable oil in a wok over a medium-high heat. Prepare a tray or plate lined with clean kitchen paper. Allow the oil to reach 170C (if you don't have a thermometer, test the heat by dropping one caper into the wok; if it bubbles and fries, it's good to go). Don't add the capers all at once as the temperature of the oil will drop too low – instead, fry them in 2 or 3 batches, removing them once they have split and flowered and the oil stops bubbling (this will take 2–3 minutes). Remove with a slotted spoon and transfer to the kitchen paper to absorb some of the oil.

Toss the rocket in the dressing and arrange it in clumps over and around the coppa. Scatter the warm, crisp capers over the top and serve.

CURED FAT SWEET MUSTARD POTATOES

Cured fat is a vital part of a good slice of jamón, a silky handkerchief of prosciutto, or soft chunk of salami – it ensures the mouthfeel is luscious and adds a great deal of flavour too. In fact, many aficionados go the whole hog and seek things like lardo or salo (cured back fat) and pancetta and ventrèche (belly), which have barely a hint of meat on them. These marble-coloured hunks of fat look unapproachable until sliced thinly and served at body temperature, when suddenly they're a smooth, sensual, gently porky bite. Even better, allow them to melt in the residual heat of hot toast or over warm vegetables, thereby becoming the ultimate seasoning.

SERVES 6 AS A SIDE, 4 AS A STARTER

600g baby potatoes
80g cured fat, for example pancetta,
*   ventrèche or lardo, thinly sliced*
1 tablespoon wholegrain mustard
1 teaspoon runny honey
½ teaspoon balsamic vinegar
1 tablespoon extra-virgin olive oil
40g rocket

Put the potatoes in a saucepan of well-salted cold water and bring to the boil over a high heat. Reduce the heat and simmer for 15–20 minutes or until the tip of a knife or prongs of a fork slide easily in.

About 10 minutes after the pan of potatoes has reached a simmer, remove the fatty cured meat from the fridge and cut each length to pieces around 8cm long (or thereabouts). If you have a rolled piece of pancetta, you will need to unravel the slices first.

When tender, drain the potatoes and immediately return them to the warm pan with a tablespoon's worth of cooking water. Add the mustard, honey and balsamic vinegar, olive oil and four or five turns of the pepper mill. Tumble the potatoes around the pan so that they become glossy, then add the rocket and allow it to wilt for 20–30 seconds. Divide into soup or pasta bowls and drape the cured fat on top. Try to ensure almost all of it is touching a hot potato.

Serve within a few minutes, watching the fat melt into ghostly shrouds over the potatoes.

'NDUJA, MOZZARELLA AND GREENS ON TOAST

'Nduja is a fully cured yet spreadable salumi from Calabria, Italy. There is some meat in there, from the shoulder and belly, but mostly fat and roasted hot red chillies, which give it a distinctive bright red colour and fiery yet sweet taste. It's addictive, and is typically spread on crackers or bread, or melted into a ragu or onto hot toast.

This dish does the latter, and is a great example of a quick lunch or supper for two that uses market produce - quality cured meat, some dairy, and seasonal greens. Ensure all components are prepared before you start cooking as the assembly should be quick in order for the 'nduja to melt.

There is authentic Calabrian 'nduja at the Market, courtesy of **De Calabria**, as well as British-made versions. Spanish sobrasada is a non-spicy alternative, where the redness comes from pimentón (paprika) rather than chillies.

SERVES 2

300g cime di rapa, purple sprouting broccoli,
    rainbow chard or cavolo nero
3 tablespoons olive oil, plus extra for drizzling
finely grated zest and juice of 1 lemon
1 teaspoon caster sugar
2 thick slices of sourdough
125g mozzarella
50g 'nduja
chive flowers, to garnish (optional)

Prepare the greens first. If using cime di rapa or rainbow chard, chop the stems into 4cm lengths up to the leafy part, then cut through the leaves 2–3 times. Keep the stems and the leaves separate. If using cavolo nero, strip the leaves from the woody stems, discard the stems and split the leaves in 2 lengthways. If you're using purple sprouting broccoli, trim the leaves from the florets and cut the widest stems to a similar size as the smallest.

Make a dressing in a medium-large bowl by whisking together the olive oil, lemon juice and sugar, and adding a generous pinch or two of flaky sea salt and a few grinds of the pepper mill.

Bring a saucepan of salted water to the boil. Toast the bread until it's crisp and fully browned. Drain the mozzarella from any water it is standing in and tear it in half.

When the water is boiling and everything else nearly ready, add any stems and cook for 90 seconds, then add the leaves and cook for up to 1 minute more. Drain completely – to avoid soggy toast – then transfer to the bowl with the dressing and mix well.

Spread the 'nduja immediately after the toast is taken from the toaster. Top with torn chunks of mozzarella, sprinkle with the lemon zest and some freshly ground black pepper, then add the greens, avoiding dripping any liquid on the toast. Drizzle with an additional glug of olive oil and serve immediately.

CARLIN PEA, SALAMI AND CHICORY SALAD

There are a number of different styles of salami available at the Market. Any will work in this salad, whether it's a classic Spanish chorizo, **Taste Croatia**'s version, or Jésus du Pays Basque from **The Ham & Cheese Company**. That said, an Italian finocchiona (pork and fennel seed) is particularly good. Carlin 'black badger' peas are a British grain alternative to a chickpea, often stocked in **Spice Mountain**, and you can buy a tinned pre-cooked version online. Chickpeas work perfectly well as an alternative.

This salad keeps well if made in advance, so is a good feasting dish. But it is also particularly agreeable when served warm, and shared between two people with crusty bread in one hand and a glass of red wine in the other.

SERVES 2–6, DEPENDING ON WHETHER YOU SERVE IT AS AN INDIVIDUAL SALAD OR A GRAZING PLATTER

120g dried carlin peas or chickpeas (or 240g cooked carlin peas or chickpeas)
2 chicory (about 250g each), leaves separated
80–100g salami, thinly sliced
a few dill fronds or parsley leaves (optional)

FOR THE DRESSING

1 tablespoon cider vinegar
2 tablespoons extra-virgin olive oil, plus extra for drizzling
½ teaspoon flaky sea salt
1 teaspoon golden caster sugar
1 garlic clove, crushed
1 teaspoon fennel seeds, bruised in a pestle and mortar

If cooking the carlin peas (or chickpeas) from scratch, soak them in water overnight then drain, bring to the boil in fresh water and simmer for 1–2 hours until tender. You will have twice the quantity necessary, but can use them in a different meal that week (for example the goat curry and carlin pea pilaf on page 150 or saffron couscous on page 285).

Reheat the cooked carlin peas in a saucepan with 2 tablespoons water over a gentle heat for 5 minutes. Whisk together the dressing ingredients in a bowl and season with black pepper. Drain the carlin peas and toss them in the dressing while they are still warm. Leave the carlin peas to cool in the dressing before adding to the meat.

Lay the chicory and salami over a platter. Pinch the slices of salami as you lay them on the plate, to create a bit of texture, and to make them easier to scoop up. Spoon carlin peas over the top, then any dressing that remains in the bowl, dripping much of it into upturned chicory leaves. Garnish with a few sea salt flakes, some additional extra-virgin olive oil, and fresh herbs (if using).

SEASONAL SHOPPING

SYBIL KAPOOR

Spring can be found in the strangest places. As the buses splash through the April showers on Borough High Street, shoppers step under the arches of Borough Market to seek out the first delicate white St George's mushrooms, frilly dark morels and great bundles of English asparagus. The Market's winding paths draw them deeper in, tempted by further glimpses of spring produce on every stall. There are hot cross buns, lemony-tasting fresh cheeses, wild garlic leaves and, for a brief period at the end of April, gulls' eggs to buy.

The Market overloads the senses. Amongst the clatter and shout, visitors find themselves pulled in every direction, bewitched by the myriad different culinary possibilities. What to buy? What to cook? Rosy cuts of lamb provoke thoughts of country walks, green fields and fragrant Sunday roasts, while the silvery wild salmon conjures up images of rural rivers, pocket-picnics of fruit cake and the last of the winter apples.

An alluring scent of coffee, spice and cheese drifts on the morning air, drawing the daydreamers back to reality. The vista opens to reveal shafts of sparkling sunshine. Many pause and take stock. This is part of the pleasure of market shopping. There is no point in hurrying or even taking a shopping list; every week is different. Who can predict when the first morello cherries will arrive in summer, or when the Kent cobnuts will be ready in early autumn? It all depends on the weather. Better by far to be inspired by the constantly changing seasonal produce.

The Market has become a haven for keen cooks. Each month brings fresh delights, ranging from tart gooseberries for a few brief weeks in June to golden quince in October. Once commonplace, many such foods have slipped from widespread sale, becoming hard-sought delicacies for city dwellers. Yet, here, amongst the brightly coloured tumble of produce, it is possible to get a sense of time and context. Summer mackerel, tart sorrel and unpasteurised cream, for example, are all in season at the same time as gooseberries. Even for those unfamiliar with traditional British cooking, they suggest themselves as natural partners to the gooseberries, just as venison, pears and wet walnuts lend themselves to the downy quince.

Regulars will carefully walk around the market, eyeing up each stall, before committing to a single purchase. It's easy to be seduced by the fat, hand-dived scallops on a bright January

day, but then there is sweet-fleshed cod, not to mention pheasant and partridge, both of whose seasons ends on 1 February. The Seville oranges have to be bought (they will only be around for a few weeks), while the lush leeks, winter greens and beautiful Italian winter chicory all look equally irresistible.

Shopping in the fresh air changes the cook's perspective. It links each visitor to the natural world, in much the same way as it has for centuries. If fingers and noses are nipped by the cold damp January weather, all thoughts will be turned to creating warming dishes such as leek soup, game pie or steamed citrus pudding. However, pale wintry sunshine can equally inspire many to make lighter, clean-tasting dishes such as truffled leek vinaigrette, chicory risotto, or seared scallops with a chilli soy Seville orange sauce.

The sheer variety of produce from around the world allows cooks to draw inspiration from a much wider range of seasonal recipes. At the height of summer, for instance, it is possible to buy plump wood pigeon, sour cherries and Moroccan spices. In the depths of winter, there is sweet-tasting salsify to accompany grilled steak, lumpy yellow citrons to be candied and pungent Vacherin Mont D'Or cheese to eat gooey and hot with La Ratte potatoes and cornichons.

Unfamiliarity is never a problem within the Market. Discussions start spontaneously as fellow shoppers listen to conversations between buyer and seller. What's the best way to cook salsify? Are Australian black truffles (sold in summer) as good as the Italian ones sold in winter? Everyone has an opinion and culinary ideas from around the world are gladly exchanged.

Every ingredient sparks ideas about another potential dish. A jar of borage honey, for example, can send the seasonal shopper in search of summery herbs for a leafy honey-and-lemon dressed salad, or creamy yoghurt and sweet strawberries for an idyllic weekend breakfast.

Slowly but surely the joy of shopping seasonally takes hold. The sadness of summer drawing to a close is softened by the delight of finding the first damsons of the year. Soon intense autumnal colours will dominate the market stalls, from apricot-yellow chanterelles to plum-coloured beef, before gradually transitioning into the glorious multi-coloured abundance of winter. As the Market's ingredients ebb and flow with the changing seasons, so cooks create a deeper, richer sense of the world within their homes.

SYBIL KAPOOR is an award-winning food writer and broadcaster, author of eight cookbooks and a regular contributor to Borough Market's website and Market Life magazine.

SUM

MER

SUMMER

Summer provides a vivid, luscious display. The greengrocers' shelves are populated by punnet upon punnet of berries and stone fruits (both conventional and specialist). There are verdant jungles of lettuces, leaves and fresh herbs, and tumbling mounds of greens, yellows and purples in the form of peas in their pods, beans, artichokes, courgettes and summer squash. Warm waters ensure fish counters are bountiful, full of the treasures of the sea. And late summer is arguably the optimal time to enjoy animals fed on pasture, these having now fully gorged on thick grasses and wild flowers.

This is the season when we need (and want) to do as little as possible to the ingredients we pick up; a happy coincidence, given what is on offer. Think crisp and peppery salads slicked with zinging dressings, lightly cured fish and seafood platters, perhaps a quiche or tart made in advance, or lean meat or fish quickly grilled on the barbecue. Precious sunlight hours should be spent eating, ideally outside, rather than hunched over the stove. Platters of cured meats and picnic baskets packed with fresh breads and deli treats are ideal – the Market provides for all tastes. And there are experts on hand to suggest precisely which bottle of rosé, cider or craft beer will match best.

Though much of the site is under cover, Borough is an al fresco space. There's shade and a breeze if you need it, but none of the cooped-up-inside feeling that city dwelling can foster. It's somewhere to wander and mingle in shorts and sandals, whether on holiday or wishing that you were; indeed, many workers and local residents take lunch in the sun whilst watching a cookery demonstration, or linger on a bench or street kerb long into the night, having attended a talk or event in the Market, eaten at a local restaurant, or simply taken in the atmosphere of the area.

SEASONAL HIGHLIGHTS

Apricots
Artichokes
Aubergines
Bilberries
Blackcurrants
Cauliflower
Chard
Cherries
Courgettes
Green beans
Greengages
Loganberries
Mangetout
Nectarines
Peaches
Peas
Peppers
Radishes
Raspberries
Redcurrants
Romanesco broccoli
Runner beans
Strawberries
Summer squash
Tomatoes
White currants
Yellow beans

Grouse (from 12 August)
Lamb
Venison
Wood pigeon

Crab
Dover sole
Haddock
Halibut
Mackerel
Plaice
Sardines
Sea trout
Lemon sole

COCOA DUTCH
BABY PANCAKE
WITH CHERRIES

Also known as a Bismarck pancake, this recipe is less hands-on than standing over a pan flipping pancakes; something that seems like a good idea from lifestyle photos, but in reality rarely leads to a calm breakfast or brunch.

This cocoa-powered version is filled with cooling yoghurt and warmed cherries (a fruit so fine during British summertime that they are incomparable to those sold out of season) – look out for them on **Paul Crane**'s stall. If sugar overload is not a concern, you could serve the pancake instead with drizzles of runny honey or maple syrup, or a spoonful of dulce de leche (see page 306). Swap the yoghurt for ice cream and suddenly this morphs into a dessert.

SERVES *2*

2 large eggs
1 tablespoon golden caster sugar
heavy pinch of flaky sea salt
30g plain flour
15g unsweetened cocoa powder
90ml whole milk
20g salted butter
Greek yoghurt, to serve

FOR THE SAUCE

60g caster sugar
100ml water
½ teaspoon cornflour
1 tablespoon tepid water
120g fresh cherries, de-stoned

Find a skillet or ovenproof frying pan with a 20–23cm diameter base. You could also divide the pancake mix between two 10–12cm ovenproof pans – just cook in the oven for 2–3 minutes less.

Preheat the oven to 220C fan/240C/460F/gas mark 9 and place the pan inside to get very hot.

When the oven and pan are up to temperature, put the eggs, sugar, salt, flour, cocoa powder and milk in a blender and blitz for 30 seconds (you could do this by hand in a bowl with a balloon whisk, but the air the blender generates is helpful).

Remove the pan from the oven (remembering the handle is hot) and place it over a high heat. Add the butter, let it melt and foam, then swirl it around the pan. Pour the pancake batter into the pan and return the pan to the oven immediately. Cook for 15 minutes, avoiding the temptation to open the oven door.

To make the sauce, combine the sugar with 100ml water in a small saucepan. Place over a medium heat and bring to a simmer. Mix the cornflour with 1 tablespoon tepid water and stir it into the syrup. Add the cherries, cook gently for a minute then remove from the heat and leave to cool and soften in the residual heat of the pan.

The pancake will be slightly crisp at the edges and billowing when you first take it out, though will inevitably deflate as it cools. Don't feel let down by that – fill with cherry sauce and yoghurt, then eat straight away (from the pan).

SCRAMBLED EGGS AND SUMMER TRUFFLES

What a way to start the day: golden, silken scrambled eggs infused with the earthy pheromones of fresh truffle and then showered with fine gratings or shavings of the same, prized nugget.

Though truffles are generally thought of as an autumn and winter ingredient, you can buy them all year round at Borough Market courtesy of **Tartufaia**. Summer truffles, some of which grow in England, are nuttier and more subtle than the highly prized Piedmont white truffles and Périgord black truffles that arrive later on; there are black winter truffles in summer too, gathered from the other side of the world. As it happens, those available in summer tend to be more affordable, so are a great choice if you're trying them for the first time.

Buy the truffle 2–3 days before making this breakfast and store it in an airtight container lined with kitchen paper, in which both the truffle and your 6 eggs (or more) will fit. You could also fill the gaps with carnaroli or arborio rice and make a truffle-infused risotto later on.

SERVES 2

15g butter, plus extra for spreading
6 large eggs – the richer the yolks, the better

TO SERVE

2 slices of sourdough bread
10–15g summer, white or Australian black
  truffle (sliced or grated at the last minute)

Put a medium heavy-based saucepan over a low-medium heat. Add the butter and allow it to melt. It shouldn't be so hot that the butter foams or browns.

Beat the eggs in a mixing bowl and season generously with flaky sea salt and black pepper. Tip the eggs into the pan and cook very, very slowly, stirring continuously – it should take longer than 4 minutes, and easily up to 8. Try to avoid the eggs catching on the base of the pan and cooking quickly: lower the cooking temperature and even remove the pan from the heat from time to time if necessary.

Toast and butter the bread and once the eggs have thickened but are still loose and glossy, scoop them onto the hot toast. Cover with fine gratings of summer or white truffle, or wafer-thin slices of winter black truffle.

BURRATA WITH TOASTED SEEDS AND OLIVE OIL

Burrata is a fresh Italian cheese made by wrapping stretched fresh milk curd (stracciatella) and cream in mozzarella. Some think that buffalo milk in spring and summer months makes the best burrata, and certainly it should be eaten as soon as possible after it's made. **The Parma Ham and Mozzarella Stand**'s burrata comes direct from the dairy and is blissfully milky and buttery.

Still, that bright white treat benefits from a few embellishments – always a grassy extra-virgin olive oil, good bread and sea salt, but perhaps another contrasting flavour and texture too. Roast peppers, lemon zest, chilli, tomatoes and balsamic-dressed rocket are classic matches, though a savoury and nutty crunch from toasted seeds is a moreish alternative.

SERVES 2

*40g pumpkin seeds and/or
    sunflower seeds*
200–250g burrata
4 tablespoons extra-virgin olive oil
fresh sourdough or ciabatta, to serve

Gently dry-toast the seeds in a small, heavy-based frying pan or saucepan over a low-medium heat, shaking the pan from time to time. Don't be impatient and turn the heat up or leave the pan unattended. Tip the seeds out into a cool bowl once their oils start to leach and they turn golden brown (the seeds will continue to cook and may burn if left to cool in the pan).

Put the burrata on a small plate or wide bowl. Slice the top knot away then cut and open the cheese to expose the creamy middle. Drizzle the olive oil liberally around the burrata and sprinkle flakes of sea salt, freshly ground black pepper and the toasted seeds all around the cheese. Eat straight away, scooping up the seeds, cheese and oil with fresh bread.

TOMATOES ON TAHINI

In late summer in particular, the colourful tomatoes plucked from eye-catching grocery displays such as **The Tomato Stall**'s need very little done to them – though they should always be served at room temperature, well salted and with good extra-virgin olive oil.

If, however, you seek a change from pairing those tomatoes with mozzarella and basil, consider taking the lead from Middle Eastern (and specifically Israeli) cooking and try spooning chunky, sharply dressed tomatoes on top of whipped tahini.

At Borough Market, **Arabica** stock an excellent tahini paste, as well as a really good, citrusy sumac for the final flourish.

SERVES 4–6

80g tahini
60ml chilled water
juice of ½ lemon
400–500g tomatoes (mixed colours if you can)

FOR THE DRESSING

1 small shallot, finely diced
1 small garlic clove, crushed
1 teaspoon sugar
3 tablespoons extra-virgin olive oil
juice of ½ lemon
leaves picked from 4 sprigs of parsley,
  finely chopped

TO SERVE

1–2 teaspoons sumac
a handful of picked parsley leaves (optional)
crusty bread

Whisk the tahini in a bowl with 60ml chilled water and the lemon juice. Initially it might appear as though the tahini and liquids won't combine, but a little perseverance with a balloon whisk will result in a light, thick yoghurt-type texture. Cover and refrigerate until required.

Cut the tomatoes into 3–4cm chunks. Transfer them to a mixing bowl and sprinkle generously with flaky sea salt. Mix and leave to rest at room temperature for 20 minutes.

Whisk the dressing ingredients together in a bowl, including 3–4 grinds of the pepper mill. Drain away the excess juices from the tomatoes, then stir the dressing through the tomatoes.

Remove the tahini from the fridge 5 minutes before serving. Dollop it onto a large plate or platter, then tumble the dressed tomatoes on top. Sprinkle with the sumac and parsley (if using) and serve with crusty bread.

GREENGROCER GREEN SALAD

Bagged mixed salads, which inevitably end up rotting in the fridge, are neither a good reflection of lettuce's potential, nor good value. Consider instead the selections of verdant leaves of various textures sold by the likes of **Chegworth Valley**, and the impressive heads of lettuce at **Elsey & Bent** and other Market grocers.

Leaves cut from the core, washed and refreshed in a bowl of cold water and dried thoroughly need only a sharp, well-seasoned dressing to complete a summer's meal. Choose from a mix of mild, crisp and flavourful lettuces, and the addition of handfuls of fresh herbs.

Most lettuces bought whole last for 4–5 days in a fridge if the leaves are left on the core until required, and sprinkled with water occasionally.

DRESSING (FOR A SALAD TO SERVE 2–4)

Add a teaspoon of golden caster sugar and heavy pinch of flaky sea salt and black pepper to a mixing or salad bowl, then one part moscatel vinegar, sherry vinegar or lemon juice to three parts extra-virgin olive oil. Whisk briefly, before tossing the salad leaves in the dressing. Serve immediately.

SUMMER LETTUCE CHARACTERISTICS

MILD
Butterhead lettuce – floppy, sweet in the middle and excellent carriers of a vinaigrette
Lamb's lettuce and land cress – mild, tender leaves

CRISP
Romaine or cos lettuce – a crunchy bite, with slightly bitter, herbal taste
Baby or little gem – a miniature, sweeter version of the Romaine lettuce, with a crisp core

FLAVOURFUL
Mustard leaves – fiery and mustardy(!): chop roughly as large leaves can overwhelm
Watercress – a fiery mix of pepper and horseradish
Nasturtium leaves – nose-tickling with a hint of mustard. You can also add the striking and similarly punchy flowers
Wild rocket – peppery and versatile
Frisée – wild, jagged leaves: this is a member of the endive family, though its bitterness is mild relative to others

HERBS
Sorrel – sharp, citrus flavours: as with mustard leaves, the flavour is powerful so shred roughly
Parsley and chervil – pick leaves and use whole in the style of a salad leaf rather than a herb
Mint – pick and shred the leaves

BARBECUED COURGETTES, BURNT LEMON AND ZA'ATAR

Courgettes are a great vegetable to barbecue, especially when grilled briefly so they are browned on the outside yet remain relatively raw and crunchy within. Fortunately, they're also a summer vegetable, and you'll find mounds of them at the Market, of all different shapes and sizes: straight, dark greens and yellows, of course, but also pale and speckled varieties, spherical, and long and bendy ones.

This charred, herby salad, dressed with mellowed and jammy burnt lemons, shows how you can use a barbecue to cook and assemble exciting platters of seasonal food. Bolster it with ricotta, feta or fresh goat's cheese to turn it into a more substantial dish.

Try the same method with summer squash (patty pans) which you might stumble upon in August and September. If the weather's inclement, you can also prepare this using a griddle pan.

SERVES 6–8 AS A SIDE DISH

1.2kg courgettes (different shapes, colours and
*   sizes), cut into chunky 2–3cm-thick*
*   triangular wedges*
sunflower or vegetable oil, for cooking
1 lemon
1 mild red chilli, finely diced
leaves picked from 4 sprigs of mint, shredded
20–30 basil leaves
4 tablespoons extra-virgin olive oil
2 tablespoons za'atar

Toss the courgette pieces in a tablespoon or two of cooking oil. If using a barbecue, thread the courgette pieces onto skewers (to avoid losing too many through the grill), ensuring the cut faces will be exposed to the heat, rather than the edges with skin. Lay over a hot barbecue and allow to blister and brown. If the courgettes have not softened too much (they should retain some bite), turn the skewers and colour them on another side, too. At the same time, cut the lemon in half and place the halves cut side down on the barbecue for a few minutes, leaving them to colour, soften and become sticky.

(You can also cook the courgettes and lemon on a hob, either on a griddle pan, frying pan or heavy roasting tin over a high heat on the hob, setting the courgette pieces cut side down and charring them for 5 minutes. Turn them over and colour the other sides a little too, but ensure they don't cook through, so they remain crunchy. Do this in batches if necessary and blacken the lemon halves at the same time.)

Transfer the cooked courgettes to a bowl or tray. Squeeze the jammy lemon juice over and add lots of flaky sea salt, black pepper, the diced chilli, three quarters of the fresh herbs and all the extra-virgin olive oil. Toss and leave for the flavours to mingle for 3–5 minutes, then tip onto a serving platter where the courgette pieces can be spread out. Add the remaining fresh herbs and sprinkle the za'atar liberally over the salad.

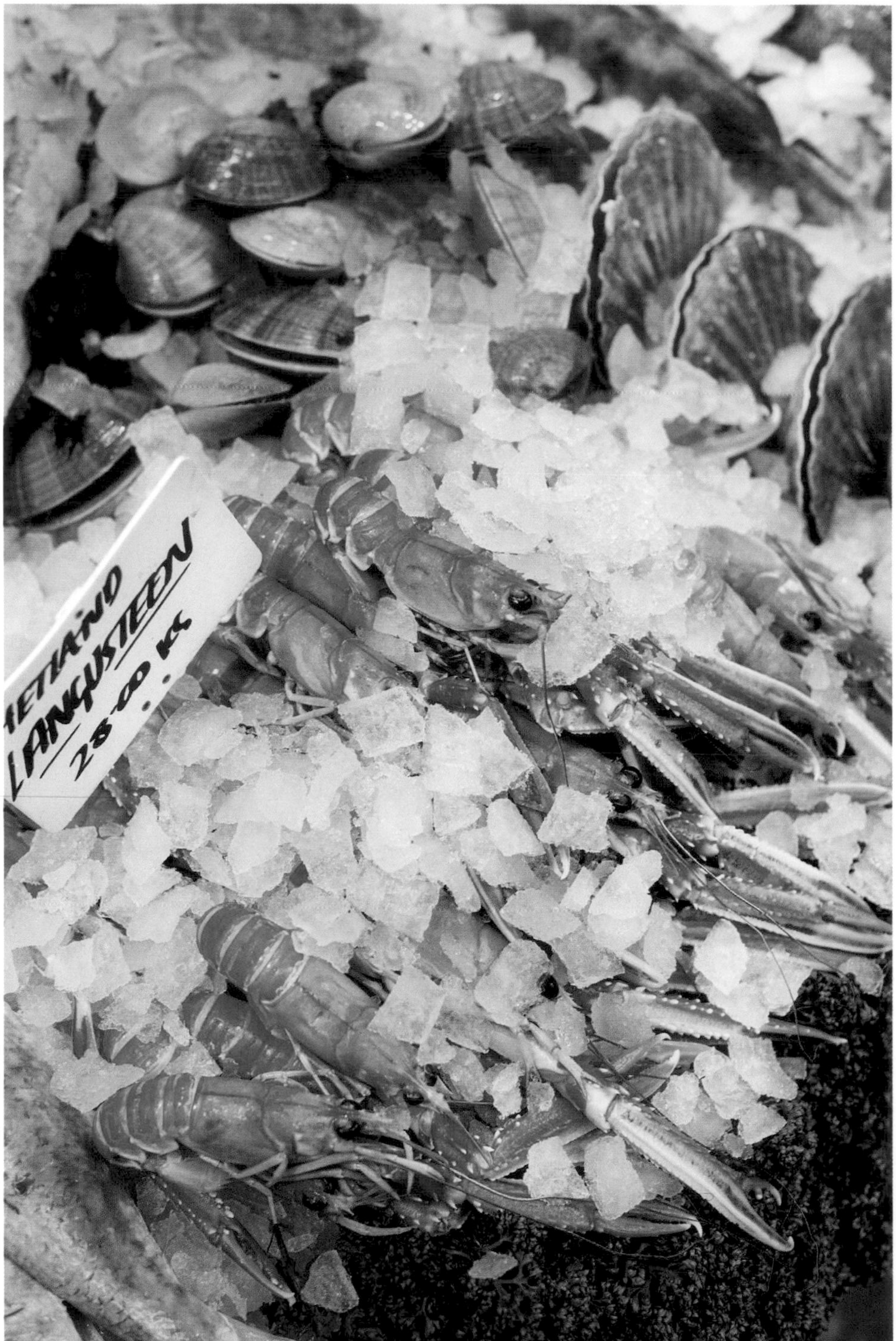
LANGUSTEEN
28.00 kr

A SEAFOOD PLATTER WITH SAFFRON MAYONNAISE

You might consider a groaning platter of cooked and chilled seafood as a treat reserved for holidays in France or a decadent restaurant experience, but if you find a good fishmonger with a range of fresh seafood and already prepared or smoked fish, such as **Furness Fish Markets** in the Market, then dining like this at home is simple. Shrimps, langoustines, lobsters, crabs, whelks, clams, oysters, mussels, sea urchins and oysters – choose the seafood for your platter according to your preference and budget. Most fresh molluscs can be kept and served raw, whereas crustaceans, such as langoustines, need to be boiled in advance.

ENOUGH LANGOUSTINES FOR 2–8, DEPENDING ON WHAT ELSE IS ON THE PLATTER

20g flaky sea salt
800g uncooked langoustines
prepared seafood of choice

FOR THE SAFFRON MAYONNAISE

4 large egg yolks
1 teaspoon Dijon mustard
juice of ½ lemon
1 tablespoon cold water
350ml sunflower oil
100ml extra-virgin olive oil
10–15 saffron threads
2 tablespoons boiling water

If your langoustines are still live, place them in the freezer for 20–30 minutes before cooking.

To cook the langoustines, fill a large 4–5-litre saucepan with water and bring it to the boil. Add the salt and, when the water reaches a rolling boil, add the langoustines. Place the lid on top. When you hear the water boiling again, the langoustines should be cooked (this should take about 2–3 minutes). Remove the langoustines from the water and leave to cool.

To make the mayonnaise, whisk the egg yolks, mustard, lemon juice, 1 tablespoon cold water and a heavy pinch of salt in a bowl for a couple of minutes until light in colour and texture. Gradually add the sunflower oil in a thin stream while continuously whisking, then drizzle in the olive oil. A little cold water will bring the mayonnaise back together if it splits. You can make the mayonnaise in a blender if you prefer.

Put the saffron in a cup and add 2 tablespoons boiling water. Leave to infuse and cool for 10 minutes, then stir the saffron and its soaking liquid into the mayonnaise using a spatula. Taste and add a little black pepper, and more salt if needed.

Place the langoustines and other prepared seafood on a platter and serve alongside the saffron mayonnaise.

(You can roast or fry the langoustine shells – and prawn, lobster and crab shells – once the meat's been plucked from them, and use them as the base for a good bisque or bouillabaisse.)

LIME, CORIANDER AND CHILLI BAKED SCALLOPS

As with all good-quality fish and seafood, very little needs to be done to plump, fresh scallops, providing you don't overcook them. These scallops, baked in their own shells with butter and a few aromatics are a good example of that maxim. Two or three scallops per person make a delectable starter, depending on their size and your appetite, which **Shellseekers Fish & Game Ltd** hand-dived scallops should whet.

SERVES 2–3

6 plump scallops with their bottom shell
a few sprigs of coriander
60g butter at room temperature
1 mild red chilli, finely diced
15g piece of fresh ginger, finely grated
finely grated zest of 1 lime, plus juice to serve

Remove each scallop from its shell (you might find a teaspoon useful for persuading it to come free from its base), setting them aside on a cool plate. Clean the bottom shells, scrubbing them under warm running water, then place the shells on a baking tray, cup side facing up. Put 2 coriander leaves in each shell and place the scallops on top.

Preheat the oven to 230C fan/250C/480F/gas mark 10.

Mash the butter in a bowl with the back of a fork. Add half the diced chilli, and all the ginger and lime zest. Beat thoroughly and put a heaped teaspoonful onto each scallop.

Place the tray towards the top of the oven and bake for 3–4 minutes, until the butter is bubbling and singeing. Remove, season the scallops with a pinch of the remaining diced chilli, freshly ground black pepper, a squeeze of lime juice and 1–2 more coriander leaves, and serve immediately (encouraging others to slurp the buttery juices from the shell).

HERITAGE TOMATO, OLIVE TAPENADE AND BELPER KNOLLE TART

This tart makes for a colourful summer lunch, or an easy centrepiece to an al fresco supper. It's a celebration of the heritage tomatoes that form such amazing displays at Borough Market and farmers' markets across the country.

In addition to the seasonal bounty, there's a potent but complementary tapenade and crème fraîche layer between the puff pastry and tomato, plus shavings of the salty, hard Swiss cheese Belper Knolle from **Jumi Cheese**. You could use pecorino instead, or omit the cheese sprinkling altogether, but do use a good-quality fresh tapenade – **Borough Olives**' is perfect.

SERVES 4–6

750–800g selection of heritage tomatoes
¼ Belper Knolle cheese
60g fresh black olive tapenade
90g full-fat crème fraîche
320g pack ready-rolled all-butter puff pastry
basil leaves, to garnish
extra-virgin olive oil, for drizzling
well-dressed green salad, to serve

Preheat the oven to 200C fan/220C/425F/gas mark 7.

Slice the tomatoes thinly – no more than 5mm thick – and arrange them in one layer on a platter or across 2 large plates. Sprinkle with a few good pinches of flaky sea salt and leave for 15 minutes. This will allow the salt to draw the juice out of the tomatoes.

Shave the Belper Knolle very finely using a mandoline or truffle slicer. Set aside the best looking half and combine the remaining shavings in a bowl with the tapenade and crème fraîche.

Lay the puff pastry flat on a baking sheet. Use the blunt edge of a knife to score a border 2cm from the edge. Spoon the tapenade, cheese and crème fraîche mixture into the middle of the pastry and spread it thinly, up to the border.

Discarding the juices, arrange the tomatoes over the tapenade in one overlapping layer, placing the thickest, juiciest slices at the edges to avoid a soggy-bottomed middle. Season with black pepper and place on the top shelf of the oven for 15 minutes, then reduce the oven temperature to 180C fan/200C/400F/gas mark 6 and bake for a further 15 minutes. The pastry edge will be puffed and golden, the tomatoes soft and beginning to dry out.

Remove the tart from the oven, scatter basil leaves over the tomatoes, drizzle with olive oil, then finish by sprinkling the remaining Belper Knolle shavings over the top. Allow to cool for 10 minutes, then serve with a well-dressed green salad.

BAKED AUBERGINES AND MOZZARELLA

As with many vegetables, aubergines are available all year round but do have a peak season, when they look and taste in their prime, and are plentiful (and therefore cheaper). For those that are grown in the Mediterranean, that season is summer.

This dish uses some of the components of a classic aubergine parmigiana, but with a lighter, more summery touch: the aubergines are baked whole, not sliced and fried, so require less oil; the tomatoes are sweet and tart and near-bursting, yet not stewed; and the creamy mozzarella is cold, not cooked, and torn fresh at the last minute, providing a contrast to the warm baked veg. It's an excellent way to eat great mozzarella when at its oozing, milky best. You could also try using smoked mozzarella, which is available from **The Parma Ham and Mozzarella Stand**.

SERVES 2 AS A MAIN, 4 AS A SIDE DISH

2 medium-large aubergines (about 300g each)
cooking oil, for drizzling
2 tablespoons dried oregano
extra-virgin olive oil, for drizzling
500g cherry tomatoes (ideally a mix of colours)
4 garlic cloves, flattened and peeled
6–8 salted anchovies in oil, chopped (optional)
30g pine nuts
1 tablespoon balsamic vinegar
20 basil leaves
250g buffalo mozzarella

TO SERVE (OPTIONAL)

crusty bread
well-dressed green salad

Preheat the oven to 200C fan/220C/425F/gas mark 7.

Place the aubergines in a small roasting tin, drizzled with just a little cooking oil, and bake in the oven for 30 minutes, until the flesh has started to sink and the skin split a little, but they aren't fully cooked. Remove from the oven and use a sharp knife to split the aubergines in half lengthways.

Place the halves cut side up in the tin, score the flesh in a criss-cross pattern and season generously with flaky sea salt, black pepper, half the dried oregano, and a few glugs of extra-virgin olive oil. Return to the oven for a further 10 minutes, then arrange the cherry tomatoes and garlic around them. Mix into the tomatoes the remaining oregano, anchovies (if using), pine nuts, and a little more salt and black pepper and return the tin to the oven for a further 20–30 minutes, until the tomatoes are bursting, collapsing and caramelising at the edges, and the aubergine flesh is soft and translucent.

Carefully stir the balsamic vinegar and half of the basil leaves into the tomatoes, then pile them onto the aubergines with a few spoons of cooking juice. Bake for 5 minutes more, then remove from the oven, spoon the cooking juices over the top again and leave for 5 minutes so all the flavours mingle.

Transfer the aubergines to plates or a serving platter, tear mozzarella on and around them, and spoon any extra tomatoes and juices over the top. Garnish with the remaining basil, plus more olive oil and serve with crusty bread and a green salad, or as a side dish for barbecue-style lamb, chicken or beef.

FENNEL, SOFT SALAMI AND LEMON LINGUINE

There are not many quicker or more satisfying meals than those made with fresh pasta bought from a deli or your local farmers' market. This might be in the form of filled shapes such as tortellini, tortelloni and ravioli, slicked with extra-virgin olive oil, or plain pasta such as tagliatelle or linguine with a simple sauce stirred through; the award-winning **La Tua Pasta** has all bases covered for commuters passing through the Market on their way to the train and Underground.

This buttery sauce is one way of embellishing the likes of linguine with two layers of anise (fresh fennel and fennel seed), warmed-through soft salami from **The Ham & Cheese Company**, and a squeeze of lemon. It's quick, low admin and ideal on a warm summer's eve.

SERVES 2

35g butter
150g fennel, diced
2 teaspoons fennel seeds
1 large garlic clove, finely sliced
250g fresh linguine
2 x salami campagnole
   (or 150g similar soft salami)
grated zest and juice of ½ lemon
60g finely grated parmesan

Bring a saucepan of heavily salted water to the boil.

In a separate large frying pan or saucepan, melt 15g of the butter over a medium-high heat. Add the diced fennel and cook for 3 minutes, stirring occasionally. Add the fennel seeds and garlic, reduce the heat to low and cook for another minute.

Put the pasta in the boiling water and cook for 3–4 minutes, draining it while it's still al dente.

Meanwhile, use the tip of a sharp knife to open the casings of the sausage, then crumble and pinch the meat into marble-sized pieces. Add the salami to the pan of fennel for 2 minutes to warm a little and for the fat to render, but avoid browning the meat at the edges. Add the lemon zest and remaining butter, allowing the butter to melt before adding 2 ladles of water from the pasta pan. Shake the pan so the liquids emulsify, then add another ladleful of water and 40g of the parmesan. Let this melt for 30 seconds before shaking the pan again to emulsify the sauce (you will need to drain the pasta at about this time – when you do, reserve another ladle or two of pasta water).

Grind plenty of black pepper over the fennel and sausage, then decant the drained pasta into the pan with one more ladle of cooking water. Shake the pan and toss the linguine so the lengths of pasta are glossy with the buttery sauce. Remove from the heat, stir in the lemon juice and divide between 2 dishes with the remaining parmesan sprinkled over the top.

ROAST RED MULLET WITH ROSEMARY AND PROSCIUTTO

This is so simple, and yet so, so enjoyable – a perfect example of how you need do little more than combine market-fresh ingredients to make a great meal. A single red mullet – so often a by-catch when fishermen are netting for other species – is typically the perfect size for one person. Here it is seasoned and flavoured by the addition of rosemary and a cloak of prosciutto.

The recipe is easy to scale up or down, so super whether eaten solo, in a pair or a larger group.

SERVES 2

4 sprigs of rosemary
2 red mullet (200–250g each), gutted and scaled
olive oil, for cooking
6 slices of prosciutto (60–80g)
1 fennel bulb
1 large orange
extra-virgin olive oil, for drizzling

Preheat the oven to 180C fan/200C/400F/gas mark 6.

Bend the rosemary sprigs in half and stuff in the cavity of each fish. Rub a little olive oil over the outside of one fish and season it with black pepper (not salt – there's plenty of that in the ham). Lay 3 pieces of prosciutto flat on a chopping board, slightly overlapping. Place the fish across the prosciutto (perpendicular to the direction of the prosciutto), head and tail poking out, then wrap the ham around the fish. Repeat with the second fish.

Cut the woody tops off the fennel and reserve. Shave the fennel bulb vertically into 1–2mm-thick slices with a mandoline (making sure you use the guard) or as finely as you can with a sharp knife. Cut the skin and pith from the orange, and cut the flesh into 3cm chunks. Combine the fennel slices, orange chunks and any juices in a bowl with a pinch of flaky sea salt and a tablespoon of oil and place on a small baking tray or low-sided roasting tin in a flattened layer not much bigger than the two fish. Place the woody bits of fennel on top, a little like a trestle, then balance the fish on top of those, the joins in the prosciutto facing down.

Roast towards the top of the oven for 15–20 minutes, depending on the thickness of your fish, until the eyes are white and the prosciutto is crisp. Remove from the oven and leave to rest the fish for 3 minutes, discard the woody parts of fennel and use a fork to mix the fennel slices and orange around in the cooking juices. Some of the fennel will be crisp at the edge, some translucent and juicy. Pile the fennel and orange onto plates with the fish next to it. Drizzle both with peppery extra-virgin olive oil.

SHREDDED CHICKEN, CARROT AND ORANGE BLOSSOM SALAD

The default approach for a whole chicken is to use it as the centrepiece of a roast. But there are alternatives. You could, for example, poach the bird with a few aromatics, so that you're left with reliably tender, juicy meat and the bonus of a flavoursome stock to use for another meal.

Here, that poached chicken is pulled from the bone by hand, shredded, and added to a fragrant carrot salad with North African notes. It's buoyed by perfumed orange blossom water, which you can get from **Arabica**, and is particularly well suited to summertime eating (whether the weather matches hopes or not). The star anise, ginger and coriander in the stock make for a fragrant and herby broth or noodle soup.

SERVES 4–6

1.6–1.8kg chicken
1 star anise
6cm piece of fresh ginger, quartered
1 garlic bulb, halved through the middle
leaves picked from 25g coriander, stalks reserved
2 teaspoons cumin seeds
½ teaspoon ground cinnamon
½ teaspoon ground ginger
juice of 1 lemon
1 tablespoon runny honey
2 tablespoons extra-virgin olive oil
2 tablespoons orange blossom water
800g carrots, peeled
30g golden raisins or sultanas
leaves picked from 40g mint, shredded
50g toasted flaked almonds

Put the chicken in a large, high-sided saucepan or flameproof casserole dish. Cover with cold water, ensuring there's 4–5cm of water above the top of the meat. Add the star anise, fresh ginger, garlic and the coriander stalks, bring to the boil then reduce the heat and simmer for 1 hour. Transfer the chicken to a bowl or plate and leave to cool for 30 minutes.

Meanwhile, toast the cumin seeds in a heavy-based dry pan for 2–3 minutes until they release their aroma. Grind them to a powder in a pestle and mortar with a pinch of abrasive sea salt, then combine with the other spices in the base of a large mixing bowl, along with the lemon juice, honey, olive oil and orange blossom water. Use a julienne peeler or the grater attachment of a food processor to turn the carrots into thin strips, then mix these and the raisins or sultanas into the dressing. Leave for 15–30 minutes so the flavours mingle.

Pull the meat from the chicken carcass by hand, tearing into bite-sized pieces along the grain of the flesh. Mix the meat into the carrots while the chicken is still warmer than room temperature. Stir in the coriander, mint and almonds at the same time. Check the seasoning, then serve immediately.

Later on, return the chicken carcass to the stock and simmer for another 30 minutes to extract all the flavour. Strain and reserve for another occasion.

CHARRED BREAM WITH GREEN SAUCE

If you enjoy cooking outdoors, consider grilling whole fish like sardines or bream instead of the usual burgers, sausages and chicken thighs. Those bought from quality fishmongers, like **Sussex Fish**, don't need much more than a lick of flame for the crisp skin and meaty flesh to impress, save perhaps some new potatoes, a salad and a puddle of piquant green sauce on the side. It's a good reminder that 'a barbecue' can be a delicious meal, rather than an event.

SERVES 4

*4 small bream, gutted and scaled (sea, gilt
    head or black bream)*
1 lemon, cut into 8 slices
cooking oil

FOR THE GREEN SAUCE

leaves picked from 25g mint
*leaves picked from 25g tarragon,
    stalks reserved*
*leaves picked from 25g parsley,
    stalks reserved*
20g salted anchovies in oil
10g brined capers, drained
1 teaspoon Dijon mustard
1 small garlic clove
juice of ½ lemon
100g light olive oil
1 tablespoon tepid water

TO SERVE

couscous or new potatoes
well-dressed green salad

Put all the green sauce ingredients (except the tarragon and parsley stalks) in a blender with 1 tablespoon tepid water and blitz for 1 minute or more, until completely smooth and silky. This can be made a few hours in advance and stored in an airtight container at room temperature.

(The green sauce is best made in a high-powered blender. If your blender isn't particularly effective, and little bits of leaves are still evident after a minute of blitzing, pause for a moment to prevent the motor overheating, then continue blitzing.)

Prepare the fish while the barbecue or griddle pan reaches peak temperature – the barbecue should be hot but no longer flaming – and the metal of the grill is also extremely hot. Pack each fish cavity with the herb stalks and 2 lemon slices. Brush the skin with cooking oil and season generously with flaky sea salt and black pepper.

Place the fish directly on the grill and cook for 3 minutes without disturbing them, ideally with the lid down if you have one (don't worry if not – it may just take a minute or two longer to cook them). After that time is up, the skin should be crisp and golden, and it should be easy to lift them from the grill without the skin catching. If so, flip the fish and cook them on the other side for a further 3 minutes (again with the lid down if you have one). Now the fats and juices should be dancing and sizzling out of the fish, and the flesh easy to pull from the spine. Cook for another minute per side if necessary but avoid turning the fish too many times or you will lose the crisp skin to the barbecue.

Serve the charred fish with generous servings of green sauce, some couscous or simple new potatoes and a well-dressed green salad.

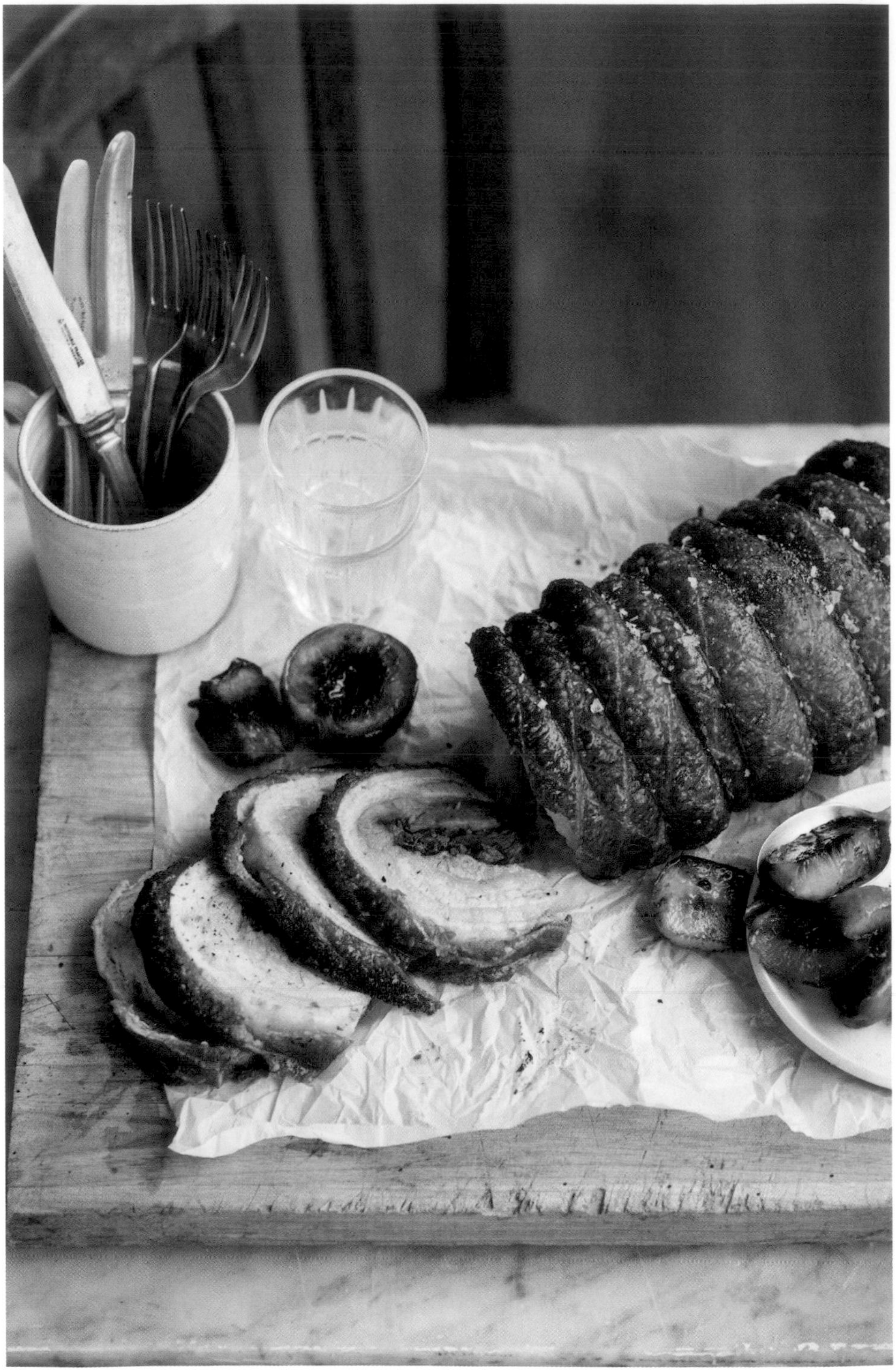

ROLLED PORK BELLY AND STICKY NECTARINES

This is a princely summertime joint: pitch-perfect crackling, aromatic and unctuous pork, served with sweet, sticky nectarines that have been baked in the roasting juices. It's also one that is undeniably and exponentially better when the cut of meat has been bought from a butcher's or farmers' market; in fact, you're unlikely to find belly big enough to roll elsewhere, let alone one with skin that's ripe for crackling.

You can take a couple of shortcuts if you wish: ignore seasoning and stuffing the pork belly and instead ask the butcher to roll it for you; or skip the first stage of salting, and just salt the skin an hour before cooking, leaving it uncovered in the fridge. The outcome will be fine, maybe even really good. But for the very best result, do try going the whole hog.

Serve with a loose, cheesy polenta or white beans and their cooking broth, plus a seasonal green such as rainbow chard sautéed in garlic-infused olive oil at the very last minute.

If you're rolling the belly yourself, you'll need uncoated cooking string or twine.

SERVES 8 (WITH LEFTOVERS)

*2.5kg pork belly, skin scored and ribs sheet-boned
    for you (weight includes ribs)*
30g flaky sea salt
1 heaped teaspoon fennel seeds
1 garlic clove, crushed
1 tablespoon extra-virgin olive oil
1 heaped teaspoon chilli flakes
leaves picked from 10 sprigs of thyme
6 ripe nectarines, de-stoned and quartered

TO SERVE

cheesy polenta or white beans
seasonal greens

Set the pork belly flesh side down on a tray and completely coat the skin with a layer of sea salt. Leave uncovered in the fridge for at least 2 hours.

Grind the fennel seeds and a pinch of salt with a pestle and mortar. Mix in the garlic, continuing to crush with the pestle until you have a smooth paste. Stir in the olive oil, chilli and thyme. Scrape the salt off the skin of the pork, reserving it for later. Turn the pork over and rub the paste all over the flesh. Cut one of the nectarines into 1cm-thick slices. Roll and tie the belly, using evenly spaced slip-knots, starting in the middle and working outwards, tying off the knot each time (how to tie butchers' knots is easily searchable online). Push the nectarine slices into the fold of the belly as you tie.

Sit the ribs at the bottom of a roasting tray that will fit the joint snugly and place the pork belly on top of them, with the join facing down. Re-apply the salt to the outside and leave in the fridge for 1–2 hours to continue to dry that skin out.

Preheat the oven to 240C fan/260C/500F/ gas mark 10 or as high as it will go. Brush the salt off the pork skin again, then roast in the top half of the oven for 1 hour. Check after 45 minutes to ensure the skin is blistering evenly – rotate the roasting tray if necessary. After a further 15 minutes reduce the oven temperature to 120C fan/140C/275F/gas mark 1. Arrange the nectarine quarters around the pork and cook for a further hour, opening the oven every 20 minutes to let steam escape (to ensure the crackling remains toffee-hard).

Remove the pork from the oven and leave it to rest for 15–20 minutes, then remove the string and carve the pork in 1–2cm-thick slices. Ensure everyone gets at least 3 nectarine quarters. The ribs can be served with the belly, or left as a treat for the chef, and there'll be lots of dripping and juices from which to make a gravy, if you wish. Serve with cheesy polenta or white beans, and seasonal greens.

GOOSEBERRY CRUMBLE SLICE

Gooseberries are only available for a few weeks across June and July. So, if you see either the green or the more unusual blushing pink varieties, pick up a punnet or two. From afar they're bright gems, but up close less promising: fuzzy on the outside with irritant brown tops; and if you bite into raw gooseberries it's a tart, sharp, face-puckering experience. Gently stewed with sugar to taste, though, and they reward cooks with one of best and unique flavours of summer.

These crumble-topped slices are a great way to enjoy gooseberries, not least as a relatively transportable item to enjoy at the end of a picnic. Lightly cooking the fruit in advance helps avoid a soggy bottom and also leaves you with a gooseberry syrup for use in a drink later on (see page 124).

MAKES 10 SLICES

600–650g fresh gooseberries
250g caster sugar
1 tablespoon water
200g plain flour
150g salted butter
1–2 tablespoons cold milk

FOR THE CRUMBLE

100g plain flour
80g jumbo oats
40g demerara sugar
100g salted butter, melted

Put the gooseberries and 180g of the caster sugar in a small saucepan with 1 tablespoon water. Heat to a very gentle simmer. Once a third of the gooseberries have burst, remove the pan from the hob and set it aside for 15 minutes – the rest of the gooseberries will split and soften in the residual heat. Strain through a sieve, without pushing on the fruit. Reserve the syrup for adding to drinks (see page 124).

Preheat the oven to 180C fan/200C/400F/gas mark 6. Line a 24 x 18cm baking tray or low-sided roasting tin with baking parchment.

Rub together the flour, remaining caster sugar, butter and a pinch of flaky sea salt in a bowl until the mixture resembles breadcrumbs (or pulse in a food processor), then add 1 tablespoon of milk and stir (or pulse) until it begins to come together (add more milk if necessary, though it shouldn't need it). Press the mixture evenly into the lined baking tray or tin – it should be 1–2cm thick. Bake in the middle of the oven for 20 minutes until lightly golden, then remove and leave to cool for 10 minutes.

Combine the crumble ingredients in a bowl.

Spoon the gooseberries evenly over the baked base (a few gaps are fine), then distribute the crumble over the top, occasionally compressing the crumble so there's a mixture of clumps and loose crumbs.

Bake in the oven for 30 minutes, until the crumble topping is golden. Remove from the oven and leave to cool to room temperature before slicing.

WHITE BALSAMIC BERRIES WITH ALMOND SEMIFREDDO

White balsamic vinegar, which can be found on **The Olive Oil Co.** and **Gastronomica**'s shelves, is delicate, less intense and cloying, and neither caramelised nor aged for as long as its more familiar dark cousin can be.

As it happens, both types of balsamic make a surprisingly good dressing for summer berries (something to do with the sharp and sweet elements of fruit and vinegar riffing off each other), but the subtler white balsamic has the edge. And a punnet or so's worth of vinegar-sharpened berries cuts through a light and creamy semifreddo rather well.

SERVES 8–10

FOR THE SEMIFREDDO

150g fresh raspberries
80g caster sugar
80g blanched almonds
600ml double cream
2 teaspoons vanilla extract
3 large eggs, separated

FOR THE BALSAMIC BERRIES

250–450g mixed berries – redcurrants,
*   raspberries and white or blackcurrants are*
*   particularly good*
2–3 tablespoons caster sugar
2–3 tablespoons white balsamic vinegar

Preheat the oven to 140C fan/160C/325F/gas mark 3.

Mix the raspberries with 1 tablespoon of the caster sugar and leave to macerate for 20 minutes before mashing to a purée with the back of a fork. In the meantime, put the almonds in an ovenproof dish in a single layer and toast in the oven until golden. Roughly chop or pulse to a coarse crumb in a food processor and set aside.

Line a 900g/2lb loaf tin or other freezable container of similar capacity with cling film or greaseproof paper.

Fetch 3 mixing bowls. Decant the cream and vanilla extract into the largest bowl and whisk to ribbon stage. In another bowl, whisk the egg yolks and remaining sugar for 1–2 minutes until pale and light. And in the third bowl, or using a stand mixer, whisk the egg whites until they form stiff peaks.

Mix the egg yolks and chopped or blitzed almonds into the cream, then add the egg whites and quickly fold them in with confident, decisive swoops of a large metal spoon or spatula. After 4–5 swoops, spoon the raspberry purée over the top and ripple these through the mixture with a few more swoops. Pour into the lined container and freeze overnight.

An hour before serving, prepare the balsamic berries. Put the mixed berries in a bowl with 2 tablespoons of caster sugar and 2 tablespoons of the white balsamic vinegar. Leave to macerate, tasting just before you serve in case more sugar and vinegar are needed. At the same time as you mix the berries with the sugar, remove the semifreddo from the freezer and turn it upside down onto a wide plate or platter. Leave to thaw gently in the fridge so that it's 'semi-frozen'. Slice and serve on side plates or shallow bowls with the tart balsamic berries spooned next to it.

GOOSEBERRY SYRUP GIN COCKTAILS

These two gin-based cocktails are a smart way of using the surplus syrup left after stewing the gooseberries for the crumble slices (page 120). You could also use rhubarb syrup (page 243) or quince syrup (page 163) to similar effect.

It's absolutely worth exploring the different, aromatic and floral 'new wave' artisanal gins now available, such as those produced and sold at Borough Market by the **East London Liquor Company.** Alternatively, keep the drink soft and use the fruit syrups as a cordial mixed with still, sparkling or soda water.

1 *GOOSEBERRY GIMLET*

50ml gin
30ml gooseberry syrup
10ml lemon juice

Measure the ingredients into a cocktail shaker with a handful of ice cubes and shake until very cold, before straining into a chilled coupe.

1 *GOOSEBERRY G&T*

50ml gin
50ml gooseberry syrup
90ml tonic water

Measure the gin, syrup and tonic water into a low ball glass over 3–4 large ice cubes. Stir and drink.

ROSÉ-POACHED PEACH MELBA JELLY

This is jelly and ice cream for adults – specifically those who are fans of a glass of blush on a summer's evening. Try to find a light, Provençal-style wine that claims to contain hints of strawberries, such as **Borough Wines**' barrel rosé, to which you can return empty bottles for a refill.

Poaching the peaches before adding them to the jelly has the double benefit of softening the fruit and infusing it with the flavours of rosé; while those peaches impart their perfumed flavour to the wine by return.

SERVES 6–8

1 x 750ml bottle of rosé
100ml water
1 tablespoon golden caster sugar
2 ripe peaches
3 lemon slices
1 sprig of mint (optional)
7 gelatine sheets (10.5g)
10 fresh raspberries, halved

TO SERVE

vanilla ice cream
toasted flaked almond

Pour the rosé and 100ml water into a small saucepan and add the sugar. Pop the peaches and lemon slices into the pan and make a 'cartouche' of crumpled greaseproof paper to help the peaches remain below the liquid's surface. Place the pan over a medium-high heat, bring to the boil, then reduce the heat and simmer gently for 12–15 minutes. Once bubbles begin to emerge in a steady stream from the dimple at the top of the peaches, they are poached and ready. Remove the pan from the heat.

Remove the peaches from the rosé and set aside. Place the sprig of mint (if using) in the rosé liquid and leave to infuse. Peel the skin from the peaches once they are cool enough to touch (the skin should come away easily), and cut the flesh into 1–2cm dice.

'Bloom' the gelatine sheets in a bowl of cold water for 3–4 minutes then squeeze excess water from the softened sheets and add them to the saucepan of still-warm rosé. Strain the rosé through a sieve (there may be bits of lemon and mint floating around) into a jug or other vessel and leave to cool to room temperature.

Place half the diced peach in the base of a 1-litre jelly mould with the halved raspberries. Fill with half the tepid rosé liquid and place in the fridge to set for 2 hours before arranging the remaining fruit on top and pouring the second half of the liquid over the top. Chill for a further 3 hours or more.

You may need to dip the jelly mould in a bowl of warm water to loosen the sides. Serve with vanilla ice cream and a sprinkle of toasted flaked almond.

AFTER HOURS

from Borough traders. Others are intrinsically linked to the environment in which they sit: Padella, Bedales of Borough and Maria's Market Café (for the early mornings) all adding to the buzz of the locale.

There's activity underneath the covers of the Market, too, as a number of traders based around Jubilee Place and Cathedral Street present opportunities to acquire new skills. It seems such a natural and obvious option to take butchery classes at Ginger Pig or slice jamón with Brindisa Ltd. Bread Ahead Bakery & School is at the heart of it all, as their thriving baking school imparts the secrets of sourdough on a daily and nightly basis.

Though traders shut up shop by 5pm most nights (6pm on a Friday), Borough Market and the bars and restaurants at its edges are a hive of positivity and recreation for many hours more.

The area has become a magnet for Londoners in search of refreshment and restoration. Shoppers and traders linger, catching up on the daily events with drinks and snacks in hand, as a clutch of traders on Stoney Street set up seating and offer chilled oysters and hot empanadas, and pubs such as The Globe Tavern and The Rake draw fans of both traditional and contemporary craft and cask ales. A number of restaurants have evolved out of market stalls, for example Arabica Bar & Kitchen in this instance, which began life as a trestle table laden with spices and produce from the Levant, and of course the iconic Tapas Brindisa, which stands like a gatekeeper at the Market's Southwark Street entrance. The likes of Roast Restaurant and Elliot's are bastions of British cuisine and produce, sourcing many of their ingredients

In fact, the bakery is a 24-hour operation, and one example of a handful of businesses that use their Borough Market base as a hub for wholesale trade. This is probably an aspect that generally goes unseen; however, those leaving classes and dinner late in the evening will experience Borough Market in a whole new light, as Grovers, Ted's Veg and Turnips receive, manage and send out new deliveries of fresh fruit and vegetables. In the early hours, Jubilee Place resembles a real-life version of Tetris, as forklifts work hard to ensure the pallets all stack and all is in place for the start of another day.

Through all of this, and indeed the normal opening hours too, the Market's operational team are found cleaning up, packing down, and helping things get going again when the early shifts begin. In many ways, the crew wearing green jackets are the oil that ensures this engine keeps going.

THE MARKET LARDER

Borough Market is a one-stop-shop for speciality store cupboard ingredients. Within a few steps you can taste the difference between extra-virgin olive oils from Greece, Spain and Italy thanks to Oliveology, Brindisa Ltd and The Olive Oil Co. There are vinegars and nut oils at Fitz Fine Foods and Nut Farms, truffle pastes at Tartufaia and Taste Croatia, and more chutneys and pickles than you can imagine, due to the presence of Pimento Hill, Temptings, De la Grenade and Rosebud Preserves.

You can taste, before you buy, extraordinary raw honeys collected in Italy, Greece, Cornwall and London and while learning about them from traders at From Field and Flower and the Local Honey Man. Stock your larder with unusual flours, pasta (both fresh at La Tua Pasta and dried from Gastronomica), fresh olives, Food & Forest's sustainably sourced nuts and Butter Nut of London's nut butters. Spices come courtesy of Sweet Roots, Cool Chile Co and indeed Spice Mountain, which is a veritable treasure trove of both the unusual and the essential.

MAGALI RUSSIE, SPICE MOUNTAIN

We knew from the very start that we wanted to grind all our spices, and to make blends and stock things you just can't get at a supermarket. A few items – the basics like cumin and coriander – you can get from anywhere of course, though I would say that we source the top-quality versions of them, with higher levels of essential oils than is typical. But our USP is the blends – a whole range of different curry mixes, rubs and marinades – and the really unusual spices, from tonka beans to dill seeds, dried kaffir limes and their leaves, annatto seeds and amchur.

I used to have an office job, but got the itch to do something different. I didn't have a background in food; the one thing I wanted to do was to have a shop that people would walk into and feel really happy. My partner and I were on holiday in India and went to a spice plantation. When there I pictured the souks in Morocco and I thought this is something that would make people smile. And it does. Some people walk past my stand and don't bat an eyelid, because they're here for cheese, for charcuterie, for bread, for that special piece of meat for the Sunday roast. But others, people planning to cook from scratch, seem to have an instant connection. Our displays catch their eye and they're drawn in. The number of times I've heard: 'I'm like a kid in a sweet shop!' They want flavours that'll make their food stand out. And that's where we come in. That might be because the spice blends make things just a little easier, or because we're providing manageable amounts of freshly ground spices that really taste like they're supposed to.

As well as all the blends, one of my specialities is to offer multiple types of one thing.

fingers in like sherbet, and you can use it as a cooking ingredient or seasoning too, sprinkled over yoghurts and ice cream and so on. They're quite seasonal, as they require a really sizeable volume of fruit to make them, so things like rhubarb powder aren't always available, for example.

Spices change in popularity through the year. In summer, for example, people reach for things like fennel seeds, sumac – flavours that are light and citrusy. And spices get used for different purposes too, like cumin, paprika and chilli, for example, which are essential in stews and slow-braised dishes in the winter, but are more associated with rubs and marinades in warmer months.

Specialist larder shops are one of the reasons to come to a market like this. Food markets should be a place of discovery, a place to source both the type and quality of ingredient you can't find elsewhere. And that is the case at Borough; you can get pretty much everything you need. My stall has the spices for your curry, stew or dessert, unusual pulses and other intriguing ingredients. I have to be very thorough when training staff to work here because customers want a lot of information; not just how you cook with an ingredient, but where's it from, how's it grown, what it smells like, what it goes well with… there's a lot of detail over a lot of items. But it works because I find that the people who apply to work here want to be here, want to sell these amazing products. It's a special place.

I should reduce the range – and from a purely business operations point of view that would make sense – but I love having a full shop. So there are different types of cardamom, tens of chillies and chilli powders, just about every type of peppercorn, and the best vanilla pods. And it's important to me that while you get the spices you're looking for, you can also stumble across the other bits on your list and beyond too, like creamed coconut, tamarind paste, Iranian limes and so on.

People also like discovering unexpected ingredients. We stock a number of different fruit powders, which are created from freeze-dried fruits. They're amazing, so intense, and unfamiliar to most shoppers. But people love trying them out because the whole character of the fruit is intact. My friends' kids dip their

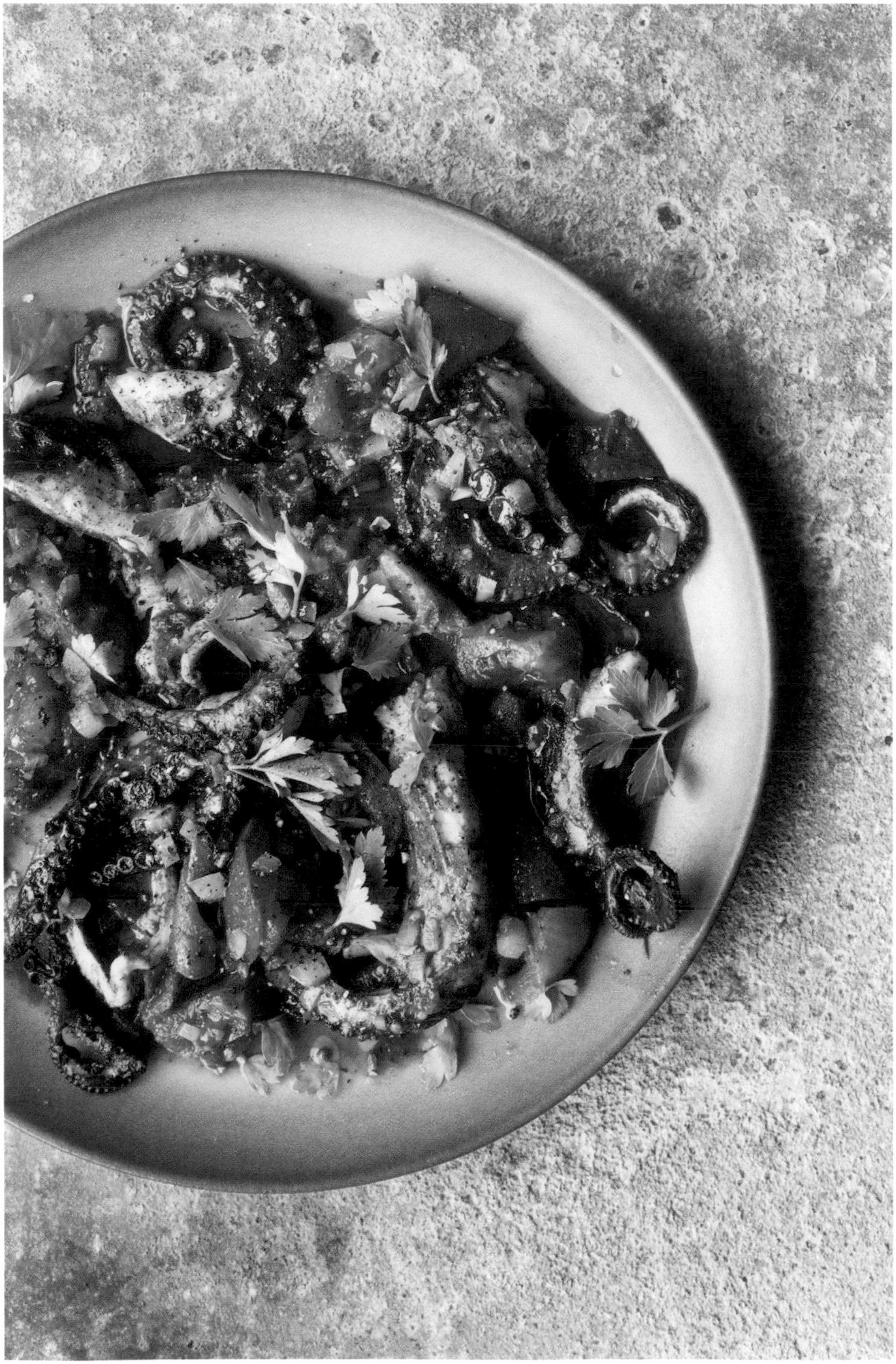

RED WINE AND BALSAMIC VINEGAR OCTOPUS

Balsamic vinegar and red wine are indisputably worth having to hand at all times. Both vary massively depending on terroir, grape quality, environment, craft and age, so it's best to shop for them where there's an expert at hand to discuss how you plan to use them - as you can at **The Olive Oil Co.**, **Bianca Mora** and **Borough Wines**.

On occasion it's good to use these as ingredients in a dish, rather than simply enjoying them in their own right. Here, for example, they help create a rich stew layered with flavour. Try making this with the smaller, pale white octopus found in British waters - they're perhaps a little more approachable than the larger Mediterranean variety (still grand if cooked like this). Use a balsamic vinegar that's not too viscous.

Accompany the dish with something like lemon-and-parsley-dressed pearl barley, couscous or rice.

SERVES 4

2 British coastal octopus (about 600g each)
  or 1–1.2kg Mediterranean tentacles
500ml red wine
3 tablespoons red wine vinegar
3 garlic cloves, 2 halved
3 bay leaves
2 tablespoons cooking oil
2 onions, finely sliced
250g tomatoes, roughly chopped
1 teaspoon dried oregano
1 tablespoon honey
50ml water
3 tablespoons balsamic vinegar

TO SERVE

extra-virgin olive oil, for drizzling
handful of chopped parsley

Clean, freeze and defrost the octopus in advance of cooking – this helps to ensure a tender bite.

Put the defrosted octopus (or tentacles) in a pan with the red wine, red wine vinegar, the 2 halved garlic cloves and the bay leaves. Bring to the boil, then reduce the heat and simmer, with the lid ajar, for 40 minutes–1 hour, until the thickest tentacles are tender (you will be able to easily push a fork or tip of a knife through). Remove the octopus from the pan, leave to cool, and reserve the cooking stock separately (you can cook the octopus well in advance of eating if it suits).

Heat the cooking oil in a large, heavy-based frying pan or sauté pan over a medium heat. Add the onions and cook for 5 minutes, stirring occasionally. Crush the remaining garlic clove to a purée and add it to the onions, along with the tomatoes, oregano, honey and 50ml water. Let this cook down for a further 5 minutes then add the balsamic vinegar – much of it will quickly evaporate. Pour in the octopus stock. Cut each baby octopus into 4 pieces and add these (or the tentacles if you have been cooking a larger beast) to the pan. Simmer for a further 5 minutes, which will be enough time to reheat the octopus and ensure the sauce is rich.

Serve the octopus on a big platter, drizzle with a glug of peppery extra-virgin olive oil and scatter over the parsley.

ROSEMARY AND CITRUS OLIVE OIL CAKE

The Market's olive oil specialists import high-quality, cold-pressed extra-virgin olive oil from Greece, Spain, Italy and elsewhere, and all the oils have distinct characteristics. It's genuinely worth having a selection of different types at home. Taste and experiment with them, and you'll find that some work best for drizzling over salads, others in a dressing (such as for the bream crudo on page 247), another as a dip, and another as an ingredient for things like this cake.

This dairy-free cake works well as a pudding with stewed fruit and a spoonful of cooling yoghurt (whether cow's, sheep or coconut) for contrast, but is otherwise subtle and not too sweet, so particularly good for breakfast or mid-morning with a long coffee or calming, floral tea.

SERVES 10–12

360g plain flour
1 teaspoon baking powder
½ teaspoon flaky sea salt
leaves picked from 4 sprigs of rosemary,
*   finely chopped*
1 lemon
1 large orange
1 teaspoon vanilla extract
3 large eggs
180g golden caster sugar
250g extra-virgin olive oil,
*   plus extra for brushing*
icing sugar, to serve (optional)

Preheat the oven to 200C fan/220C/425F/gas mark 7. Line a 20–22cm springform cake tin with greaseproof paper.

Mix the flour, baking powder, salt and chopped rosemary together in a bowl. Finely grate the zest from the orange and lemon into the flour mix. Juice the fruits, combine the juices and measure the volume of liquid – you should have approximately 120ml. If you have much less, soak the fruit skins in water and squeeze again to achieve the volume required. Add the vanilla extract to the juice and set aside.

Cream the eggs and sugar together in a stand mixer fitted with the paddle attachment on a medium-high speed for 2 minutes, until light and voluminous. Reduce the speed a little and gradually pour in the olive oil in a steady stream, leaving the mixer running for another 2 minutes once all the oil is in. Slowly pour in the fruit juice, then lower the speed again, gradually adding the dry ingredients until well incorporated. Scrape any flour around the edges of the mixing bowl into the batter, mix for 10 seconds, then decant the batter into the lined cake tin. You could use a hand-held electric mixer if you don't have a stand mixer.

Put the cake tin on a tray and place it in the middle of the oven. Immediately reduce the oven temperature to 160C fan/180C/350F/gas mark 4 and bake the cake for 50 minutes. Check the cake is fully cooked by inserting a metal skewer into the middle of the cake: it should come out clean. Return to the oven for a further 5 minutes if necessary.

Remove the cake from the oven and leave to cool in the tin for 15 minutes before unclasping the cake tin, and leaving to cool completely, ideally sliding the cake away from the base and onto a wire rack. Store in an airtight container at room temperature, and sprinkle with icing sugar for a touch of extra sweetness just before serving.

HONEY-ROAST PINEAPPLE, CHILLED RICE PUDDING AND BEE POLLEN

Though most mass-produced British honeys are relatively unadulterated, the difference in flavour between often disarmingly cheap supermarket jars and sustainably produced and collected honey is genuinely extraordinary. Small-batch honeys have character. They're interesting. They genuinely taste of the flowers and crops from which the bees collected pollen. So it's absolutely worth exploring what the likes of **From Field and Flower**, **Oliveology** and **Local Honey Man** offer and choosing your favourite to enjoy at home. Using it to flavour a dessert, such as this chilled rice pudding, also helps to make the honey go further.

Most of this dessert can and should be made ahead, so you only have to assemble the various components at the last minute.

This would work just as well with halved peaches, apricots and plums, if those fruits are in season and catch your eye.

SERVES 6

900ml whole milk
4 tablespoons runny honey
180g short-grain pudding rice
1 teaspoon vanilla extract or 1 vanilla pod
finely grated zest and juice of 1 lime
1 medium-large pineapple
120g Greek yoghurt
1 heaped tablespoon bee pollen
3 tablespoons roughly chopped pistachios
   (optional)

Measure 800ml of the milk into a large saucepan. Add 2 tablespoons of the honey, the rice and vanilla extract (or cut a vanilla pod in half lengthways and scrape the seeds into the milk using the blunt edge of a small knife – put the empty pod in a tub of caster sugar rather than the bin). Place the pan over a medium heat, bring to a gentle simmer and cook for 25 minutes, stirring increasingly regularly to encourage a creamy texture. Remove the pan from the heat when it's similar in texture to a loose risotto and the rice grains are swollen and tender. Pour in the remaining cold milk, stir and refrigerate until required. Don't worry if you think it's too wet – it will firm up as it cools.

Whisk together the remaining honey and the lime zest and juice. Trim the skin from the pineapple and cut the fruit in half lengthways, then each of those halves into 3 lengths through the core. Place these in a strong sealable food bag or wide bowl, pour the honey and lime marinade over the pineapple and leave for at least 1 hour, occasionally turning the bag and basting the fruit.

Preheat the oven to 200C fan/220C/425F/gas mark 7. Set the pineapple on a small baking sheet in one layer, reserving the marinade. Roast for 10 minutes, then spoon half of the remaining marinade over the top. Cook for a further 10 minutes and baste with the remaining marinade, before a final 10 minutes of roasting. Cut into chunks.

Stir the yoghurt through the cold rice pudding. Divide the rice pudding between 6 bowls, sprinkle with the bee pollen and pistachios (if using) and place the roast pineapple pieces on top.

CHAI ICE CREAM

Tea has always been a popular product at Borough Market. Current specialists include **Tea2You**, who import fine teas from Darjeeling in northeast India, and **Organic Life** whose tea comes from a single estate in Sri Lanka. Both, as it happens, have a subtly spiced chai in their range, and warm cups of it to drink while you shop. This ice cream is inspired by that.

The flavour of the ice cream will vary according to the bags of chai you use. Ultimately, the infused milk should be strongly flavoured but not astringent. Add more teabags instead of increasing the steeping time if you think it necessary. A scoop goes particularly well with the brownies on page 303, but is enjoyable on its own, too.

MAKES 1–1.2 LITRES

400ml whole milk
8 chai teabags (20–25g)
400ml double cream
4 large egg yolks
80g golden caster sugar

Pour the milk into a medium heavy-based saucepan and place over a medium heat. At the point little bubbles appear and it comes to a simmer (if you have a cooking thermometer it should read 85–90C), turn off the heat, add the teabags and leave to infuse for 15–20 minutes. Squidge the bags occasionally to encourage flavour distribution. It should be really flavoursome (as there's cream to come), but not bitter or overly pronounced. Strain the milk through a sieve into a jug, add the cream and return the liquid to the saucepan. Warm gently for 1–2 minutes and taste to see if you're happy with the flavour (though note it seems to strengthen further when churned).

Whisk the egg yolks and sugar together in a bowl until light and fluffy. Pour 3–4 tablespoons of the warm liquid onto the yolks, and whisk to combine before adding the remaining liquid (this avoids scrambling the yolks). Clean the saucepan, then transfer the liquid to it. Heat very gently for 10–15 minutes, stirring almost constantly, until the liquid is thick enough to coat the back of a spoon. Remove from the heat, press a layer of cling film or greaseproof paper to the surface of the custard and cool to room temperature, then refrigerate for a few hours (ideally overnight).

Churn the fridge-cold custard in an ice cream machine for 10–20 minutes until well thickened and voluminous (how long this takes will depend on your machine) before scraping into a suitable-sized container. Freeze for at least 4 hours before serving.

FRUIT POWDER MARSHMALLOWS

Fruit powders are one of **Spice Mountain**'s many highlights. They're the essence of the fruit they derive from (strawberry, rhubarb, banana and more) and are simply that ingredient freeze-dried and ground to a dust. Their effect is a sherbet-like burst of flavour and colour when stirred through a yoghurt, or as a dusting for a meringue, panna cotta, cream or these marshmallows.

Proper marshmallows are infinitely more pleasurable than the shop-bought versions, and are surprisingly simple to make, provided you have a sugar thermometer and a stand mixer. These are particularly good when raspberry or sour cherry flavoured, but experiment with whichever fruit powder you wish.

MAKES AROUND 20 DEEP
MARSHMALLOWS

flavourless oil (such as groundnut or sunflower),
 for brushing
440g granulated sugar
1½ tablespoons golden syrup
200ml water
12 gelatine sheets (20g)
2 large egg whites
3 tablespoons fruit powder

FOR DUSTING

3 tablespoons icing sugar
3 tablespoons cornflour
2 tablespoons fruit powder, plus extra
 for sprinkling

Line a cake, loaf (or even a biscuit) tin approximately 20 x 15cm and at least 5cm deep with cling film or baking parchment, and brush the film or parchment with flavourless oil.

Put the sugar, golden syrup and 200ml water in a small, high-sided saucepan and place over a medium heat, stirring until the sugar has dissolved. Increase the heat, bring to the boil and continue letting it bubble for about 8–10 minutes until the sugar syrup reaches 122C (the 'hard ball' stage of candy-making).

Meanwhile, soak the gelatine sheets in a large bowl of cold water for 4–5 minutes.

Once the sugar syrup passes the 116C mark, begin whisking the egg whites in a stand mixer at a medium-high speed until they reach soft peaks. (Stop whisking if the whites peak before the syrup has reached 122C.) When the syrup reaches 122C, continue whisking the whites until they form stiff peaks, then keep the machine whisking while you gradually pour the syrup into the bowl (avoiding the spinning whisk). Squeeze any excess water from the gelatine and add the softened sheets 2 at a time. Finally, add the fruit powder and continue to whisk on a medium speed for 8–10 minutes, until the marshmallow is like stretchy bubble gum. Transfer it into the lined tin and use a slightly wet or lightly oiled palette knife or similar to smooth the top, then leave to cool at room temperature for 3 hours.

Dust a baking tray with the icing sugar, cornflour and fruit powder. Tip the marshmallow onto the powder and rotate to dust it evenly on all sides. Cut it into thick strips and then chunks, each time turning the newly cut edges in the dusting ingredients. Sprinkle with generous pinches of fruit powder to finish.

Store for up to 3 days in an airtight container at room temperature, layered with excess dusting powder.

SHARING KNOWLEDGE

A market is more than an arena accommodating the sale of provisions: it's a meeting of minds as much as a physical space, a community in which stories, gossip and, importantly, knowledge can be traded. Conversations about every facet of food are as constant at Borough today as they would have been hundreds of years ago. There's no better way to understand where your food is from, what it tastes like, what it goes well with and how to cook it, than to speak to the people selling it to you. The traders are experts, and are happy to pass on their experience.

Borough Market as an organisation is also very conscious that it has a responsibility to foster that community spirit, and to connect its visitors with the origins and processes of food and cooking from scratch. Multiple events and publications run throughout the year to help achieve these aims.

In addition to the voices of the traders, each week resident cooks, well-known chefs and food writers share their skills and recipes from the cookery Demonstration Kitchen in the Market Hall. These sessions are free to attend, generally running over lunch hour, and cover a wide range of topics and cuisines.

The Borough Market Cookbook Club meets monthly – a cross-generational group, they cook from a specified tome, discuss their experiences and share their interpretation of the recipes. Meanwhile, on weekday evenings between April and September, Borough Talks, a popular series of public debates held in Three Crown Square, feature prominent names in the food industry discussing issues as diverse as the future of food, sustainability and waste, food writing, media and business.

Among the most cheering regular happenings are the Young Marketeers sales held at various points in the year in partnership with the charity School Food Matters. At these, children from local primary schools gather to sell vegetables that they have grown from seed, raising money in the process for the charity FareShare, which provides meals for vulnerable families. Regular traders are on hand to pass on the art of creating a winning market stall, and the children return the gesture with their enthusiasm and energy. On separate occasions, secondary school students make and sell bread from scratch, and soup from surplus vegetables. So far, money raised by the Young Marketeers project has produced more than 17,000 meals, and more than 7,000 pupils have spent time at school learning how to grow food from seed and avoid food waste. Across the country, markets are following Borough's example, inspiring new generations to find out more about the provenance of their food. It's well worth seeking out your local market and joining the conversation.

MARKET LIFE MAGAZINE, WEBSITE AND RECIPES

*Community spirit and knowledge sharing takes place both online and in print. For news of upcoming community events and the Demonstration Kitchen schedule, visit **www.boroughmarket.org.uk** and follow **@boroughmarket** on social media. In addition to calendar information, the website hosts original recipes and topical articles about people, ingredients and occasions, with new content uploaded on a daily basis. Some of those articles and recipes are taken from Market Life, an award-winning magazine that is freely available when you visit the Market. It's packed full of stories, trader tips and seasonal recipes from both regular contributors and friends of Borough Market.*

PREPARED FOR YOU

Bustling restaurants, pubs and bars, freshly prepared sandwiches, oysters and clams opened in front of you, hot and cold pies and pasties, plus award-winning and iconic street food – it's hard to leave hungry having visited Borough Market. The likes of Borough Wines, Cartwright Brothers Vintners Ltd, Bedales of Borough, Utobeer, The Cider House and East London Liquor Company provide an opportunity for shoppers to learn about and buy fine and unusual wines, craft ales and ciders, and locally distilled spirits in a low-key, convivial environment, while non-alcoholic fruit juices from Total Organics, Turnips and Chegworth Valley, and coffee and tea from, among others, Change Please, Flat Cap Coffee Co, Tea2You, The Colombian Coffee Company and Monmouth Coffee Company ensure no shopper need to be without flavourful refreshment.

This Market is a bustling centre of food to go, and there are a number of traders whose dishes are renowned across London and beyond. Take, for example, Kappacasein Dairy's humble yet extraordinary raclette and cheese toasties.

BILL OGLETHORPE, KAPPACASEIN DAIRY

I have always been fascinated by the transformation of raw ingredients into a product, by the whole process of making food. I was born in Zambia, trained in agriculture in Switzerland and eventually ended up in England about 25 years ago, via time spent on a dairy farm and cooking in the South of France. In London I got a job as a cheesemonger at Neal's Yard Dairy, which kind of embodied all the things I was interested in; we were really involved with the people who make the cheese, controlled much of the maturation process, and took that product to retail.

While there I started an occasional hot-food stall. It kind of happened by accident. We wanted to animate the front of the shop, so I set up a raclette machine, which I had from my days in Switzerland, and I put together a toastie using ends of Montgomery's cheddar which would otherwise have gone unused. Both were amazingly popular, and I eventually left to set up my own dairy, making cheeses in a railway arch in Bermondsey, which I now sell, and some of which I use in the hot food too. So I've gone some way to closing the circle, but I guess the idea of controlling the farm the cows are on is a dream I'm still entertaining.

Raclette is both a style of cheese and a dish. It's a semi-hard cow's milk cheese made in Switzerland and the Savoie area of France, known for melting well. Historically, Swiss farmers and cow herders would have heated it by an open fire, scraping the cheese onto bread or potatoes once cooked – and that's the dish that's known by the same name. But at my Borough stall we use either Ogleshield, a cheese made from Jersey cow milk, which I had some role in developing with James Montgomery, one of Britain's pre-eminent farmhouse cheesemakers; or another cheese

If you deconstruct it on a pure business basis it's a terrible sandwich – no one would develop this if they were thinking about costs, as the cheeses and the bread are pretty much the most expensive of their kind! But at the beginning it was about finding a way to use up cheddar scraps, so it made sense then. The scale of our sales has changed the emphasis a little, and surplus alone won't keep us in cheese. Still, people love it so we won't change, though we do add either Ogleshield or London Raclette in there too because they melt so well, and we also include Comté from the Borough Cheese Company from time to time.

The raclette is good in winter as it's so comforting, but the toastie is great all year round. It's enriching and invigorating, and it's got all the things people crave. Michael Pollan talks about cheese as 'flirting with taboo', something to do with all the flavours and smells that come out of cheeses, which I think become amplified when in the toastie format, and customers find it irresistible.

I've developed in my Bermondsey dairy, which I call London Raclette. The choice depends on stock levels, maturity and ultimately which cheese is at its optimum at the time. Both work really well because you get multiple layers of flavour and texture as they cook. They've each got a really high fat content, which allows the top of the cheeses to roast and turn golden, rather than burn. Creamy and crusty – that's the desired result.

The toastie became a bit of a thing from 2005 when the American food writer Ruth Reichl described it as 'the Platonic ideal of toasted cheese'. Since then it's always been popular. There's something special going on, I think: the umami of the cheese; the sweet-savoury alliums; the sourness of the Poilâne bread; also that crisp sheen on the outside, which is the melted then grilled cheese. It's so good.

CHORIZO AND PIQUILLO PEPPER TRAY BAKE

This is an homage to **Brindisa Ltd.**'s legendary chorizo, piquillo pepper and rocket roll; one of the first and still one of the best street foods in London.

This one-tray sausage dish is rich, piquant and deceptively luxurious. It's simple to cook, though the specific sausages are essential. These can be found at good market delis and online if you can't make it to Borough. Also note that the addition of the ingredients to the roasting tin are staggered to ensure everything peaks at the same time.

SERVES 6

12 Brindisa dulce cooking chorizo
400g spring onions
7 tablespoons light olive oil
1 ciabatta loaf (about 250g)
leaves picked from 10 sprigs of thyme
1 lemon
2 garlic cloves, very thinly sliced
225ml fino sherry
200ml chicken or vegetable stock
1 x 390g tin whole piquillo peppers (or roasted
* peppers in brine), each split in two*
wild rocket, to serve

Preheat the oven to 200C fan/220C/425F/gas mark 7.

Find a roasting tin that snugly fits the sausages and spring onions in a single layer. Cut any stringy roots from the spring onions and roughly chop the dark green ends, to leave onions around 8–10cm in length. Add these, the chopped spring onion ends and the sausages to the roasting tin. Roll the sausages and onions in 2 tablespoons of the olive oil until glossy. Cook towards the top of the oven for 10 minutes.

Meanwhile, tear the ciabatta into thumb-width croutons. Place in a mixing bowl and toss with the remaining olive oil, thyme leaves, the finely grated zest of the lemon, and a good pinch of flaky sea salt and black pepper.

Remove the roasting tin from the oven and shuffle the sausages and spring onions to hide the browner spots. Reduce the oven temperature to 180C fan/200C/400F/gas mark 6. Add the garlic slices to the roasting tin, pour in the sherry and stock, and place on a slightly lower shelf in the oven for a further 15 minutes, turning the sausages once during that time.

Push the pepper halves among the sausages and onions and scatter the croutons over the top – where possible ensuring they sit on dry land, rather than in a puddle. Place the tin on the top shelf of the oven this time, cooking for 15 minutes more so that the croutons turn crisp and golden.

Serve with a wedge of lemon on each plate, plus fistfuls of peppery wild rocket to mop up the juices.

LONDON RACLETTE AND MONTGOMERY'S CHEDDAR AND ONION QUICHE

As mentioned by Bill Oglethorpe (see page 142), **Kappacasein Dairy**'s toastie is of international renown. You'll find it's always cooked perfectly - slowly enough that the inner core is molten, while at the edges it's golden and crisp. But the key to its success is surely the combination of quality ingredients: mature, unpasteurised, meaty and characterful Montgomery's cheddar; creamy Ogleshield or Bill's own London Raclette, which tempers the cheddar and melts so well; and leeks and spring onions, warm but still slightly raw. These ingredients combine to stellar effect in a quiche, too.

SERVES *4–6*

1 quantity shortcrust pastry (see Swede
*   and stilton pie on page 262)*
well-dressed green salad, to serve

FOR THE FILLING

20g butter
150g trimmed, washed leeks, very thinly sliced
*   (trimmed weight)*
2 garlic cloves, thinly sliced
80g trimmed spring onions, thinly sliced
4 large eggs
100ml whole milk
200ml double cream
100g London Raclette or Ogleshield cheese,
*   grated*
150g Montgomery's cheddar, grated

Blind-bake the pastry case in a deep 24cm tart tin or pie dish, according to the method for the Swede and stilton pie on page 262.

To make the filling, melt the butter in a large, heavy-based frying pan or saucepan over a medium-high heat. Add the leeks and a pinch of flaky sea salt and sweat for 3–4 minutes until soft and sweet but still vivid green and with an oniony edge. Add the garlic, cook for 1 minute more, then stir in the spring onions. Remove the pan from the heat and leave the onions to warm through in the residual heat – there should be a slight raw edge to the onions, as is the case in Bill's toastie.

Preheat the oven to 140C fan/160C/325F/gas mark 3.

Beat the eggs in a large bowl, add the milk, cream and lots of black pepper. Whisk together then add the grated cheeses.

Scrape the leeks and spring onions into the base of the pastry case (still within the tart tin or pie dish). Pour in the cream, egg and cheese mix and bake in the centre of the oven for 45 minutes until just set, with the hint of a wobble in the centre. Remove from the oven and leave to cool for 10 minutes before attempting to remove from the tin.

It's up to you whether you like it warm, room temperature or fridge-cold (though the colder the quiche, the easier it will be to cut and serve). But do make a well-dressed green salad to go with it.

ROAST FISH WITH BEURRE BLANC

The experience of buying wine from the likes of **Bedales of Borough** and **Cartwright Brothers Vintners Ltd** is very different to a grab-and-go from the supermarket – they really add value when providing advice as to whether you should be drinking a chardonnay, albariño, muscadet, pinot blanc or otherwise with your meal.

On which note, the glass required in this classic beurre blanc sauce is both a handy way of using up the end of one bottle, and a reason to open another. Though it works with most fish, it's particularly good next to the stars of a fishmonger's display – turbot, john dory, monkfish, brill and ray – when they've been roasted whole on the bone.

BEURRE BLANC SERVES 4

turbot, john dory, ray wing, monkfish tail,
*   or brill on the bone*
olive oil, for rubbing
125g butter, cubed and fridge-cold
1 banana shallot, finely diced
125ml dry white wine
2 tablespoons white wine vinegar
2 tablespoons water

TO SERVE

well-dressed green salad, shaved fennel
*   or wilted spinach*
cooked potatoes of choice

Preheat the oven to 200C fan/220C/425F/gas mark 7. Put your fish on a baking tray or very shallow-sided roasting tin, rub with olive oil and season with plenty of flaky sea salt and black pepper. Cook towards the top of the oven for 12–25 minutes, depending on the size of the fish – it's ready when the flesh is opaque and comes away easily from the bone. Rest for 5 minutes before serving.

While the fish is cooking, make the beurre blanc. Put one cube of butter in a small, heavy-based saucepan over a medium heat. Once melted, add the shallot and a pinch of salt and soften without colouring for 5 minutes.

Add the white wine, vinegar and 2 tablespoons water, bring to the boil and reduce the liquid by half – this could take 5 minutes. Strain the liquid through a fine sieve, wipe the pan clean and return the liquid to it. Heat to a simmer and add a cube of cold butter, whisking continually to emulsify the fat. Keep adding the butter, one cube at a time, each time waiting until the butter has melted and been incorporated into the liquid before adding the next (you can add 2–3 cubes at a time once two thirds have been added). Keep warm until required.

Serve with a simple well-dressed green salad, shaved fennel or wilted spinach, and a potato dish for bulk.

GOAT AND POTATO CURRY, KALE AND CHICKPEA PILAF

Amongst the new generation of traders, **Gourmet Goat** is firmly established as a prominent Borough Market business, thanks to their award-winning commitment to sustainability. They champion high welfare British goat and English rose veal, both derivatives of the dairy industry which might otherwise be wasted. The ethos continues in their salads and sides, which though Cypriot in spirit are based on seasonal British ingredients seen as surplus to requirements elsewhere. Tellingly, all their takeaway hot food is utterly delicious.

Rather than ape their star dishes, this recipe uses **Gourmet Goat** as inspiration, slow cooking kid goat meat with Indian rather than Eastern Mediterranean spices, and serving it with a pilaf based on their chickpea and kale salads. You could, if you prefer, use a pre-ground curry powder instead of the individual spices.

SERVES 4

25g ghee or butter
3 onions, thinly sliced (about 400g)
4cm piece of fresh ginger, peeled and finely grated or cut into thin matchsticks
3 garlic cloves, crushed
1 mild green chilli, finely diced
20g fresh coriander, leaves picked and stalks finely chopped
1 teaspoon black mustard seeds
1 teaspoon coriander seeds
1 teaspoon cumin seeds
½ teaspoon ground cardamom
½ teaspoon chilli powder
500g diced goat leg or shoulder
2 tablespoons tomato purée
3 pieces of cassia bark or 1 cinnamon stick
500ml chicken, duck or lamb stock
150ml water
500–600g waxy potatoes, peeled and cut to golf-ball-sized

FOR THE PILAF

200g basmati rice
200g bunch of kale
10–20g ghee or butter
handful of fresh or dried curry leaves
1 tablespoon black mustard seeds
240g cooked chickpeas

TO SERVE

yoghurt
pickles
fresh green chilli

For the curry, melt the ghee or butter in a large, high-sided saucepan over a medium heat. Add the onions with a pinch of flaky sea salt and cook for 10–15 minutes until golden and much reduced in volume. Then add the ginger, garlic, chilli and coriander stalks, stir and cook for a further 3 minutes.

Meanwhile, lightly toast and grind the spice seeds, then mix them with the ground cardamom and chilli powder (or use 3 teaspoons of a pre-ground Spice Mountain curry powder).

Brown the diced goat meat in a very hot, separate pan for 3–5 minutes. Add to the onion mix along with the dry spices. Cook for 2 minutes more then stir in the tomato purée and add the cassia bark or cinnamon stick, stock and 150ml water. Cook with a lid on for 45 minutes before adding the potatoes and simmering with the lid off for a further 45 minutes, until both the goat meat and potatoes are tender, and the sauce reduced and intense.

To make the pilaf, boil the rice for 3 minutes less than the packet tells you to. Drain, rinse with boiling water, return it to its saucepan, place a lid on and leave to steam for 5 minutes.

Strip the kale from its woody stalks and roughly chop the leaves (discard the stalks). Place a separate, large saucepan over a medium-high heat. Add the ghee or butter, heat for a few seconds and add the curry leaves and mustard seeds. When the seeds begin to pop, throw in the kale and cook for 2 minutes, stirring occasionally. Add the chickpeas, season with plenty of salt and black pepper and turn the heat right down. Add the cooked rice, mix well and leave to warm through for 2 minutes.

Serve the curry and pilaf with the coriander leaves, some yoghurt and pickles and some extra fresh green chilli for those who want heat.

STONE FENCE COCKTAIL

This cocktail – a popular drink during the American War of Independence – is simply a mix of dry cider and dark rum or rye whisky. So its success depends on the quality of these ingredients.

Borough Market hosts a number of specialist alcohol providers: **Bedales of Borough**, **Borough Wines** and **Cartwright Brothers Vintners Ltd**; **Utobeer**'s brilliant selection of UK and world craft beers; rum, gin and whisky distilled by the **East London Liquor Company**; and the best of the cider and perry world via **The Cider House**. As with all market shopping, it's worth speaking to the traders so you can choose the best ingredients to suit your needs.

MAKES 1 STONE FENCE

50ml dark rum or rye whisky
150ml dry cider
large ice cubes

Pour the rum or whisky into a low ball glass over 4 large ice cubes. Stir, add the cider and serve.

To make more than one serving at the same time, measure the appropriate quantities of spirit and cider into a jug filled with ice, stir well and serve immediately (before the cider loses its fizz).

A THOUSAND YEARS OF TRADING

MARK RIDDAWAY

Borough Market is a survivor. For 1,000 years it has stood at the foot of London Bridge, serving the people of Southwark. It has endured through food shortages, bubonic plague, wartime bombs, legislative threats and fundamental shifts in the way we eat. Chaucer has supped here, Shakespeare has shopped here, Charlie Chaplin has sponsored the sports day. Much has changed – its voices have evolved from Old English to cockney to today's orchestra of international accents – but over the centuries the Market has remained a source of fresh produce, a place of noise, colour and heady aromas, a landmark by the bank of the Thames.

After the construction of the first medieval bridge, probably in the mid-990s, the road we now know as Borough High Street acted as a vital artery joining London – a walled metropolis on the north side of the river – to the ports and towns of the south, making it a magnet for farmers, bakers, brewers and fishermen hoping to sell their wares to travellers. By the 1270s, the presence of these hawkers beside the highway, on land owned by the crown, was providing stiff competition to London's markets and causing considerable irritation to the City authorities, who responded by banning citizens from crossing over to Southwark to buy 'corn, cattle, or other merchandise'.

Any disgruntlement was eased in 1406, when Henry IV granted London 'assay and assize of bread, wine, and ale and other victuals' traded at Borough Market, and completely assuaged in April 1550, when Edward VI sold control of Southwark to the City for £1,000, creating the wonderfully named Ward of Bridge Without, at the heart of which stood this busy bazaar.

An engraving from 1616 shows traders plying their wares in the shadow of the grand gateway to London Bridge, atop which sway the severed heads of eighteen 'traitors', planted on spikes. The traders were supervised by bailiffs and constables, who enforced price controls, inspected goods, collected fees and unleashed a battery of petty regulations. One set of rules from the 16th century positioned the stalls with the fish sellers closest to the bridge, followed by the butchers, the poulterers from the countryside, the oatmeal makers, the fruiterers and herb sellers, then finally the local bakers and poulterers. A further set of ordinances from 1624 aligned everyone in a completely different order, with the added stipulation that fishwives weren't allowed to sit down.

BOROUGH MARKET TRUST.

THROWING FRUIT, VEGETABLES, &c. IN THE MARKET.

Complaints having frequently been made of persons throwing Fruit, Vegetable and other Refuse in and about the Market, to the danger and annoyance of persons passing through; the Trustees have issued special instructions to the Beadles on duty to prevent such practices in the future.

NOTICE IS HEREBY GIVEN that any persons found so offending will be prosecuted in accordance with the Act of Parliament.

By order of the Trustees,

ARTHUR MUSGRAVE,
Superintendent & Clerk.

MARKET OFFICES,
BOROUGH MARKET.
October 3rd, 1904.

H. PERKINS, Printer, 12, Newcomen Street, Borough, S.E.

Borough Market Trust notice, 1904

Borough Market traders in Middle Road, 1920s–1930s

In an era before refrigeration, meat was brought to market both whole and very much alive, so irritable goats and wandering cattle were a constant menace. One ordinance attempted to force butchers to stop entering local shops or slaughterhouses with oxen, bullocks or cows 'that are so wild, that they will not quietly enter but run away (as often it happeneth)'.

Eventually, the City would tire of having the only southern route into London completely blocked by bakers and bullocks. In 1754 a bill went before Parliament declaring that as 'the market obstructs much trade and commerce', it would have to cease trading by 25 March 1756.

Stunned by this injunction, local residents petitioned to be allowed to start a new market away from the high street, independent of the City. Parliament agreed that 'for the convenience and accommodation of the public' the parishioners of St Saviour's Church could set up a market, to 'be and remain an estate for the use and benefit of the said parish for ever'. The parishioners raised £6,000 and bought an area called The Triangle. In February 1756, advertisements were

Borough Market and South London Fruiterers' Charity Sports, Herne Hill Athletic Ground, 1930s

placed stating that a 'commodious place for a market is now preparing on the backside of Three Crown Court'. Borough Market had found a new home.

In the 19th century, the character of the Market – previously busy but parochial – rapidly evolved. Driven by urbanisation, a population boom and the arrival of the railway (a branch of which was constructed through the middle of the Market in 1862), Borough was transformed into a crucial hub of the fruit and vegetable wholesale trade, selling to the greengrocers who fed the capital. Blanchard Jerrold, in his evocative London: A Pilgrimage (1872), described a place 'choked with market carts and costers' barrows, and crowded with unclassable poor, who seem to linger about in the hope that something out of the mighty cupboard may fall to their share'.

By the mid-1930s, 188 pitching stands were being let to 81 merchants in the central area of the Market, with a further 203 stalls around the periphery manned by individual farmers. Trading took place through the night and into the following day. One 1950s guidebook described the early morning as a 'veritable hive of industry', the sight of which made instantly apparent 'what a highly important and essential service is given in order that a vast population served shall have its daily requirements so efficiently met'.

Borough Market's status as a wholesale hub was sabotaged in part by the construction of the huge New Covent Garden Market in the 1970s, but mainly by the relentless growth of the supermarkets which, by killing off independent greengrocers, destroyed the entire ecosystem in which the market had thrived. Its decline was swift and sad.

In the 1990s, a few pioneering artisan food businesses began moving into the area's abandoned warehouses. With the encouragement of these newcomers, a three-day Food Lovers' Fair was held at the Market in 1998, gathering together around 50 of Britain's finest food producers. The event was a roaring success, with many traders selling out within hours.

This clear evidence of public demand led to a decision by the trustees to hold a regular monthly retail market, with British traders joined by those offering produce from around the world. This soon became a weekly affair. In the blink of an eye, Borough Market became an institution of international renown, open six days a week, as vibrant and relevant as it had ever been in its 1,000 years at the foot of London Bridge.

Here it will remain, not just for years, nor even for centuries, but – as its 18th century constitution made clear – for ever.

MARK RIDDAWAY is CEO of LSC Publishing and editor of Borough Market's award-winning Market Life magazine.

Borough Market wholesale traders, Three Crown Square, 1920s–1930s

AUT

AUTUMN

London doesn't let go of a hard-earned summer without a fight, and indeed September, though heralding the first days of autumn, is normally relatively warm. The colours at the greengrocers skirting the Market's edge, which do so much to shape its decor and vibe, reflect that reluctance to move on, as bright reds, yellows and greens of the best of the year's tomatoes jostle with late courgettes, a final flourish of chard and end-of-summer squashes. Plums provide a range of purples and light greens, and a sunset-pink hue emanates from stacks of peaches and nectarines (including the flat version of both) whilst the annual mountain of British corn-on-the-cob shines its own ray of light across shoppers. The yellow-green hops snaking their way up the walls of the Market Hall are at their peak now, too.

In early October, the cheery rainbow flips to a palette of beige, golden brown and orange almost overnight. This is not a melancholic lens, though, as the new ingredients provide reason to celebrate. Wild mushrooms, cobnuts, wet walnuts, chestnuts, Jerusalem artichokes, winter squash and pumpkins match the sudden and often surprising appearance of fallen leaves on the pavement; a variety of brassicas provide a dusky, hardier green on the shelves than there's been for a while, and by late October, British apples and pears abound. As the redecoration takes place, traders layer up too: loose change is counted and returned via gloved palms, branded jackets and aprons squeeze over thick hoodies, and there's a particular shuffle of the feet (the Borough two-step) that helps toes stay lively throughout the day as the temperature drops.

Whisper it, but this might actually be the best time for ingredient shopping and seasonal cooking. The British game season gets going in earnest, and native oysters, plump scallops, clams and cold-water fish return to the fishmongers' displays. And as produce arriving from the farms and fisheries changes dramatically in this season, so too do our cravings. Longer nights mean tray bakes, casseroles, roast vegetables, pulses and braised meats – comfort food for both the belly and the soul. Oh, and by the end of this period, those hops will have been harvested, fully fermented and siphoned off into bottles of Borough's annual ale. Cheers.

SEASONAL HIGHLIGHTS

Apples
Beetroot
Blackberries
Cavolo nero
Damsons
Figs
Jerusalem artichokes
Kale
Native nuts
Pears
Plums
Quince
Sweetcorn
Turnips
Wild mushrooms
Winter squash

Grouse (until 10 December)
Mallard (until 31 January)
Partridge (until 1 February)
Pheasant (until 1 February)
Wild rabbit

Clams
Gurnard
Hake
Mackerel
Mussels
Oysters
Plaice

APPLE AND QUINCE OVERNIGHT OATS

There's not much to do here, but you do need to start making this well before breakfast: the quince, which you can find on greengrocers' shelves from September through December, takes six hours to cook and cool; the oats should be stirred together just before you go to bed. The advance preparation is worth it, though, as the uniquely perfumed, sunset-pink quince yields to the touch of a spoon and makes a classy start to any autumnal morning, while the sweetly sodden muesli is both comforting and enlivening.

There's enough fruit to last a couple of days here, either for breakfast again, or serving as a simple pudding with yoghurt or ice cream, and the overnight oats recipe is scalable down or up, depending on how many mouths you are feeding. Save some poaching liquor to use as a cordial, or a syrup for a cocktail (see page 124).

SERVES 4 (WITH FRUIT LEFTOVERS)

FOR THE QUINCE

130g granulated sugar
1 litre just-boiled water
juice of 1 lemon
2 large French or Turkish quince or about 800g small English quince

FOR THE OVERNIGHT OATS

juice of ½ lemon
1 large, sharp juicy apple (Cox's orange pippin, Discovery, Spartan, Worcester Pearmain)
120g rolled oats (not jumbo)
40g sunflower seeds
50g dried pitted prunes, roughly chopped
300ml quince poaching liquor
200ml whole milk

TO SERVE

extra milk and Greek yoghurt
honeycomb (optional)

Preheat the oven to 120C fan/140C/275F/gas mark 1. Put the sugar for the quince in a pan or jug and pour the just-boiled water over the top so the sugar dissolves.

Squeeze the lemon juice into a mixing bowl. One at a time, peel and halve the quince lengthways, then cut each half into three segments through the core. Cut the core from each of the segments and drop the quarters into the lemon juice to prevent them browning. Put the peel and cores into the base of a heavy, ovenproof non-reactive dish (Pyrex or ceramic). Cover with greaseproof paper then place the quince segments in one layer on top. Pour the lemon juice and hot sugared water over the top, place another sheet of greaseproof paper over the quince and tuck it in around the fruit, then place a lid on top (or cover tightly with foil) and cook in the oven for 3 hours, gently disturbing the peel once or twice over that time to help draw out the colour. Remove from the oven, leave to cool for a few more hours or overnight, again occasionally prodding the peel and turning the fruit.

Transfer the quince and the poaching liquor to a fridge-friendly container and chill, ensuring the fruit is submerged in the liquor (and discard the peelings and cores). The poached fruit will keep for at least 3 days. Don't worry if the fruit seems soft or overcooked – it will firm up in the fridge.

To make the overnight oats, squeeze the lemon juice into a mixing bowl then grate the unpeeled apple into the bowl and toss to combine (this will help prevent too much discoloration). Add the oats, sunflower seeds, prunes, quince liquor and milk and mix. Cover and place in the fridge overnight.

The next morning, give the Bircher a good stir and serve. Top each bowl with a few pieces of poached quince plus a spoon or two of poaching liquor or milk, plus a large dollop of thick Greek yoghurt.

EGGY BREAD AND ROASTED GRAPES

It's easy to forget that grapes are seasonal, such is their ubiquity throughout the year. But autumn is the time of the European grape harvest, and it's worth taking home a bunch or two of premium French or Italian grapes (such as the black muscat variety) if you come across them in September and October. In fact, if you do see grapes that appear different to the generic, year-round varietals, try roasting them for a particularly sweet, juicy and intense experience and serve them for breakfast with a lightly spiced eggy bread.

Tonka beans, available from **Spice Mountain**, are an intriguing spice which provide an intoxicating mix of almond, vanilla, nutmeg, the high notes of liquorice, cherry, cinnamon, caramel and dark honey too. It's totally recognisable, yet unique at the same time, and excellent here. Use nutmeg if you can't get hold of tonka beans.

The recipe is for two but scales up easily – though one tonka bean (grated like nutmeg) will still be enough for up to four eggs.

SERVES 2

2 large eggs
2 tablespoons whole milk
1 tonka bean, finely grated (or ⅓ nutmeg)
1 teaspoon golden caster sugar
300g sweet red or black grapes
1 tablespoon extra-virgin olive oil, plus extra
    to drizzle
2 x 2.5cm-thick slices of pain rustique
    or white sourdough
20g butter
Greek yoghurt, to serve

Use a whisk or fork to combine the eggs, milk, grated tonka bean (or a heavy grating of nutmeg), sugar, a heavy pinch of flaky sea salt and grind or two of black pepper in a bowl. Leave to infuse for at least 15 minutes.

Preheat the oven to 200C fan/220C/425F/gas mark 7.

Remove the grapes from the bunch (leaving them on the vine looks pretty, but isn't so clever when eating). Tip the grapes onto a small baking tray with a couple of pinches of flaky sea salt and the extra-virgin olive oil. Shake the tray until all grapes are glossy, then roast in the top of the oven for 15–20 minutes, until the grapes are split and a little wrinkled, but still juicy.

Meanwhile, tip the egg mix onto a plate or a tray with a lip. Lay the bread slices in the liquid and leave them to soak for 1 minute, then flip them over and leave for another minute. Repeat until two thirds of the liquid has been absorbed.

Put the butter in a heavy-based frying pan over a medium-high heat. Once the butter begins to foam lay the eggy bread slices in the pan. Fry for 1 minute, then flip the bread and cook for 1 minute more. While it's cooking on the second side, pour half of the remaining eggy liquid over the partially cooked bread. Repeat, so each side has been slicked with the eggy mix, cooked twice and is golden brown (around 4 minutes in total). Consider browning the thick edges too.

Serve the eggy bread with the warm roasted grapes and their juices spooned over, plus a heavy pinch of salt and extra-virgin olive oil drizzled onto the grapes, and a dollop of yoghurt nearby for contrast.

CUCUMBER DILL PICKLES

It's one of the joys of market shopping to have cured meats sliced onto waxed paper in front of you, whether you're putting together a selection of meats, or maxing out on your favourite. But what to serve alongside? Pickles, of course.

While you can buy the likes of caper berries, cornichons and olives to cut through the salt, fat and protein, it's not too much bother to make your own. Proper gherkin cucumbers appear fleetingly at the end of summer and in the early days of autumn; the brine method below would also work with chard stalks, green tomatoes, mild chillies and young turnips. If you make the beetroot, carrot and drinking vinegar on page 199 the pickled gratings are an excellent match for cured meat, too.

FILLS A 3-LITRE JAR
OR FERMENTATION CROCK

1.5 litres water
55g flaky sea salt
15 gherkin cucumbers
8–10 sprigs of dill
2 teaspoons dill seeds
2 teaspoons yellow mustard seeds
2 teaspoons black peppercorns
½ teaspoon cloves
½ teaspoon juniper berries

You will need a clean and sterilised 3-litre jar or fermentation crock. There are various methods for sterilising preserving jars, including running them through a dishwasher cycle, but given the size of the jar here, the best method is to wash it with hot soapy water then leave it in a low oven (120C fan/140C/275F/gas mark 1) to dry completely.

Make a brine by warming 1.5 litres water and dissolving the salt in it. Leave to cool to room temperature. This brine is 3.5% salt, so if you have a bigger (or indeed smaller) quantity of cucumbers, calculate the salt and water quantities according to that ratio.

Wash the cucumbers and then pack into the sterilised jar or crock, along with the aromatics. When the brine is at room temperature, pour it into the jar or crock, ensuring the contents lie beneath the water. You can help submerge them by adding a layer of clean vine leaves, or a clean freezer bag filled with non-salted water. Seal with the lid and leave in a warm place out of direct sunlight. Remove the lid to 'burp' the contents twice a day, or use a jar with an air lock.

Check the pickles for sourness every day or so from 10 days onwards, then decant them (with the brine) into vessels that will fit in your fridge once they're at a level of sourness you enjoy. Use within a month.

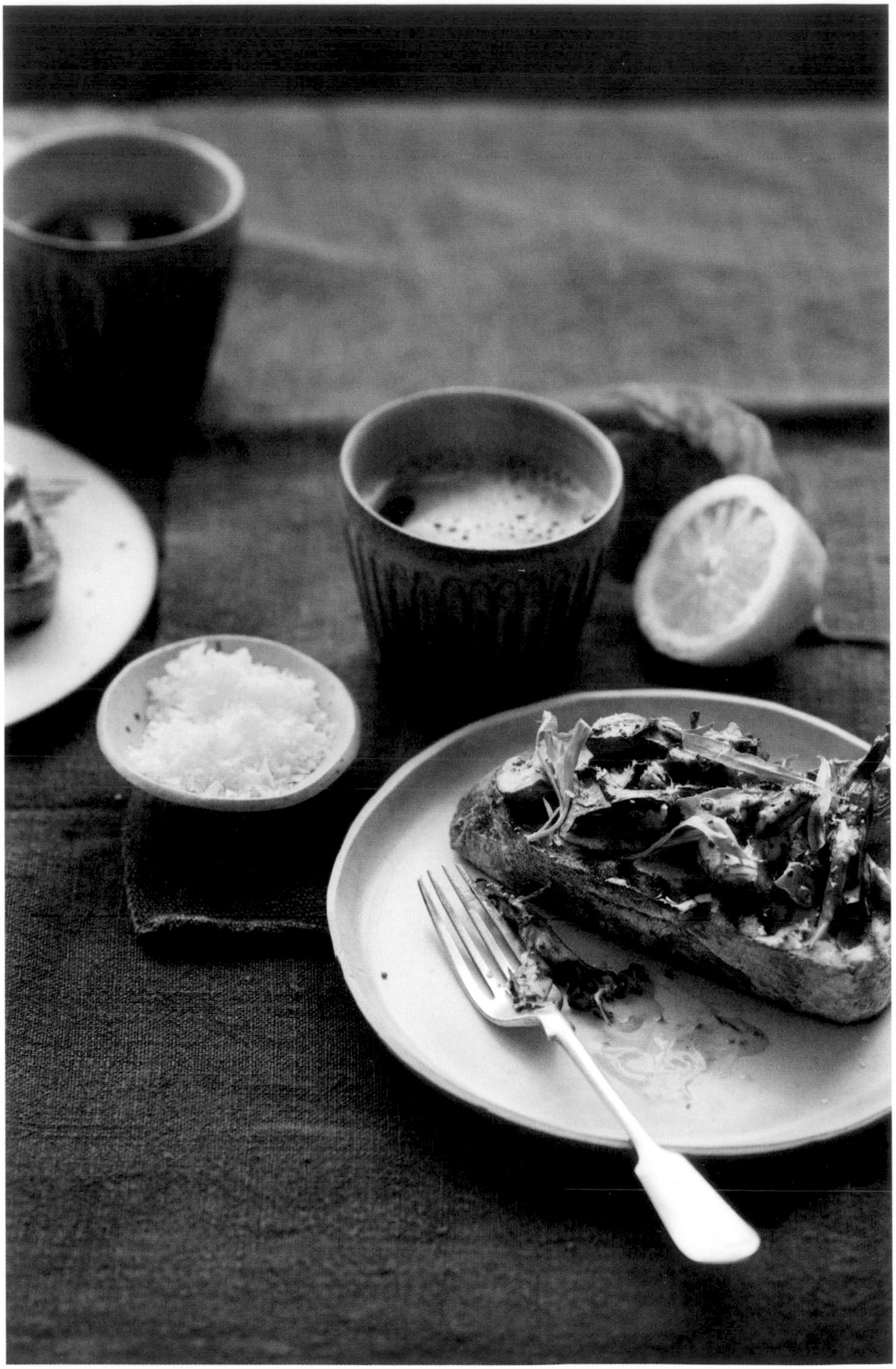

TARRAGON AND MUSTARD MUSHROOMS ON TOAST

There are mushrooms for most seasons, but in early autumn the likes of chanterelles, girolles and trompettes de la mort come to the fore – plucked from the woods and brought to market by the box-load. Look, for example, at the ultra-seasonal mushrooms display at **Fitz Fine Foods** and **Tartufaia**.

This simple celebration of them works equally well for breakfast, brunch, lunch or supper. Flavours like tarragon and mustard are a well-established match and shouldn't overwhelm the 'shrooms, given how prized and pricey they can be. On which note, the recipe includes chestnut mushrooms to add bulk and an alternative texture. But feel free to go all out with only wild mushrooms; using only ceps (also known as porcini or penny bun), for example, would make a particularly decadent but rewarding toast topper.

SERVES 2

150–200g wild mushrooms – a mix of
*   chanterelles, girolles, pieds de mouton*
*   and/or trompettes de la mort*
2 tablespoons water
100g full-fat crème fraîche
2 thick slices of fresh sourdough bread
2 tablespoons cooking oil
250g chestnut mushrooms, quartered
40g butter
1 large garlic clove, finely sliced
leaves picked from 6 sprigs of tarragon,
*   roughly chopped*
2 teaspoons wholegrain mustard
juice of ¼ lemon
extra-virgin olive oil, for drizzling

Brush any mud off the wild mushrooms with a damp cloth, cut away any woody bits at the base and, if necessary, tear any particularly large ones so they're a similar size to the rest. Add 2 tablespoons water to the crème fraîche and mix well. Toast the bread.

Heat the cooking oil in a large frying pan or wok over a high heat and wait until the oil is almost smoking hot. Add the chestnut mushrooms and fry them for 1 minute, stirring just once or twice, then add half the butter, which will froth immediately if the temperature is right, and cook for a further minute: the mushrooms should look shiny as they begin to release their juices and some edges should be taking on colour. At this point add the wild mushrooms, the rest of the butter and the garlic, and lots of flaky sea salt and black pepper. Fry for another 60–90 seconds, then scrape in the crème fraîche and add the tarragon and mustard. Stir and allow to bubble for a final 30 seconds, remove from the heat and add the lemon juice – just enough to cut through the sauce, but not so much that you only taste citrus.

Drizzle the toast generously with olive oil and spoon the mushrooms over the top. Eat immediately.

CORN ON THE COB WITH HONEY, THYME AND PAPRIKA BUTTER

British sweetcorn is most plentiful in September: at Borough there's a seasonal trader, **Crouch Cobs**, which sells grilled and buttered cobs picked that day in Essex, for only as long as they're in harvest. Elsewhere around the Market, other greengrocers like **Jock Stark & Son** will offer English cobs encased in their natural green wrapping too, in deals of two, three or four, depending on the glut.

You don't need to do much with fresh cobs: just blanch them in boiling salted water, possibly chargrill, and definitely gloss with oil or butter. A sweet and aromatic flavoured butter is an easy and neat twist, and will taste particularly good if you use top-quality paprika and honey. It's an enticing starter or snack, and a good side dish too, particularly next to things like roast partridge, guinea fowl and chicken.

SERVES 4 AS A STARTER, SNACK OR SIDE DISH

70g butter at room temperature
30g runny raw honey
leaves picked from 10 sprigs of thyme
½ teaspoon sweet smoked paprika
    (Pimentón de la Vera)
4 sweetcorn cobs

Cream the butter in a small bowl using the back of a wooden spoon. Add the honey, thyme and paprika, plus a heavy pinch of flaky sea salt and many grinds of the pepper mill. Continue to prod and stir until all the ingredients are combined and the butter is smooth. You can either use the butter immediately, scraping it over just-cooked corn and allowing it to melt, or spoon it onto a piece of greaseproof paper and roll it into a sausage shape to store in the fridge until required.

Bring a large pan of salted water to the boil.

Cut each corn cob into 2 or 3 pieces, drop them into the boiling water and cook for 4 minutes. By this time the kernels will be plump, juicy, piping hot and ready for that butter.

CAVOLO KRITHARAKI

Kritharaki is a form of pasta, cut short to look like a grain of rice. It's the Greek version of Italian orzo and is brought to Borough by **Oliveology** (orzo would work perfectly well if easier to find). The shape enjoys glossy, loose sauces – such as this creamy option, which is rich with the umami of parmesan and anchovies.

This dish is packed with cavolo nero – it's almost the reverse of a typical pasta dish, where the carb dominates the sauce. You will be able to find this brassica from June through to March, but the summer crop can be a bit straggly, so it's better to go for the wider, fully-textured leaves harvested from autumn onwards. Much of Britain's crop is grown in the east of England, so make Lincolnshire farmer **Ted's Veg** your first port of call if you're at Borough.

SERVES 4

650g cavolo nero
220g kritharaki dried pasta (or orzo)
20g butter
½ onion, finely diced
6–8 salted anchovies in oil, roughly chopped
2 garlic cloves, very thinly sliced
100ml white wine
300ml double cream
100g grated parmesan
¼ nutmeg
finely grated zest and juice of ½ lemon

Bring a large saucepan of salted water to the boil.

Pull or cut the dark green leaves away from the hard central ribs, leaving you with long ribbons of kale. Discard the ribs, and if the remaining ribbons are longer than 10cm, cut them in half. Blanch them in the boiling water for 90 seconds, then remove using tongs, rinse under cold running water to cool then leave to drain.

Cook the pasta in the salted water used to blanch the cavolo nero, following the packet instructions. Drain, reserving 3 tablespoons of the cooking water.

Melt the butter in a large, high-sided frying pan or sauté pan over a medium-high heat. Once it's frothing, drop in the diced onion and a pinch of flaky sea salt, stirring occasionally for 3 minutes before adding the anchovies and garlic. After about 1 minute, when the anchovies start to melt, increase the heat and pour in the wine, allowing it to bubble and reduce by half. Add the cream and three quarters of the parmesan, then reduce the heat a little before adding the cavolo nero to the pan. Grate in all the nutmeg, grind plenty of black pepper into the cream and cook for 2 minutes, occasionally shuffling the contents around the pan.

Transfer the drained pasta to the pan, mix it through the cavolo nero ribbons and add the reserved cooking water, a spoonful at a time, while stirring or shaking the pan, until there is a loose but creamy sauce. Turn off the heat, mix in the lemon zest and a squeeze of juice. Divide into bowls and sprinkle over the remaining parmesan.

AUTUMN PANZANELLA

An authentic panzanella involves tomatoes, which this does not. This does, however, mimic the piquant soaked bread nature of the Tuscan summer salad, while firmly placing itself in autumn – with the spotlight on kale, broccoli, roast shallots, thyme and tarragon.

The kale, which will be ever-present at the greengrocers from now until spring, is massaged but still raw and adds plenty of ballast. This could be a one-dish meal on its own merit, but it's also particularly good accompanied by bresaola, and is even better as a side dish, or part of a banquet or buffet alongside rich meats and oily pink fish.

SERVES 4–6 AS A SIDE DISH

250g kale
leaves picked from 8 sprigs of tarragon, roughly chopped
leaves picked from 25g parsley, roughly chopped
40g brined capers, drained and roughly chopped
4 tablespoons extra-virgin olive oil, plus extra to serve if needed
2 tablespoons red wine vinegar, plus extra to serve if needed
8 tablespoons cold-pressed rapeseed oil
1 teaspoon caster sugar
5 banana shallots, peeled and halved lengthways
1 small romanesco broccoli and its leaves
250–300g sourdough or ciabatta loaf, torn into thumb-sized chunks
leaves picked from 8 sprigs of thyme
2 garlic cloves, finely sliced

Preheat the oven to 200C fan/220C/425F/gas mark 7.

Tear the kale from the central rib of each leaf, discarding the rib. Roughly chop the leaves and transfer to a mixing bowl with ½ teaspoon of flaky sea salt. 'Massage' the leaves for 2–3 minutes so the kale dampens and reduces in volume. Add the herbs, capers, olive oil and red wine vinegar, mix well and set to one side.

Splash 2 tablespoons of the rapeseed oil into a small roasting tray. Sprinkle with sugar, plus a couple of pinches of salt and place the shallot halves in the tray cut side down. Rub them around the oil, tumble them until glossy, then place them cut side down again. Roast on the middle shelf of the oven for 20 minutes.

Remove the leaves from the romanesco and cut the broccoli itself into small florets. Cut the core and stem into a similar size as the florets, then put everything (including the leaves) in a small roasting tin with 2 tablespoons of the rapeseed oil and lots of black pepper. Place at the very top of the oven, above the onions.

Put the chunks of bread into a mixing bowl with thyme leaves, garlic, a heavy pinch of salt, a generous grind of black pepper, and the remaining 4 tablespoons of rapeseed oil. Once the onions have been roasting for 20 minutes, flip them over and lay the bread on top. Swap the onion tray with the romanesco, and cook at the top of the oven for 15 minutes until the bread is golden and crisp-edged.

Remove the romanesco from the oven after 25 minutes, by which point the florets, stems and leaves should be charred at the edge and moreish, but not totally dried out. Leave on their warm tray until the bread is golden, then tip everything into the kale (including the cooking juices). Mix well and let the bread soak up some of the juices for a few minutes.

Taste and add more olive oil or red wine vinegar if you think it needs it. It's best eaten straight away while it's still warm.

PARSLEY MALFATTI WITH WILD MUSHROOMS AND SAGE

Malfatti means misshapen or badly formed, which is just the thing you want to read when making something for the first time. These dumplings are essentially a filled pasta without the pasta shell. They take very little effort to put together, though you need to allow them to cool and form a bit of a skin for a few hours.

Once cooked, the ricotta, parsley and lemon shapes go perfectly with a quick, buttery fry of sage and the wild mushrooms which are so prevalent at produce markets during autumn. Use whatever variety you fancy or can find - most can be cooked in exactly the same way as button and chestnut mushrooms (i.e. fried in butter).

If you are a real fan of fungi, replace 100g of the ricotta with 100g of mushroom pâté from **Tartufaia** or **Pâté Moi**.

SERVES 4 AS A MAIN, 6 AS A STARTER

250g mix of wild mushrooms of your choice
40g butter
2 garlic cloves, finely chopped
12 sage leaves
juice of ½ lemon

FOR THE MALFATTI

500g ricotta
4 large egg yolks
80g '00' flour
30g picked parsley leaves, very finely chopped
60g finely grated parmesan
finely grated zest of 1 lemon
½ nutmeg, finely grated
fine semolina flour, for dusting

Start by making the malfatti. Put the ricotta, egg yolks, flour, parsley and 40g of the parmesan in a bowl. Add the lemon zest, grated nutmeg, 2 good pinches each of flaky sea salt and freshly ground black pepper and mix well.

Dust a baking tray or small roasting tin with a generous layer of semolina flour. Use a teaspoon to scoop up some ricotta mix and another to help you shape it into an oval shape. You don't need to be too precise. Scrape the dumpling onto the semolina and roll it like a snowball to the other end the tray or tin. Repeat until you've used up all of the mixture – you should have enough to make around 20 malfatti. Once done, add another dusting of semolina over the top of the malfatti dumplings, cover and chill in the fridge for at least an hour.

Brush any mud off the wild mushrooms with a damp cloth, cut away any woody bits at the base and, if necessary, tear any particularly large ones so they're a similar size to the rest.

When you're ready to cook, bring a large saucepan of salted water to the boil. Drop the malfatti in and cook for 2–3 minutes (they're done when they float on the surface). Remove from the water with a slotted spoon and set aside. You may need to do this in batches.

Place a large frying pan or wok over a high heat. Add two thirds of the butter and, when it's frothing, add the mushrooms, garlic, sage and a good pinch of salt and black pepper. Cook quickly, shuffling the mushrooms around the pan as required. When they start to release their juice add the rest of the butter, the lemon juice and half a ladle of malfatti cooking water.

Shake the pan to help the liquids emulsify, then add the cooked malfatti. Gently roll them around in the sauce to ensure they're warm and glossy, then serve with the mushrooms and buttery juices spooned on top, plus a sprinkling of the remaining parmesan.

WATERCRESS, RUSSET APPLE AND COBNUT SALAD

Kentish cobnuts have made something of a comeback in recent years and are often spotted at Borough in autumn, thanks to **Nut Farms**. The nuts, which come in threes, shrouded in pale green-golden husks, are similar to hazelnuts, but sweet and creamy too. They are ripe and ready to eat when green, but those left to turn brown on the trees in September are easier to shell and perhaps taste better, too.

This salad works well as a partner to pork chops or belly, beef, or roast game birds, with Russet apples adding a sharpness, and the peppery watercress a touch of heat. It could become a dish in its own right if you have also visited the cheesemonger and returned with a sharp blue cheese or a curd.

SERVES 4–6 AS A SIDE DISH, OR
2 AS A SALAD TO SERVE WITH CHEESE

80g brown cobnuts (including husk)
  (or 40g hazelnuts)
200g watercress
2 Russet apples
juice of ¼ lemon

FOR THE DRESSING

2 tablespoons extra-virgin olive oil
1 tablespoon cider vinegar
1 teaspoon tepid water
1 teaspoon golden caster sugar

Preheat the oven to 140C fan/160C/325F/gas mark 3.

Crack the cobnuts on a solid surface using a rolling pin. Discard the shells and any leafy husk. Arrange in one snug layer in a small tray and roast on the middle shelf of the oven for 40 minutes–1 hour until golden and hard. Leave to cool, then tap or roughly chop so they've mostly broken into halves.

Whisk the dressing ingredients together until emulsified and season with flaky sea salt and black pepper. Pick the watercress leaves and stems so they're not longer than 6cm.

When you're ready to eat, quarter the apples, remove the cores and chop those quarters in half, tossing them in the lemon juice, then mix the watercress, apples, nuts and dressing together and serve.

PARTRIDGE WITH CELERIAC AND PEAR REMOULADE

The partridge season runs from 1 September to 1 February, with plucked, oven-ready birds available at a number of the Market's butchers. This bird receives very little fanfare, relative to other feathered game, but it is arguably the most pleasing: plump and with a meat that's lighter both in colour and flavour than grouse, and less 'gamey' than pheasant. It's also best when the meat is just blushing, so is less of a gamble to cook than those birds that really need to be served quite rare.

The brining method ensures a juicy, flavoursome bite, and the simple celeriac and pear remoulade is an excellent and sprightly accompaniment. Ask your butcher to spatchcock the birds for you if you prefer.

SERVES 4

4 partridge
watercress sprigs, to serve

FOR THE BRINE

50g flaky sea salt
50g granulated sugar
pared zest of 1 lemon
8 sprigs of thyme
10 black peppercorns
750ml warm water

FOR THE GLAZE

2 tablespoons runny honey
1 tablespoon Dijon mustard
2 tablespoons cold-pressed rapeseed oil
leaves picked from 10 sprigs of thyme

FOR THE CELERIAC AND PEAR REMOULADE

400g celeriac, peeled
grated zest and juice of ½ lemon
2 conference pears
1 heaped teaspoon wholegrain mustard
1 tablespoon yoghurt

Combine the brine ingredients with 750ml warm water, stir to dissolve the sugar and salt and leave to cool to room temperature.

To spatchcock each partridge, use sturdy scissors to remove the breastbone, cutting either side of it. Flip the bird over and flatten it. You may need to clean away a few innards from within the ribs too, and run the birds under a cold tap to get rid of bloody remnants.

Place the spatchcocked birds in a non-reactive container (Pyrex or ceramic) that fits them snugly, pour the cold brine over the top, cover (ensuring the birds are fully submerged) and refrigerate for at least 6 hours (but no more than 24). An hour before cooking, pour away the brine, dab the birds dry with some kitchen paper then leave uncovered on a plate in the fridge to dry out.

Combine the ingredients for the glaze and massage it over the birds. Preheat the oven to 220C fan/240C/460F/gas mark 9 and line a baking tray with greaseproof paper or foil.

Cut the celeriac into 1–2mm-thick strips, using a julienne peeler if you have one. Otherwise, slice as thinly as you can and cut the slices into thin matchsticks. Place in a bowl with a heavy pinch of salt and the lemon juice and zest. Toss, then cut the pears (unpeeled) into similarly thin matchsticks and add to the celeriac along with the mustard, yoghurt and a few grinds of the pepper mill. Mix well.

Lay the partridge breast side up on the lined baking tray and roast at the top of the oven for 12 minutes. Remove from the oven and leave the partridge to rest on the tray for 5 minutes before serving with the remoulade and a few sprigs of watercress.

BEETROOT DAL

A good dal makes for an excellent informal supper - perhaps with some chutneys or lime pickles from Mrs Sandhu's **Temptings** stall. This version uses the English-grown yellow split pea, a pulse that's similar to but not quite the same as chana dal (made from yellow gram peas). Cooking the onions for a long time is essential to create a base flavour, though there is also fresh beetroot (so good in the autumn) and dried beetroot powder added at the very last minute - both give the dish a burst of colour and a surprising sweetness. The split peas and beetroot powder can be found at **Spice Mountain**.

This dal doesn't necessarily need anything else with it, besides yoghurt and chutney, but flatbreads can be a welcome companion. See page 38 for a recipe if you'd like to make your own.

SERVES 4

300g yellow split peas
2 litres water
2 bay leaves
35g butter
3 onions, thinly sliced (about 400g)
3 garlic cloves, thinly sliced
thumb-sized piece of fresh ginger (about 35g),
*   peeled and grated*
1 teaspoon cumin seeds
½ teaspoon ground turmeric
1 heaped teaspoon garam masala
10 sprigs of coriander, leaves picked and stalks
*   finely chopped*
1 mild green chilli, finely diced
450g beetroot, peeled and cut into 1cm dice
3 tablespoons desiccated coconut
1 tablespoon beetroot powder

TO SERVE

Greek yoghurt
mango chutney

Put the split peas in a bowl, cover with cold water, drain immediately and repeat until the water is clear – you may need to do this 10 times. Place the peas in a saucepan with 2 litres cold water and the bay leaves, bring to the boil then reduce the heat and simmer for 45 minutes. After this time about half of the split peas will be mushy. Skim off any froth that forms on the surface of the water, and add extra water if it looks necessary.

Melt the butter in a separate, large heavy-based saucepan over a medium-high heat. Add the onions and a heavy pinch of flaky sea salt and cook for 15–20 minutes, stirring occasionally so the onions just catch (but don't burn), and reduce and intensify in flavour. Lower the temperature, then add the garlic, ginger and cumin seeds. Cook for a further 3–4 minutes, then add the turmeric, garam masala, finely chopped coriander stalks and fresh green chilli. Place a lid on top and cook the spices for 3 minutes, then remove the pan from the heat.

While the split peas and onions are cooking, place the diced beetroot in a separate small saucepan with cold water that just covers them. Bring to boil, reduce the heat and simmer for 20–25 minutes until tender, but with a little bite. Remove from the heat (reserving the cooking liquor) and put aside one third of the beetroot plus the same amount of onions to use as a garnish.

When half the lentils have broken down, add the remaining onions and beetroot with its cooking liquor, plus the coconut. Let the flavours mingle over a very low heat for a final 10 minutes, adding more water as required – the addition of spices and coconut will dry things out a little, but this is best as a robust soup, rather than a stodgy porridge.

Finally, sprinkle the beetroot powder over the dal, mixing it in thoroughly to ensure the vivid purple spreads throughout. Serve immediately, dividing the reserved onions and beetroot between the bowls, plus a dollop of yoghurt and chutney on each.

CREAMED CORN WITH LIME AND CHILLI SQUID

This loose creamed corn purée is made without dairy or vegetable stock. Instead, it makes use of the naturally milky husks of corn, and is so flavourful, with both colour and sweetness bouncing off the lime- and chilli-dressed squid. That squid should be charred as quickly as possible, and squid fresh from a fishmonger will always taste best.

You may want to serve it with bread or homemade flatbreads (page 38) in order to scoop up the last smudges of purée.

SERVES 4 AS A STARTER

2 large sweetcorn cobs (350–400g each),
*   husks and string removed*
1 banana shallot, peeled and quartered
1 garlic clove, peeled and halved
½ teaspoon cumin seeds
5 black peppercorns
2 bay leaves
600ml water
15g butter
leaves picked from 6 sprigs of coriander,
*   to garnish*

FOR THE LIME AND CHILLI SQUID

2 whole squid (about 600g total weight),
*   cleaned and 'pen' removed*
grated zest and juice of 2 limes
a little flavourless cooking oil
2 tablespoons extra-virgin olive oil
2 mild red chillies, very finely diced

Stand a corn cob upright in a wide bowl and cut the kernels from it. Repeat with the second cob, then scrape each cob with the back of a knife to release the milky liquid into the kernels. Set to one side. Cut each cob into three pieces, then arrange them in a saucepan that fits them snugly in one layer. Add the shallot, garlic, cumin seeds, peppercorns, bay leaves and 600ml water. Bring to the boil then reduce the heat and simmer for 30 minutes before straining through a sieve – yielding around 200ml of liquid (top up with water if necessary). Discard the cobs and aromatics.

Combine the warm corn stock, butter and three quarters of the corn kernels. Blitz to a smooth, silky purée using a hand-held or stand blender. It should be the texture of a loose porridge – add a dash more water, or gently cook it to achieve that consistency. Mix in the remaining whole corn kernels, season well with salt and black pepper and keep warm.

Prepare the squid by cutting the tentacles off, then slicing open the tubes so that they sit flat. Score the inside of the squid in a diamond criss-cross patttern, with the lines about 1cm apart (this will be pleasing when charred, and helps the squid curl). Toss with the lime zest, a little flavourless oil and plenty of black pepper.

Make a dressing for the squid in a large bowl by whisking the olive oil and lime juice together. Season with salt and black pepper, add the diced chilli and set to one side.

When ready to eat, place a heavy-based frying or griddle pan over a high heat until it just begins to smoke. Lay the squid pieces scored side down and push flat. Cook for 60–90 seconds, then flip the squid over (they should curl, though you might need to prompt them) then remove from the griddle pan soon after. Leave to rest for 30 seconds, before cutting into bite-sized curls and tossing in the dressing.

Spoon the corn purée onto each plate, divide the squid pieces and dressing evenly, and sprinkle with coriander and black pepper.

ROAST MALLARD
AND MADEIRA FIGS

Wild mallards can be shot from 1 September to 31 January. During that period, these lean but richly flavoured ducks are found, plucked and oven-ready, at a number of stalls in the Market, including **Wyndham House Ltd** and **Furness Fish Markets**. It's imperative that they're cooked and eaten when the flesh is still crimson and tender; the method here, which involves browning the birds then finishing them very gently in a low oven, is one of the most reliable ways of achieving the best result.

The striking red flesh is best enjoyed with sweet accompaniments, such as this squash purée and warmed figs with Madeira. You'll also want something earthy and savoury alongside, perhaps some blanched or steamed kale, cavolo nero or cabbage.

SERVES 4

400g Delica, Crown Prince or other winter
*   squash, peeled and diced into 2–3cm chunks*
1 sprig of rosemary
1 garlic clove, peeled
45g cold butter
8 black peppercorns
6 juniper berries
2 mallards, wishbone removed
2 tablespoons vegetable oil
4 fresh figs, halved
60ml Madeira
blanched greens of choice, to serve

Put the squash in a saucepan and cover by 2cm with just-boiled water. Add the rosemary, garlic and a good pinch of flaky sea salt and simmer for 20 minutes or until tender. Drain the squash, discarding the rosemary but reserving the cooking water, then use a blender or food processor to purée the squash and garlic with 50ml of the cooking water and 20g of the butter until completely smooth – it should be closer to a thick and silky soup than a mash. Taste and season with salt and black pepper, then return the purée to the saucepan to reheat before serving.

Preheat the oven to 120C fan/140C/275F/gas mark 1.

Use a pestle and mortar or spice grinder to grind the peppercorns, juniper berries and a pinch of salt into a powder. Season the mallards with the spice mixture inside and out.

Place a heavy-based frying or sauté pan, ideally with an ovenproof handle, over a medium-high heat and add the vegetable oil. When the oil is hot, add the mallards and brown them for 45 seconds on each breast. Add 15g of the butter to the pan and sear the breasts for another 20 seconds each, then set the mallards breast side up in the pan (or a separate roasting tin if your pan isn't ovenproof). Nestle the fig halves around the mallards, cut side up, and cook in the oven for about 20 minutes, depending on the size of the bird.

Remove the mallards and figs from the oven and transfer them to a warm plate. Leave to rest for 6 minutes. Place the pan or roasting tin over a medium-high heat. When hot, deglaze the pan with the Madeira and whisk in the remaining cold butter. Turn the heat right down and put the figs back in the pan, still cut side up, to reheat for 1–2 minutes.

Cut the breasts from the rested mallards and serve with the squash purée, the figs, a couple of spoonfuls of sauce from the pan, plus a mound of greens. Be sure to use the leftover legs and carcasses to make a stock.

VENISON AND BLACK BEAN CHILLI WITH WHOLE BAKED SQUASH

This rich and warming chilli takes full advantage of Borough Market traders: venison from **Shellseekers Fish & Game Ltd**, where the Sika deer shot by owner, Darren Brown, often hang behind the counter ready to be butchered; three layers of Mexican chillies, which **Cool Chile Co** stock; and a dark London porter from the craft beer specialists, **Utobeer**, which adds a deep savouriness to the stew. You should be able to find equivalent ingredients elsewhere, though, and it is very much something to sink into when the nights are lengthening and you've turned the heating back on. The chilli is mighty on its own, but better if paired with the sweetness of butternut squash, and a cooling splurge of sour cream.

SERVES 6–8

200g dried black turtle beans (or 2 x 400g tins of cooked beans, drained – about 480g drained weight)
2 dried ancho chilli peppers
1 x 400g tin chopped tomatoes
3 tablespoons cooking oil
200g smoked lardons
1 onion, diced
1 garlic clove, crushed
800g minced venison (shoulder, or a mix of shoulder, leg and trimmings)
1 teaspoon ground cumin
1 teaspoon chipotle chilli powder
1 teaspoon Mexican pasilla chilli powder
330ml dark porter beer
2 bay leaves
2 pieces of cassia bark or 1 cinnamon stick
1 tablespoon golden caster sugar
1 large butternut squash
extra-virgin olive oil, for drizzling

TO SERVE

sour cream
coriander (optional)
flatbreads and/or rice (optional)

If using dried beans, rinse them with cold water, then put them in a heatproof bowl or pan, cover with just-boiled water and leave to soak for 1 hour. Drain and set aside. At the same time, place the ancho chillies in a small heatproof bowl, cover with just-boiled water and soak for 30 minutes. Then put the chillies, their soaking water and the tomatoes in a blender. Fill the empty tomato tin with water and add that too. Blitz until smooth. Preheat the oven to 160C fan/180C/350F/gas mark 4.

Put 1 tablespoon of cooking oil and the lardons in a flameproof casserole dish or ovenproof saucepan (for which you have a lid). Fry over a medium-high heat for 5 minutes, stirring occasionally. Add the onion, reduce the temperature and cook for 5 minutes, then add the garlic and cook for a further 2 minutes.

Meanwhile, heat the remaining cooking oil in a separate large, heavy-based frying pan over a high heat. Add the venison, brown it for 8–10 minutes, then stir in the cumin and the chilli powders. Cook for 1 minute then transfer to the casserole. Increase the heat, move the meat to one side and pour the beer in. Allow it to bubble for 20 seconds before adding the tomato and ancho chilli purée, black beans, bay leaves, cassia bark or cinnamon stick, sugar and a good few grinds of pepper. Stir, bring to a lively simmer, put the lid on and place in the oven for 1½ hours. Remove the lid and cook for 30 minutes more, by which time the beans should be tender and the liquid thickened and intensely flavoured. Taste and season with flaky sea salt and black pepper. (If using pre-cooked beans, add them for the last 30 minutes of cooking time.)

Wipe the squash clean and bake it whole on a small roasting tray next to or under the casserole for around 1½–2 hours, until the skin colours and sinks. To serve, slice it in half and remove the seeds. Tip any juice that's cooked out back over the flesh and season generously with salt, black pepper and extra-virgin olive oil. Serve the chilli and squash with sour cream, plus flatbreads or rice.

CONFIT DUCK TACOS WITH CORN AND GIROLLE SALSA

Confit duck legs (which you can find at both **Le Marché du Quartier** and **Wyndham House Ltd**) are a brilliant convenience food; half the work of making a delicious meal has been done – all you need to do is reheat the duck leg to a temperature where the meat falls apart at the touch of a fork, and the skin is golden. Classically, they are served on lentils, in a white bean stew or with sautéed potatoes, but that flaking, unctuous meat and crisp skin also make an ideal taco filling – the only other components required being a piquant salsa, zippy sauce and a garnish or two.

It's easy and quick to make your own corn tortillas from masa harina (corn flour). Alternatively, they're increasingly available already pressed. **Cool Chile Co** and many delicatessens sell both masa harina and tortillas.

SERVES 4

FOR THE SALSA

1 sweetcorn cob
120g small girolle mushrooms
75ml cold-pressed rapeseed oil
1 mild red chilli, very finely diced
45ml cider vinegar
1 garlic clove, crushed
1 teaspoon golden caster sugar

FOR THE TACOS

4 confit duck legs
4 limes, quartered
3 tablespoons yoghurt
*1 teaspoon chipotle powder (or ½ teaspoon
  each sweet smoked paprika and chilli powder)*
*12 ready-made corn tortillas
  (or 350g masa harina)*
leaves picked from 10 sprigs of coriander

Make the salsa in advance (it will keep for up to 3 days in the fridge), or at least an hour before serving. Cut the kernels from the cob, yielding around 200g sweetcorn. Set to one side. Brush any mud from the girolles with a damp cloth. Heat 1 tablespoon of the rapeseed oil in a saucepan over a high heat. Add the girolles, season with flaky sea salt and black pepper and fry for 2–3 minutes, stirring occasionally. Add the sweetcorn kernels and cook for a further 90 seconds, then transfer to a small container. While the mushrooms and sweetcorn are cooking, combine the red chilli, the remaining oil, the vinegar, garlic, sugar and a pinch of salt. Pour this over the warm mushrooms and corn, then leave to cool and pickle.

Preheat the oven to 200C fan/220C/425F/gas mark 7.

Arrange the confit duck legs skin side up in a shallow baking tray and cook at the top of the oven for 45 minutes until crisp.

Squeeze two of the lime quarters into a bowl and combine with the yoghurt and chipotle powder. Warm the ready-made tortillas in a dry frying pan 5 minutes before the duck legs are ready, storing them in the folds of a clean tea towel to keep them warm and pliant.

If making your own tortillas, simply mix the masa harina with 500ml just-boiled water. Cover and leave to rest for 30 minutes, then divide the dough into 25–30g balls, giving each one a quick knead before squashing into 8cm circles using a tortilla press (you could use a rolling pin, but a press is best). Cook in a dry pan over a medium-high heat for 45 seconds, flip and cook for another 30 seconds then repeat with the next tortilla.

Flake the meat from the duck legs and break up the crisp skin. Add a dollop of chilli-lime yoghurt to the centre of a taco, some meat, skin, a generous spoon of salsa, and garnish with a few coriander leaves and a squeeze of lime. Napkins are necessary.

PERSIMMON, WALNUT AND NUTMEG JAM MUFFINS

De La Grenade bring chilli pepper sauces and Grenadian jams and jellies to shoppers at Borough Market. Their nutmeg conserves are particularly intriguing, having been made from the rind and flesh of the fruit rather than the kernel we traditionally know as nutmeg, or its red covering (mace). The familiar spice flavour is there, but also a hint of grapefruit marmalade crossed with apricot jam. Use apricot or gooseberry jam if you can't get to the Market to pick up the nutmeg variety.

Persimmon arrive at the likes of **Elsey & Bent** in September and remain throughout winter. Look for the non-astringent fuyu variety, which can be eaten when firm and crisp (rather the hachiya, which must be almost jelly-like to be edible). They are similar to a pear in flavour, but with the drier, crisper texture of an apple, and ultimately bake very well.

MAKES 12

450 plain flour
150g spelt flour
2 tablespoons baking powder
½ teaspoon flaky sea salt
2 large eggs
200g granulated sugar
125g salted butter, melted
300ml whole milk
¼ nutmeg, freshly grated
2 large, firm persimmon (fuyu variety),
  peeled and cut into 1cm dice
80g walnuts, roughly chopped
150g nutmeg jam, 2 tablespoons reserved
  for a glaze
1 tablespoon hot water

Preheat the oven to 170C fan/190C/375F/gas mark 5 and line a 12-hole muffin tin with 12 paper muffin cases.

Sift the flours, baking powder and salt into a bowl and mix together.

Put the eggs and sugar in a separate large bowl and whisk together for 1–2 minutes until the eggs are lighter in colour and texture. Pour in the melted butter and whisk to combine, then add the milk and grated nutmeg and whisk once more. Fold in the dry ingredients, then the persimmon and walnuts. Do not be too thorough – just 6–12 confident swoops through the mixture with a large metal spoon or spatula will do it. It's fine to leave a few streaks of un-blended flour.

Moving quickly, as the baking powder has already started to work, use an ice cream scoop or spoon of similar volume to put a generous blob of muffin mix into each of the paper cases. This should use up about half of the mix. Slide two shallow teaspoons of jam on top of each of these blobs – in different places, so that when you bite into a muffin you find pockets of sweet jam – then use the ice cream scoop again to divide the remaining muffin mix among the cases, which should be fairly full at this point. Finally, drop another teaspoon of jam in the middle of each muffin, perhaps making a little indent as you do so that it sits in that spot.

Slide the tray into the top third of the hot oven and bake for 30–35 minutes, until the muffins have swollen, domed and cracked, and are golden brown.

Mix the remaining 2 tablespoons jam with 1 tablespoon hot water and brush over the warm muffins so they're sweet and glossy. Leave to cool for at least 15 minutes. They will keep well for a day if stored in an airtight container.

ROAST PLUM PAVLOVA

British plums tend to be found at the likes of **Jock Stark & Son**'s stall in August and September, so really they're both a summer and autumn market fruit. Finding the correct season in which to pigeon-hole plums, though, is less important than recognising that they make a very fine pavlova topping. Here they are roasted rather than stewed, so that they soften but retain their shape, and turn pleasingly tart too. The tarragon adds an extra dimension, with fresh and grassy notes cutting through the jammy fruit. Flaked almonds provide extra crunch, which feels necessary amidst all the cream.

Use whichever plum variety seems the most plump and juicy when you're picking through them, though Victoria, President and Pershore are reliably good for this. Roast them well in advance so that they can take on as much tarragon flavour as possible.

SERVES 6—8

FOR THE ROAST PLUMS

6 sprigs of tarragon
150ml water
1kg seasonal plums, halved and de-stoned
40g golden caster sugar

FOR THE MERINGUE

5 large egg whites (about 175g)
350g caster sugar (or twice the weight
 of the egg whites)
70g toasted flaked almonds

TO FINISH

600ml double cream
2 teaspoons vanilla extract
leaves picked from 2 sprigs of tarragon
15g toasted flaked almonds

Preheat the oven to 200C fan/220C/425F/gas mark 7.

Place the tarragon sprigs for the roast plums in the base of a ceramic dish or roasting tin with 150ml water. Lay the plums over these, cut side up, ideally in one layer. Sprinkle the sugar onto the plums, macerate for 15 minutes, then bake in the oven for 20–30 minutes, until soft and puffy but still plum shaped. Leave to cool for 15 minutes, then transfer the plums, juices and tarragon to a smaller vessel and refrigerate until required.

Weigh the egg whites. You will need double the quantity of sugar to whites to make a classic meringue, and ideally a stand mixer fitted with the balloon whisk to do the hard work. Set the oven to 130C fan/150C/300F/gas mark 2 and line a baking sheet with baking parchment or a silicone baking mat.

Ensure the mixing bowl is spotless. Add the egg whites and whisk at medium speed until they form stiff peaks. Increase the speed and sprinkle the sugar into the egg whites in a steady stream. Continue whisking for 9 minutes, until the mixture is glossy and, if pinched, has no hint of sugary crystals.

Scatter half the toasted almonds over the meringue mixture. Use a large metal spoon to carefully but confidently ripple through the nuts in two or three large swoops. Spoon the mixture onto the lined baking sheet, creating a circle 26–28cm in diameter, with high, wavy sides and an indent for cream and fruit in the middle. Place in the centre of the oven, reduce the oven temperature to 110C fan/130C/250F/ gas mark ½ and bake for 2 hours, then turn the oven off and leave for 1 hour more. Remove the meringue from the oven and sprinkle the remaining almonds on top.

Whip the cream and vanilla extract in a bowl until they reach loose ribbon stage, then spoon on top of the meringue. Arrange the plums and juices over the cream, then scatter with fresh tarragon and the flaked almonds.

SAGE AND HONEY BAKED FIGS WITH GINGER BUTTER BISCUITS

Figs are at their best in September and early October. The most prized, perhaps, are French black figs, which have a luscious and intense flavour, reminiscent of a blackcurrant-flavoured boiled sweet. Italian and Turkish black- and green-skinned varieties are no less enjoyable though, and their perfumed red centre is particularly sweet at this time of year.

As with any seasonal fruit, the first thing that comes to mind is to eat one raw and unadulterated. But figs are gorgeous cooked, particularly when encouraged by the natural sweetness of raw honey and enhanced by a fragrant herb – often thyme or mint, but in this case sage, which feels comforting when the temperature and light are dropping. Together with the ginger butter biscuits and crème fraîche, they make an easy and appealing dessert.

Make the biscuits in advance – they store well for a day or two in an airtight container.

SERVES 6

FOR THE GINGER BUTTER BISCUITS

100g unsalted butter at room temperature
90g caster sugar
100g plain flour, sifted
20g cornflour
1 teaspoon baking powder
1 teaspoon ground ginger

FOR THE FIGS

10 sage leaves
6 plump fresh figs
3 tablespoons raw honey
2 tablespoons warm water

150g full-fat crème fraîche, to serve

Preheat the oven to 180C fan/200C/400F/gas mark 6 and line a baking tray with baking parchment or a silicone mat.

Cream the butter with the sugar in a bowl using the back of a wooden spoon. Add the remaining ingredients, mix well and refrigerate for 20 minutes. Roll a walnut-sized teaspoon of biscuit dough quickly in your hands to make a ball, then repeat to make 6 balls (using half the biscuit dough). Space them evenly on the baking tray. The biscuits spread significantly, so don't be tempted to cram more on. Bake in the oven for 8 minutes, until they have flattened and started to turn golden. Remove, leave to cool and harden on the tray for 5 minutes, then slide them off the tray with a palette knife. Repeat the process with the remaining biscuit dough. Store in an airtight container until required.

To cook the figs, preheat the oven to 180C fan/200C/400F/gas mark 6. Put 4 of the sage leaves in the base of an ovenproof dish that will fit the 6 figs snugly. Cut a cross into each fruit from the stalk to two thirds of the way down. Squeeze each fig at its base to encourage the centre to present itself and slot a sage leaf in each of them. Place the figs in the dish. Mix the honey with 2 tablespoons warm water and pour it in and over the figs.

Bake the figs in the oven for 15–20 minutes, basting them with the honey and fig juices after 10 minutes. They should be soft and sticky, but still intact.

Carefully decant the figs into bowls. Pour a couple of spoons of juice over the top of each fig and serve with a generous dollop of crème fraîche and 2 ginger butter biscuits per person.

LINCOLNSHIRE POACHER AND APPLE PIE

The addition of cheese to a sweet pie might seem strange, but it is in fact a relatively traditional English pastry. And if you think about it, the combination of fruit and cheddar-style cheese is not controversial. The result here is a sharp and moreish twist on a conventional apple pie; the ideal way to end an afternoon spent at Apple Day, perhaps?

The tang of Lincolnshire Poacher, from **Neal's Yard Dairy**, works very well as it's not so strong nor musky a flavour that the sharp Bramley apples are overwhelmed. You could try using an aged Comté or manchego if you can't get hold of it.

Serve cream as an accompaniment to the pie. For once, vanilla ice cream and/or custard doesn't seem to be quite such a good partner.

SERVES 6–8

FOR THE PASTRY

375g plain flour
225g cold unsalted butter, cubed
80g cold Lincolnshire Poacher cheese, cubed
pinch of flaky sea salt
3 tablespoons fridge-cold water
1 tablespoon cider vinegar
3 tablespoons golden caster sugar
whole milk, for brushing

FOR THE FILLING

juice of 1 lemon
1.2kg Bramley apples
3 tablespoons golden caster sugar, or to taste,
*   plus extra for sprinkling*
6 cloves

cream or crème fraîche, to serve

You will need a 22–23cm pie dish. Note that the pastry is best made in a food processor.

Put the flour, cold butter, cold cheese and salt in a food processor and pulse until the mixture resembles breadcrumbs. Add the water and cider vinegar and pulse again until the pastry comes together. Divide into two, one half slightly bigger than the other, and squash each into a disc. Wrap and refrigerate for 2 hours. Unwrap the larger pastry disc and roll it between two sheets of greaseproof paper to a thickness of 4mm, or until it is large enough to line your pie dish with a 1–2cm overhang. (The pastry is very short and the paper technique helps to keep it from breaking as you roll it.) Repeat with the second disc and chill the pastry sheets for at least 30 minutes.

To prepare the apple filling, put the lemon juice in a mixing bowl. Peel, core and roughly chop the apples and transfer to the lemon juice. Sprinkle the sugar over the apples, toss, then transfer half the apples and the cloves to a heavy-based saucepan. Stew over a low heat for 15–20 minutes, stirring occasionally, until the apples are soft and relatively dry. Pick out the cloves if you can and taste the purée – if it's too sharp for your liking, add more sugar, then mix back into the uncooked apples.

Preheat the oven to 180C fan/200C/400F/gas mark 6.

Line the pie dish with the larger piece of chilled pastry. Fill with apple mix, then brush the edges of the pastry with milk. Lay the second piece of pastry over the top, pushing the edges of the pastry firmly together either by crimping it, or using the back of a fork. Make 3–4 small holes in the top with the tip of a knife (to help steam escape). Brush the pie with milk, then place on a baking tray and bake in the centre of the oven for 30 minutes. Remove the pie, brush it with milk again and sprinkle with golden caster sugar. Return to the oven for a final 15 minutes until the pastry is golden brown. Remove from the oven, allow to cool for 5 minutes, and serve with cream.

GOLDEN BEETROOT, CARROT AND GINGER DRINKING VINEGAR

Drinking vinegars are made by macerating vegetables and fruit with sugar, then using that to flavour vinegar (usually a raw cider vinegar). The resulting concoction can be mixed with sparkling water to make an invigorating morning drink, or even with gin or vodka and tonic for a fruity sharpener. You can also use the flavoured vinegar as part of a dressing.

A wide variety of ingredients can be used, from raspberries and blackcurrants, through to rhubarb, quince, elderflower and even parsnips. It's well worth experimenting. However, this tried-and-tested combination of golden beetroot, carrot and ginger makes for a bright start to any autumn morning, no matter how grey the sky. If you would like to try a drinking vinegar before making one, the flavoured vinegars sold by **Fitz Fine Foods** could be diluted with sparkling water too.

MAKES 500ML

500g golden beetroot, peeled
150g carrots, peeled
50g piece of fresh ginger, peeled
220g caster sugar
330ml cider vinegar
(ideally 'raw' and unfiltered)

TO SERVE

sparkling water
ice cubes

Use a box grater to shred the beetroot and carrots, and grate the ginger with a Microplane or similar. Transfer the gratings to a bowl or large Tupperware container, sprinkle with the caster sugar and mix well. Place a layer of cling film or greaseproof paper directly on top of the gratings (this will help prevent the top layer turning brown – don't be discouraged if it does, as once it's diluted the drink is a pretty one) then cover the mix with a further layer of cling film or an airtight lid and place in the fridge for 48 hours, occasionally shaking the container to encourage maceration.

Transfer the gratings and all juices into a sterilised 1-litre Kilner jar or similar (see page 167). Pour the cider vinegar over the gratings, ensuring all parts are submerged, and leave in the fridge or a cool place for a further 4–6 days. The idea is for the vinegar to sweeten and take on the flavours of the beetroot, carrot and ginger. Taste to check that is the case and leave for an additional day if you think the vinegar will benefit from that. Once to your taste, strain the vinegar through a fine sieve or muslin (via a funnel) into a clean, sealable bottle. The drinking vinegar will keep in the fridge for a number of weeks.

To serve, pour 30ml vinegar into a short glass. Add a couple of ice cubes and top with 150ml sparkling water. A similar quantity is a strangely enjoyable addition to a gin-based cocktail, too.

The residual gratings make an excellent pickle (see page 167) – use as a condiment for cured meats and cheese, as well as in sandwiches and salads. Store for up to a week in the fridge, using the jar in which they'd sat submerged in vinegar.

AN URBAN MARKETPLACE

It's hard to know where to begin when describing the physical space in which Borough Market exists. In many ways this mirrors feelings when on site; there are numerous entrances and, whether by chance or design, people arrive from all angles. But this is surely one of the attractions. Certainly it illustrates the fact that the Market is a physical and metaphorical meeting place – a confluence of producers and traders of exceptional produce who have brought their goods from near and far; of hungry home cooks, discerning chefs, inquisitive tourists, office workers and food-loving Londoners in search of a gourmet bite.

If you look at a map or floorplan, you'll see a jigsaw that has morphed and been added to over time. The architecture is an idiosyncratic meld of decorative wrought-iron coils and practical corrugated-metal sheets; of soaring cathedral-like glass ceilings, but also squat, damp brick arches, utilitarian concrete columns and the open air. The floor is a riot of differing materials, some rough, some smooth, others cobbled (something you'll hear the traders' trolleys enjoy as they're rolled out and back in during set-up and pack-down).

Many of the walls, facades and columns are painted in a distinctive Borough green. Three Crown Square is the most regal space, with soaring glass ceilings and ornate ironwork providing a grand setting for the semi-permanent stands at its edges and tributary alleyways, and the moveable stalls in the middle. Other areas, such as Green Market, are populated by colourful stalls during the day, but return to Victorian brickwork at night. There are wide, open, permanent stands on the Stoney Street edge and along Middle Road, delineated only by wire cages. Head to

London Bridge, continuing the long and intertwined history of railways and market.

It's somewhat of a maze, which enhances the feeling that this is a place to wander and to discover. The various paths and corners mean there are constant new sights and smells, and it takes multiple visits to truly get your bearings. Yet the architecture is ultimately just a backdrop to a finely detailed scene that changes on a daily basis. See, for example, how calm and serene Three Crown Square is on a Tuesday, when most of the trade is in the Green Market, compared to Fridays and Saturdays when there's a riot of yellow and red umbrellas, and throngs of shoppers moving as if in a carefully choreographed dance.

This spider's web of alleyways and squares is so different from a linear set of stalls in a classic market town. The space is dynamic and bustling, metropolitan and confusing. It's a patchwork of industrial furniture, which is brought to life only by the wares of a panoply of producers and the people who roam its paths. And therein lies its charm.

Jubilee Place, and you find a mix of on-site production and wholesale units and a seating area, where shoppers can sit and tick off their shopping lists. The modern Market Hall is a community space where events and cookery demonstrations are held, with hops growing up the glass walls in a kind of bucolic defiance of the busy road outside.

Hemmed in on the eastern side by Borough High Street and London Bridge, Southwark Street to the south, and the Thames and its surrounding footpaths to the west and north, this is a resolutely urban arena. There's a constant thrum of traffic, punctuated frequently by wailing sirens and the chatter of pedestrians. The rumble and resonance of trains dominate, however; those utilitarian columns and concrete arches support railway tracks running to and from the mainline stations of Cannon Street, Waterloo and

THE GREENGROCERS

The greengrocers set the scene – of all Borough's traders, it's their produce that varies most often, providing a constantly changing tableau according to the time of the year. From staple root vegetables and brassicas, to specialist berries, wild mushrooms, heritage apples and variegated bitter leaves, the likes of Chegworth Valley, Elsey & Bent, Ted's Veg, Paul Wheeler Fresh Supplies, Paul Crane and Jock Stark & Son offer all the fresh produce you could wish for, while the nighttime operations of Grovers, and the deliveries to all grocers in the early hours, provide a constant pulse, and are a reminder of the Market's origins.

Fred and Caroline Foster have run their business, Turnips, from under the arches for around thirty years. Their dramatic displays are an iconic landmark for many shoppers, not least the medley of wild mushrooms and mounds of multicoloured tomatoes. Behind the scenes, this is a significant supplier of quality produce to the restaurant trade.

FRED FOSTER, TURNIPS

I'm a third generation greengrocer. But when I started in the early- to mid-1980s, I wanted to take things in a slightly different direction, to find a niche, so I concentrated on selling direct to restaurants rather than retail. My wife and I needed a unit and set up here at Borough. Back then it was a small wholesale market and very different to what it is today.

The idea of the retail market came up because the central location made the logistics of a modern wholesale space difficult. There were only about eight of us left at the time, and some were unsure about it as they hadn't done retail before. I liked the idea though, and worked to convince others that a change could rejuvenate the area. Still, the fact I'd gone down the restaurant route meant it was a bit of a shot in the dark; when we opened up our fridges to the public, we were't selling the basic tomatoes and mushrooms that people expected.

As a restaurant supplier my job was working with Michelin starred chefs, the likes of Nico Ladenis and Eric Chavot. Nico would ask me to find things he couldn't get from other wholesalers but he knew he could get from France. So I learnt how to go direct to places in France and then Italy to source these specialist items. I also built up a network of independent farmers around the UK, instead of just getting the stuff from the commercial markets. Which meant I had a better grade of product than what most retailers were getting hold of. That was what made our business stand out. I think I was the first person to sell rocket on a retail basis, for example, having found it on behalf of Nico. Borough shoppers have always appreciated that. They want to get the things they eat in restaurants or see on TV or in books – years ago things like truffles, bergamot lemons; these days unusual brassicas, bitter leaves, specific squash and so on.

I like to think of our produce displays as live art. They draw people in and provide a backdrop to the Market. My daughter Rica runs our retail purchasing and displays now, and I drive her mad as she's the one who has to start at 4:30 in the morning laying all the produce out. She knows when I think it looks good and when I don't! The seasons are crucial because ultimately they affect what the displays are made from. As the seasons change, the displays change. It's continual. You can define the time of year by the colours you see.

So what's autumn? Look up at the trees. Those browns and burgundies, golds and oranges are what you get in fruits and vegetables too – all the different squash, pumpkins, mushrooms, aubergines and figs. In a sense it makes it easy for us, because those fruit and vegetables are in abundance and obviously good. That's the beauty of following the seasons.

We do go beyond local fruit and vegetables, too; I've always been an importer because of the restaurant connections, and in fact internationally-grown ingredients might be the bulk of our produce. I just try to follow the principle that if it's British, it's in season; and if it's not British, it's world class and at its peak. That's what we promote.

It's real food here, you know? We don't always have what people are looking for, because it might be the wrong time of year. And when people buy fruit and veg, guess what? It goes off! That's fine, that's proper. The supermarkets have made food bland and one track. It's good if we can help people understand that.

Sometimes I get frustrated because I think people are more inclined to become knowledgeable or interested in artisan produce: wine, cured meat, cheese. I think there's an assumption that there's less skill or effort involved in the process of growing things. They're wrong, of course. And then people say to me: 'a tomato's just a tomato'. They're missing out. Come here in late summer and see the number of varieties in our displays. Or in winter eat a Marinda tomato alongside one from a supermarket – and then tell me a tomato's just a tomato…

I hope we can help people find that out, to discover new food and its possibilities. I remember a young Jamie Oliver coming here and being astounded at what we had, even though he got to cook with top-class ingredients all the time. I'd love it if we can help enthuse everyone in the same way, so that they know, say, just like apples and potatoes, there's early-season, mid-season or main-crop varieties of squash. Butternut is wonderful because it's an all-year-round thing – first from South Africa and then Peru – but in autumn, it's the onion, acorn, spaghetti and delica squashes that are world class. They're what you want to be cooking then.

VARIEGATED KALE WITH ANCHOVY BUTTER SAUCE

One of the many benefits of market shopping is exposure to extraordinary vegetables years before supermarkets catch on (if ever). Shoppers may be both attracted and put off by ingredients that are alien to them, but few are difficult to cook. One vegetable that is making an increasingly bold appearance in autumn and winter is variegated kale – purple, white and green brassicas. They come in all sorts of shapes and sizes: some appear spiky and ornamental, others look like a flower made of colourful cabbage. They are generally more delicate than the curly kales that we are accustomed to and need only be warmed in a large pan, emboldened by a salty, buttery emulsion.

This striking side dish goes very well with a multitude of meats and fish – anything from beef, lamb, venison or chicken to white fish like cod, hake, haddock, halibut, turbot and john dory.

SERVES *4–6* AS A SIDE DISH

1 variegated kale (or 300g regular kale,
  leaves stripped from tough ribs)
8 salted anchovies in oil, roughly chopped
40g butter
2 tablespoons water
juice from a wedge of lemon

Trim the kale leaves from the base and refresh them briefly in a bowl of cold water, then remove and leave in a colander or similar to drain and dry. Unless the leaves are particularly large and considerably more than a mouthful, leave them whole.

Use the largest saucepan, high-sided frying pan or wok you have, as it's helpful to have as much pan in contact with kale at the same time as you can.

Put the pan over a low-medium heat and leave to warm up for a minute. Add the anchovies and butter and allow them to melt but do not let them fry or the butter foam. Add 2 tablespoons water and 6 or 7 grinds of the pepper mill, then shake the pan so that the water and butter comes together as a glossy emulsion. Add a touch of lemon to lighten the sauce, then add the kale leaves to the warm pan for 2–3 minutes, turning with tongs to ensure all the kale gets heated through. Remove the leaves from the pan before they turn translucent and overly floppy. If you are cooking regular kale in the butter, cook it at a slightly warmer temperature.

JERUSALEM ARTICHOKE SOUP WITH HAZELNUT OIL AND CRISPY SKINS

It's easy to walk past Jerusalem artichokes. The knobbly roots are a classic ugly duckling, appearing fiddly and unpromising when in a muddy box, yet once roasted, sautéed or boiled, they have a pronounced and appetising flavour and smell – a combination of earthy, sweet and mineral. One simple way to get acquainted with the vegetable is by turning it into a classy, velvety soup.

As with all soups, adding texture ensures interest beyond the first couple of spoonfuls. Here, the artichoke peelings are roast until crisp to become a natural crouton, and raw slices provide additional bite. It's all the same vegetable, but by using every last part, the soup is varied from first to last spoonful. To add further interest, swirl in cooling crème fraîche, plus a drop or two of hazelnut oil from **Fitz Fine Foods** (or alternatively good extra-virgin olive oil, or even a dash of truffle oil if you have it).

SERVES 6

30g butter
1 onion, chopped
2 medium leeks, trimmed finely sliced
    and washed
1kg Jerusalem artichokes, 900g peeled
    and cut into 2cm chunks (skin reserved),
    100g unpeeled
250g floury potatoes, peeled and cut into 2cm
    chunks (skin reserved)
leaves picked from 6 sprigs of thyme
parmesan rind (optional)
1.3 litres hot vegetable or chicken stock
1 tablespoon vegetable or sunflower oil
hazelnut oil, for drizzling
100g full-fat crème fraîche
3 garlic cloves, crushed
chopped chives or parsley (optional)

Preheat the oven to 220C fan/240C/460F/gas mark 9.

Melt the butter in a large, heavy-based saucepan over a medium heat. Add the onion, leek, and a pinch of flaky sea salt and cook for 4–5 minutes until softened but not coloured, stirring frequently.

Put the chunks of artichoke and peeled potato in the saucepan, along with the thyme leaves, garlic and parmesan rind (if using). Reduce the temperature to low, place a lid on top and cook gently for 15 minutes, stirring occasionally. Pour the stock into the pan and simmer for a further 30 minutes until the artichokes are completely soft. Use a hand-held blender, food processor or stand blender to purée the soup until velvety smooth.

Just after the artichoke and potatoes are added to the saucepan, toss the vegetable peelings in the vegetable or sunflower oil then scatter them over a baking tray in one layer – use a fork to spread the peelings out so they roast and crisp up, rather than clump and become soggy. Place towards the top of the hot oven and roast for 10–15 minutes until golden and crisp, shuffling them around after about 8 minutes. Remove, sprinkle with lots of salt and a few drops of hazelnut oil, mix, and try to avoid eating them before the soup is ready.

Check the soup is at a desirable consistency – it should be neither too watery nor thick like a purée; cook to evaporate liquid or add a splash more as necessary. Once happy, season generously with salt and black pepper and serve with a dollop of crème fraîche and generous swirl of hazelnut oil in each bowl, plus a scattering of chives or parsley (if using) and a handful of the peeling crisps. Slice the reserved artichokes very thinly (with a mandoline if you have one), and add a few to each bowl to garnish.

WINTER SQUASH RED CURRY

During October, greengrocers display an appealing mix of squash and pumpkins. Confusingly, the likes of acorn, Delica and onion squash are categorised as 'winter squash', yet their appearance absolutely heralds the onset of autumn. Ignoring semantics, all are compelling and flavoursome alternatives to butternut squash.

As a general rule, treat winter squash more or less as you would a butternut. Most have edible skin, and can be boiled, steamed or roasted, and they are as good as the main part of a meal as they are a side dish. The onion squash, for example, makes a fine focal point for a Thai red curry, as it is reasonably firm, and its flavour strong and sweet enough to match the aromatics and heat of the sauce.

Galangal and lemongrass are important here; happily they are increasingly available, not least at **Turnips** and **Paul Wheeler Fresh Supplies**.

SERVES *4*

6–10 dried Thai red chillies (about 7g)
120g creamed coconut or 1 x 400ml tin
   coconut milk
1 teaspoon coriander seeds
1 teaspoon cumin seeds
1 teaspoon white peppercorns
150g banana shallots, roughly chopped
40g garlic cloves, roughly chopped
3 sticks of lemongrass, roughly chopped
25g fresh galangal, roughly chopped
2 teaspoons shrimp paste (optional)
800g–1kg onion squash, woody ends cut off
25g coconut oil
2 tablespoons palm sugar or golden caster sugar
2 teaspoons fish sauce
140g string beans, woody tops cut off
   and beans halved
about 20 Thai holy basil leaves (or a handful
   of coriander leaves)
2 long red chillies, thinly sliced
jasmine or basmati rice, to serve

Put the dried chillies in a heatproof bowl or mug and cover them with just-boiled water. If using creamed coconut rather than tinned milk, put the coconut in a separate heatproof bowl and pour 400ml boiling water on top. Leave both for at least 15 minutes.

Dry-toast the spices until fragrant then grind into a powder.

Put the ground spices in a food processor or blender with the shallots, garlic, lemongrass, galangal, shrimp paste (if using), the rehydrated chillies and 4 tablespoons of their soaking water. Pulse and blend until smooth – this may take a few minutes. Pause from time to time to prevent your blender or processor from overheating. You could be more authentic and pound each ingredient into a paste in a pestle and mortar, but the machine replaces romance with efficiency, and the taste is not too different.

Cut the squash in half (from top to bottom) and scoop out the seeds and mushy fibres. Place each half cut side down on a board and use a large knife to cut them into 2–3cm-thick slices.

Put the coconut oil in a wok placed over a medium heat. Add the curry paste and cook for 3–4 minutes, stirring regularly. Add the sugar and fish sauce and cook for another minute then pour in the coconut cream or coconut milk and add the squash slices. Bring to the boil, ensure the squash is submerged, then simmer for 20–25 minutes until just tender. Add the green beans and cook for 5 minutes more. Remove from the heat and stir in the Thai basil and the red chillies. Serve with jasmine or basmati rice.

PARSNIP, PEAR AND PORK TRAY BAKE

Though pork is integral to this one-tray meal, the porcine treats of crackling, chops and black pudding seem to bind and play second fiddle to the parsnips, pears and shallots; these fruit and veg may be greengrocer staples, but they're as important as the meat here, if not more so.

The cooking is done in a few stages to ensure each ingredient is at its optimum by the end. Do seek out thick chops from a good butcher. A thick layer of fat is integral to the cooking process, and slow growing, sustainably reared pigs are a world away in ethics and taste compared to more commercial breeds.

SERVES 4

4 bone-in, heritage breed pork chops
   (300–400g each)
3 sprigs of rosemary
6 garlic cloves, flattened
finely grated or shredded zest of 1 lemon
2 tablespoons maple syrup
2 tablespoons olive oil
800g parsnips, peeled and cut
   into thumb-sized batons
4 banana shallots, peeled and halved
2 large or 3 medium conference pears,
   quartered lengthways
250g black pudding, cut into 1–2cm-thick chunks
peas or seasonal greens, to serve (optional)

Use a sharp knife to trim the fat and skin from each chop in one strip, leaving 0.5–1cm of fat next to the meat. Cut the strips of fat and skin into 3–4cm lengths and set aside. Bruise the rosemary with the blunt edge of a knife and put the sprigs in a sturdy freezer bag with the garlic, lemon zest, maple syrup, olive oil and a heavy pinch of black pepper. Add the pork chops, rub the marinade over them and leave for at least the remaining steps in the cooking process (you could do this 12–24 hours in advance for maximum flavour).

Preheat the oven to 200C fan/220C/425F/gas mark 7.

Put the chunks of pork fat and skin in a large roasting tin and place in the oven for 15 minutes, so that much of the fat starts to render out, then add the parsnips and shallots, shake the pan and roast for 20 minutes.

Remove the crackling pieces and set them to one side. Add the pears and cook for a further 20 minutes, using a fish slice to move the ingredients around after 10 minutes to ensure even crisping. After that time, remove the tin and increase the temperature to 220C fan/240C/460F/gas mark 9.

Shuffle the ingredients again, leaving enough space in the tin to place the black pudding directly on the tin's surface. Sit the pork chops on top, season with flaky sea salt and brush with any excess marinade. Add the marinade aromatics into the tin, and return the pork crackling too (ensuring they avoid any juice from the pears and parsnips, or the skin will soften), then roast for 15–20 minutes more, until the chops are firm and catching at the edges. Place the chops on a warm plate while the vegetables and crackling have a final 3–5-minute blast in the oven. Serve immediately, with peas or seasonal greens if you wish.

DATE SCONES WITH PEAR AND CARDAMOM BUTTER

British pears are a key part of a greengrocer's autumnal display and remain in season through many of the colder months, though they don't quite have the staying power many apples do.

If you have a glut of ripe-to-overripe pears, cooking them into a butter conserve is an excellent way of making the haul last longer (you could do the same with apples). This butter doesn't have as much sugar as traditional fruit butters do, and therefore the pears are not overwhelmed by sickly sweetness, as can sometimes be the case. It is particularly well suited to being spread on a warm, date-studded scone, with a spoonful of clotted cream on top for good measure.

FOR THE PEAR BUTTER
(MAKES 500ML–1 LITRE)

4 tablespoons lemon juice
150ml water
1kg ripe conference or concord pears
70g golden caster sugar
½ teaspoon flaky sea salt
1 teaspoon ground cardamom

Put the lemon juice and 150ml water in a heavy-based saucepan. Wash, quarter and cut the cores from the pears, dropping the segments into the liquid once they're prepared. Heat gently for 10–15 minutes, until the pears have released enough liquid that the contents of the pan can come to the boil. Reduce the heat and simmer for 30 minutes, or until mushy.

Blitz in a food processor or blender (a high-powered blender will give the best result) until completely smooth and ideally without flecks of peel, then return the purée to the pan with the sugar, salt and cardamom. Reheat, stirring until the sugar has dissolved, then simmer uncovered for 1–1½ hours, stirring with a spatula frequently to prevent the pears burning or sticking to the bottom of the pan. The butter is ready when the gold-green mix is as thick as whipped cream, holds its shape if you drag a spoon through it, and has minimal water content – if you spoon a little onto a plate, no water should seep out.

Ladle into sterilised jars (see page 167) and store in the fridge for up to a month.

FOR THE SCONES (MAKES 6—8)

225g self-raising flour, plus extra for dusting
½ teaspoon baking powder
½ teaspoon flaky sea salt
25g golden caster sugar
60g cold unsalted butter, cubed
20g dried dates, finely chopped
125ml fridge-cold whole milk

Preheat the oven to 200C fan/220C/425F/gas mark 7 and line a baking sheet with non-stick paper or a silicone mat.

Sift the flour and baking powder into a mixing bowl. Add the salt and sugar and use your fingertips to rub in the butter until the mixture resembles fine breadcrumbs. Stir in the dates, then make a well in the centre and pour in the milk. Use a spoon or knife to mix the ingredients into a dough, resorting briefly to a lightly floured hand. Avoid working the dough too much. Tip the dough onto a lightly floured surface, and push it together then use your hands to pat it to a thickness of about 3cm.

Use a lightly floured 5cm smooth (not fluted) round cutter to stamp out scones – you should get 6–8 from the dough – then transfer these to the lined baking sheet. Bake for 10–15 minutes until risen and golden. Remove from the oven and leave to cool for at least a few minutes on a wire rack. Scones are best when fresh from the oven, though these will keep in an airtight container for a day (leave to cool fully before storing).

MARKET EVENTS

APPLE DAY
AT BOROUGH MARKET

Every October, Borough Market is the setting for one of the country's most prominent and vibrant Apple Days. It's a hive of apple-themed activity. There are cider vans, mulled spiced apple juice, hog roasts with apple sauce, apple cakes and pastries and much more. All in praise of this single crop, and marking the calendar custom initiated in the 1990s by arts and environmental charity, Common Ground, who had sought to commemorate not only the richness and variety of British apples – of which there are thousands, yet barely a handful on offer in supermarkets – but also the links between food and the land.

Each year there's something new to see: visitors have been able to swap their supermarket apples for lesser-known heritage versions, there has been a display of 1,000 different apple varieties, and the likes of Chegworth Valley always provide an opportunity to buy apples such as Crimson Crisp, Egremont Russet and Cox, grown on their farm in Kent.

The Demonstration Kitchen is in constant action, with sweet and savoury recipes showing the never-ending possibilities of apple as a cooking ingredient.

Throughout the afternoon, children and adults alike try their hand at speed-peeling competitions, pause for a moment to plant a wish or listen to stories in temporary apple-tree orchards, and try a range of unusual and endangered apple varieties, including local fruits like London Pearmain and Cellini.

The performances of a local company of actors, the Lions part – whose October Plenty festival prompted and now intertwines wonderfully with Borough's – provide humour and cheer.

Perhaps the most striking part of Apple Day is the parade of the Corn Queene, a huge effigy made from wheat and barley and decorated in apples, root vegetables and foliage. At the end of the day, she is dismantled by the Berry Man – the autumnal incarnation of Green Man, an ancient pagan symbol of growth – with the edible decorations handed out to the crowds.

The Mayor of Southwark often parades with the actors; there are fantabulous plays and songs; prancing, jingling Morris men, and the whole event begins with a short service in the Market led by Southwark Cathedral. It's both a nod to Britain's fruit heritage and a real community effort.

THE APPLE

The apple comes from central Asia. As apples were used as fodder for pack animals, their seeds gradually spread along the silk route, and eventually reached Europe where they thrived. Britain's national fruit collection (NFC) at Brogdale Farm in Kent grows over 2,000 varieties of heritage apples. During the apple season – typically from late August to the end of October – there are crates of these at the entrance to Neal's Yard Dairy, including the likes of Ananas Reinette, which has the perfume of pineapple and tastes like soured-apple candy, and the crotchety sounding, but juicy and sweet William Crump.

The NFC sends a multitude of samples to the Market for tasting on Apple Day and encourages us all to keep pushing retailers to see a bigger range of British-grown apples for sale through the autumn and winter months.

THE FISHMONGERS

The glistening bounty of bright-eyed fish and plump shellfish sitting on beds of ice is impossible to miss as you walk around Borough Market. From the day-boat haul of Sussex Fish in the Green Market, to Furness Fish Markets' treasure trove of seafood along Middle Row, these displays are a sight to behold. As, in a less colourful but no less impressive fashion, are Richard Haward's stacks of oysters and clams, and the tempting wares of the cold and hot smoke specialists like Oak & Smoke.

One ebullient fishmonger is Darren Brown of Shellseekers Fish & Game Ltd. His native sustainable catch is found in the heart of the Market. Rigid, silvery mackerel sit next to line-caught sea bass, long, winding hake, pearlescent Cornish octopus and other fish from England's south-west coast. As the name suggests, though, it all began with the scallops that Darren hand-dives down in Dorset.

DARREN BROWN, SHELLSEEKERS

I started off back in 1997, when earning a living from working the sea and land was all just a bit of a dream. I was coming to the end of my career in the Royal Navy and was on night shifts four days a week, which meant I had time to go diving where I live in Lulworth Cove, Dorset. I had this idea that I might be able to set up a scallop diving business as I'd been collecting them off the sea bed and selling them to friends for years – it was a bit like picking up 50p pieces! So I tried it out as I transitioned to civilian life, and pretty quickly found myself moving quite a volume into Billingsgate, the wholesale fish market in east London.

Then, some time early in 1998, a friend of mine gave me a ring and said 'we've been asked to come to this place called Borough Market where they've started a farmers' market. Can we give it a go?' So we did. We turned up with an old van and one hundred dozen scallops, and put them on a table that we'd covered with camouflage netting. We sold the lot by 10:30am. Twelve hundred scallops in a couple of hours! It was a game-changing moment for me – not that we'd sold them all so quickly; more the revelation that I could both harvest food and sell it direct to the appreciative end user.

We stopped doing wholesale pretty much immediately and got a regular stall. My partner left the business to sell at other markets, but I stayed on at Borough and gradually added Fridays and then Thursdays and so on. And here I am, twenty years later, trading six days a week.

I have two boats now. We still dive for scallops a couple of times a week, but I have to have a decent range of fish on my stall to make the six-day-a-week trading work. So we rod- and line-fish mackerel and sea bass too, and

fish caught on
Jurassic Coast
Boat Maddy Moo

total opposite to the big commercial fishing operations. We cannot keep taking. We need reserves, areas that can't be trawled or dredged, that sort of thing. It's vital that we manage our seas.

I like it when customers ask 'what's good this week?'. Being flexible is the best way to shop for fish. What we sell is always fresh, of course, as it'll have come up from the coast overnight. But we might not have what you're after if you've come with something specific in mind. We really notice when a celebrity chef has been cooking something on television as people come and ask for it. Maybe they filmed that at a different time of year, though, or something else is at its peak that week.

It's easy to forget that seasonality is a factor with fish and seafood. The supermarkets have fed us a year-round diet of cod and salmon, but there's much more to it. In part, it comes down to breeding cycles. Once they've spawned, fish are underweight and scrawny. You want fish and seafood to be plump and appetising. Scallops, for example, spawn when the waters are warm in late summer. So they're much better when they've fattened up again, from October, November and onwards. For sea bass the early part of the year is a no go. In the months before that, though, say autumn to Christmas, they're at their best. There's also the question of water temperature: in late summer, for example, when the sea is at its warmest, the south west of England gets bream that's swum up from the Azores, and sardines from the Mediterranean; they don't stick around when temperatures drop again.

For me it's all about showcasing the finest fish and venison in its best possible condition. To be able to sell direct to people who appreciate quality food is still exciting. The next step is my new boat, which will be licensed to take people out with me. I just think offering customers the chance to come out and see the process will be a great way to complete the circle.

if I see some nice flat fish on the bottom when I'm diving, I'll bring them up with me. To supplement the catch I gather a range of fish and seafood from other fishermen in the south west of England who I know fish locally, ethically and sustainably. We also sell meat from deer that I personally stalk and shoot down here in Dorset. You can even try before you buy, as the scallops and venison are available in the shell and as burgers to eat on the spot. I think the fact we're responsible for the whole process, from sea bed and land to our stand at Borough, is vital.

Hand-dived scallops and rod- and line-caught seafood are good examples of responsible fishing: there are natural limitations on how many shells a human can collect in one dive; and with rod and line, the fish don't always bite. This means our impact on the sea bed is minimal. Plus, anything that doesn't make the grade goes back in the sea unharmed. It's the

OYSTERS, TWO WAYS

There's a strong argument – supported if you graze on oysters and clams at **Richard Haward's Oysters** stall, **Shellseekers Fish & Game Ltd** or **Furness Fish Markets** – that oysters need only lemon, Tabasco or a shallot vinaigrette. But to stick rigidly to those condiments would be a shame, not least because you would miss out on trying these fresh and fiery embellishments. The cucumber and lime granita works particularly well with native flat-topped oysters, which are in season from September through to April; whereas the sobrasada (cured, spreadable spiced sausage – you could also use 'nduja) and lemon butter is best saved for the deeper, sturdier rock varieties which are available all year round.

CUCUMBER AND LIME GRANITA

MAKES ENOUGH FOR A DOZEN NATIVE OYSTERS

1 cucumber, peeled
3 tablespoons water
2 teaspoons caster sugar
pinch of flaky sea salt
juice of 1 lime

Place the peeled cucumber in a blender with 3 tablespoons water and blitz for 2 minutes. Strain the cucumber mulch through a sieve and discard any foam (you may find that you need to repeat the straining process).

Decant the liquid into a small Tupperware or similar container, filling it to one third of its depth. Add the sugar, salt and lime juice. Stir, ensuring the sugar has dissolved, then place in the freezer for at least 8 hours. Remove every couple of hours to push a fork through the mix and break the ice into sharp flakes.

Shuck the oysters and, when ready to serve, drop a forkful of granita into each shell.

GRILLED OYSTERS WITH SOBRASADA AND LEMON BUTTER

MAKES ENOUGH FOR 6 ROCK OYSTERS

50g butter at room temperature
60g sobrasada (or 'nduja)
finely grated zest of 1 lemon

Mash the butter with the back of a fork in a bowl or in a pestle and mortar. Add the sobrasada and lemon zest and keep mashing until the mixture is soft, then transfer to a bowl and 'whip' with a wooden spoon or spatula until smooth. You can use this immediately, or spoon the butter onto a piece of greaseproof paper, roll it into a sausage shape and store it in the fridge until required.

Turn the grill to its hottest setting and move the shelf approximately 4–5cm away from the heat source. Close the door and allow the oven to heat up for 10 minutes.

Shuck the oysters, trying to keep as much juice in them as possible, and place them on a tray or ovenproof dish that fits them snugly. Put a heaped teaspoon of butter in each oyster and grill for 3–4 minutes, so that the butter melts, the sobrasada sizzles and the juices begin to boil. Allow to cool for a minute before eating.

MARKET FISH SOUP

A fishmonger's display (referred to by some as a flash) often features a selection of showpiece fish, which due to their freshness need very little done to them to make a stunning meal – turbot, john dory, sea bass, ray and halibut, for example. There are ideas in this book for these prime specimens (see pages 149, 252 and 266), but it's also possible for a humble bowl of soup made from less celebrated fish to steal the show.

The method here could be used with a wide variety of fish, and you could make it with whichever fish is plentiful at the time, but it is a particularly good use of gurnard, whose sweet flesh is flavoursome enough, yet not too fishy, and its bones are also excellent for making the stock that forms the base. If you ask nicely, good fishmongers will pass on the frames of other fish they've filleted to go with your order. Ask the fishmonger to pin-bone the fillets and remove any fish eyes and gills before giving you the bones as these add an undesirable bitterness to a fish stock.

SERVES 6

1 small leek, washed
1 small fennel bulb
2 celery sticks
5 garlic cloves
extra fish bones from the fishmonger
1 star anise
1 lemon
2 litres water
3 tablespoons vegetable or olive oil
*1.5kg gurnard (weight of whole fish), filleted
    but heads and bones kept
    (you could add red mullet, grey mullet
    and snapper to the mix, but keep at least
    50% gurnard)*
1 carrot, peeled
1 red pepper, deseeded
50g salted anchovies in oil, chopped
75ml Pernod
1 x 400g tin plum tomatoes
pinch of saffron threads
pinch of dried chilli flakes

TO SERVE

lemon wedges
fresh bread

Trim the green tops from the leek and the woody stalks from the fennel. Add the trimmings to a large saucepan along with 1 celery stick, roughly chopped, and 2 garlic cloves cut in half. Add the fish bones, star anise and 2 slices of lemon. Cover with 2 litres cold water and bring to the boil. Reduce the heat to a light simmer, skim away any foam from the surface of the water and allow to bubble gently for 20 minutes (but no longer, as it will turn bitter), then strain the liquid through a fine sieve – you should have 1.5–1.8 litres stock. Boil and reduce the liquid to that volume if you have more.

Meanwhile, place a separate large and heavy-based saucepan over a medium-high heat. Add 2 tablespoons of the vegetable or olive oil. Trim the thinner tail ends and any scrappy bits from the fish fillets, so that two thirds of the fish remain as thick fillets. Set aside these thicker bits (they get added at the end). Put the trimmings in the hot oil, skin side down, and fry for 2–3 minutes until golden. Flip onto the flesh side and cook for 1 minute more, then set aside.

Chop the remaining celery, fennel bulb, the leek, carrot and red pepper into 2cm dice and add them to the still warm saucepan with a pinch of flaky sea salt and the remaining oil. Cook over a medium heat for 10 minutes, stirring occasionally, until the vegetables are soft, sweet and just a little browned at the edges. Add the anchovies to the pan and cook for a further 2 minutes until melted. Slice the remaining garlic thinly and add to the pan. Increase the heat, pour in the Pernod and let this bubble and reduce by half before adding the tinned tomatoes, saffron, chilli flakes, the browned fish and stock. Turn the heat down and simmer for 1 hour, reducing by around one third in volume, then purée it completely with a hand-held blender. Cut the remaining fish fillets into 3–4cm pieces and add them to the soup. Warm through for 5 minutes (do not boil), season to taste with salt and black pepper, and serve the soup with a wedge of lemon each plus some fresh bread.

MUSSELS WITH OLOROSO SHERRY AND VENISON CHORIZO

British mussels are plump and in season from late August through autumn. They're easy and quick to cook, so full of flavour and remarkably economical to buy, and as such should be a lunch or starter in everyone's armoury. Give your diners a spoon to slurp up the stock, and hunks of fresh bread to mop up any remaining juices.

Often, cooks use white wine, cider and/or cream for dishes like this. This version takes a quick trip to Spain, via a glass of dry yet caramel-tinted oloroso sherry, and a hit of smoked paprika; and then back to Britain thanks to some lightly smoked venison chorizo from **Cannon & Cannon**. Other venison salamis, for example from **Alpine Deli**, or a more classic pork chorizo, would work too.

SERVES 4

2kg mussels
2 tablespoons light olive oil
2 banana shallots, very thinly sliced
2 teaspoons sweet smoked paprika
    (Pimentón de la Vera)
2 garlic cloves, very thinly sliced
10 sprigs of parsley, leaves picked,
    stalks finely chopped
1 small venison chorizo (80–100g), diced
200ml oloroso sherry
fresh bread, to serve

Purge (clean) the mussels by leaving them to soak in cold water for 30 minutes, changing the water 3–4 times. Over this time you'll see plenty of grit and dirt emerge from the molluscs. Pull off any straggly beards from the mussels and sort through the mix for shells that are open or broken – if open mussels do not close up when tapped against a hard surface, discard them.

Place a large saucepan over a high heat (you might even split the mussels between two saucepans). Add the oil, the shallots and a pinch of flaky sea salt and sauté for 1–2 minutes without colouring. Add the paprika, garlic and parsley stalks and soften for 1 minute, then tip in the mussels and diced venison chorizo. Shake the pan for 30 seconds, move the mussels to one side of the pan and pour in the sherry, letting it bubble, then place a lid on and cook for about 4 minutes, until the majority of the mussels have fully opened and they look plump and inviting. The remainder should work their way open in the residual heat as you finish the dish (which is better than waiting for the last shell to pop and overcooking the rest as a result).

Throw in the parsley leaves then ladle the mussels into bowls, ensuring everyone has a fair share of the cooking liquor. You will need extra bowls on the table for empty shells, plus a few napkins to mop messy hands. Serve with hunks of fresh bread.

FLAT WHITE FISH WITH LEEKS AND BROWN SHRIMPS

Autumn is a particularly good time to eat flat white fish like plaice, lemon and Dover sole, and indeed other lesser-known varieties native to UK coastal waters, such as dab and megrim. Each appears to offer little (how can something so flat be worth eating?), yet in fact they provide tender, juicy, subtly flavoured flesh that's easy and ludicrously quick to cook.

Fishmongers like Paul Day of **Sussex Fish** will happily guide you towards which of them is best on the day. Ask them to do the hard work and fillet it for you, too, then it'll take you barely five minutes to go from raw ingredient to gourmet meal; in this instance with the help of a sweet and nutty brown shrimp and butter sauce, and soft, aromatic leeks. Buttery, silky mashed potato works very well next to this fish and leek combo.

SERVES 2

*2 medium leeks, trimmed (about 300g), halved
    lengthways, cut into 1–2cm-wide half moons*
60g butter
50ml dry vermouth
*2 skinned plaice, Dover or lemon sole fillets
    (about 150g each)*
2 tablespoons cooking oil
*1 lemon, ½ juiced, the remaining
    cut into wedges*
40g brown shrimp
*leaves picked from 8 sprigs of parsley,
    finely chopped*

Wash the leeks thoroughly. Melt 10g of the butter in a heavy-based pan (for which you have a lid). Add the still-wet leeks and cook over a high heat for 4 minutes. Make a little space in the pan and pour in the vermouth, allowing it to bubble and reduce by half. Season generously with flaky sea salt and black pepper, cover, and remove the pan from the heat.

Meanwhile, find a heavy-based frying pan big enough to fit the 2 fillets. Add the cooking oil and place over a medium heat. Allow the pan to heat up, then lay the fish fillets on the oiled surface, the equivalent of their skin side down, and cook gently for 2–3 minutes until the flesh has turned opaque to about two thirds of its depth, the remainder still being slightly translucent. Add 20g of the butter to the pan and, once it has melted, spoon over the fish for a further 1 minute to finish cooking the top side before the bottom is overcooked.

Just prior to adding the butter to the pan, divide the leeks into two neat piles on two warmed plates. Gently slide the cooked fish out of the pan and onto the leeks.

Finally, put the remaining butter in a smaller pan over a high heat and allow it to foam then turn brown and nutty. When the middle of the pool of butter stops foaming, turn the heat off, add the lemon juice, brown shrimp and a third of the parsley and let them warm through in the butter. Spoon the brown shrimp sauce liberally over the fish. Sprinkle with the remaining parsley and serve with the lemon wedges.

SPICED BUTTERFLIED MACKEREL

Still abundant in autumn, mackerel is richly flavoured, hardy and bullish enough to stand up to heavy spicing and relatively aggressive cooking. Which is exactly what happens here. A spicy paste is applied, then the fish is grilled until the spices sizzle and the flesh just begins to flake. A salad of pickled carrots and coriander helps to cleanse the palette between each bite, cutting through the spice and oily nature of the mackerel. This is a great evening meal for two.

It's not too difficult to butterfly the fish at home, removing the fillets from the bones in one piece, and leaving the tail on to keep them together, but ask the fishmonger to do it if you prefer. Or use two regular fillets per person.

SERVES 2

FOR THE PICKLED CARROT SALAD

3 carrots (350–400g), peeled and cut
into 2mm-thick circles (use a mandoline
if you have one)
150ml apple vinegar
50ml water
70g granulated sugar
10 black peppercorns
½ teaspoon flaky sea salt
1 teaspoon yellow mustard seeds
1 teaspoon coriander seeds
leaves picked from 10 sprigs of coriander

FOR THE MACKEREL

2 mackerel, butterflied
1 garlic clove, crushed
thumb-sized piece of fresh ginger, peeled
and finely grated
1 tablespoon Spice Mountain Mauritius masala
(or alternative spice mix – see method)
3 tablespoons light olive oil

Put the sliced carrots in a container that fits them snugly. Heat the vinegar in a pan with 50ml water to just below a simmer. Add the sugar, peppercorns, salt, mustard and coriander seeds, stir to ensure the sugar has dissolved and pour the mixture over the carrots. Cover and leave to cool for at least 1 hour, ideally more (up to 8).

Line a baking tray with greaseproof paper. Lay the fish on top, skin side down. Combine the garlic, ginger, masala, oil and a good pinch of salt and spread this over the fish flesh. Refrigerate for 1 hour. (If you can't find Spice Mountain's Mauritius masala, grind ½ teaspoon each of cumin, coriander, yellow mustard seeds and red chilli flakes in a pestle and mortar, and mix with ½ teaspoon of ground turmeric and ginger, plus a few turns of a pepper mill.)

Turn the grill on to its hottest setting, set a shelf 6–8cm from the heat source and close the oven door. Allow the oven to heat up for 10 minutes, turn your extraction fan on, then slide in the tray of mackerel and close the door. Grill for 6–7 minutes, until the spice mix is sizzling and turning golden and the fish begins to release some of its oils. Remove from the oven and allow to rest for 3 minutes.

Mix the coriander leaves and pickled carrots (without their pickling juices) and serve alongside the fish.

THE NEW FOOD ETHICS

TIM LANG

What defines good food in the 21st century? First and foremost, it's whatever you enjoy eating, whatever sustains you and gives you pleasure – yet it's so much more than that. Enjoying your food should also mean knowing your food, trusting it, being happy with how it has been produced.

Our preferences are shaped – often unconsciously – by many different factors: our circumstances, incomes, backgrounds, aspirations, tastes, memories. But if we want our food choices to be better, we need to reflect on what 'better' means, and to be clear about what those values are. We might think our values are constant and firm, but they are actually affected by vast industries, flush with finance and new technologies, trying to influence what we buy. An academic colleague of mine in Brazil, who led the creation of the country's national dietary guidelines, advised the public: 'If a food is highly advertised, think very carefully about eating it.' It's not a bad rule for all of us to follow.

As a vocal champion of the kind of high-quality foods that are unlikely to feature in expensive advertising campaigns, Borough Market can help to stretch our understanding of the choices we make. Encouraging people to widen their tastes is an essential part of the Market's mission,

and that means moving beyond fatty, sweet and salty foods – the tastes with which over-processed foods seduce us – and embracing those that are bitter, mature, fermented or spicy. Yet while the taste of our food matters greatly, so too does the way it is grown. This may be out of sight, but it is real nonetheless.

Food has a huge impact upon ecosystems and, if we consumers fully understood the extent of this, it would feature in our decisions. Food production is the biggest driver of climate change, biodiversity loss and soil degradation. The 20th century scientific revolution massively increased food output – a success story, in many ways – but it did this mostly by using fossil fuels and artificial fertilisers, the use of which has almost certainly already exceeded what scientists call the 'planetary safe operating space'. It took ever more land out of nature into production for us and for animals. Water use is also a big problem. The amount of water needed to produce a 150g beefburger, for example, has been calculated as 2,400 litres, and this 'embedded' water should be a defining factor in our food choices, even here in wet Britain. Unless the food we eat receives

good husbandry, like that conducted by the best small-scale producers who sell their wares at Borough Market, our diets will be the agents of future generations' troubles. These hidden effects need to be out in the open.

The food we consume is also a major determinant of public health, influencing the incidence of heart disease, cancer and antimicrobial resistance, hunger and obesity. In fact, food is now the single largest factor in premature death worldwide, above tobacco. A century ago, the big food problem was that vast numbers of people on low incomes couldn't afford to eat enough. This is still a global problem. In affluent countries, however, food has become relatively cheap, and health problems are increasingly associated with over-consumption and the rise of non-food foods: bland, ultra-processed stuff. For the sake of our health, as well as that of the environment, we need to consume overwhelmingly plant-based diets and to eat meat both sparingly and of only the highest quality.

Knowing this, we can develop a clearer understanding of the true cost of the food we buy. People often say we live in a market economy – we don't: we live in a supermarket economy, often a hypermarket economy. Ours is now a consumer society, with over four times the number of people working in food service in the UK than make their living from growing or fishing. Those who produce primary food products get less than a tenth of the money we spend; even in a rich country like the UK, their incomes are on the edge, reliant on subsidies. So, while it may be cheap, the price of food rarely sustains those at the bottom of the chain, and does little to reflect the social and environmental costs of production. No one pays for the climate change, soil erosion or water pollution caused in production. We might all pay later for diet-related healthcare, but that's not currently added to the food bill.

If we are to make good food choices, we need the support of good governance – a clumsy but useful word that describes the work of all the decision-makers who affect our food before we see it: scientific bodies, politicians, lawyers, businesses, regulators. When food scandals erupt, warped governance is exposed. Corners are seen to have been cut, standards shaved in the name of profit, in extreme cases serious fraud committed. Since the 19th century, Britain has maintained a proud record of campaigns that pressure regulators and legislators to enforce good standards, and we must remain vigilant and questioning about any erosion of this hidden infrastructure of good food.

Surely, people sometimes say to me, having to think about all this is too much: we haven't time, life's too short, fill the trolley, pay and run. Fair enough, I reply, but happy cooking and eating comes from facing up to the effects of our food choices, not burying them. By making decisions that are guided by our values, by the environmental and public health emergencies that are continuing to unfold, by the true cost of the food we consume, we can pressurise the food system into changing. Only then will we enable the right thing to become the normal thing. Too often at present, it isn't.

TIM LANG is Professor of Food Policy at the Centre for Food Policy, City, University of London and served as a trustee of Borough Market, 2007–17.

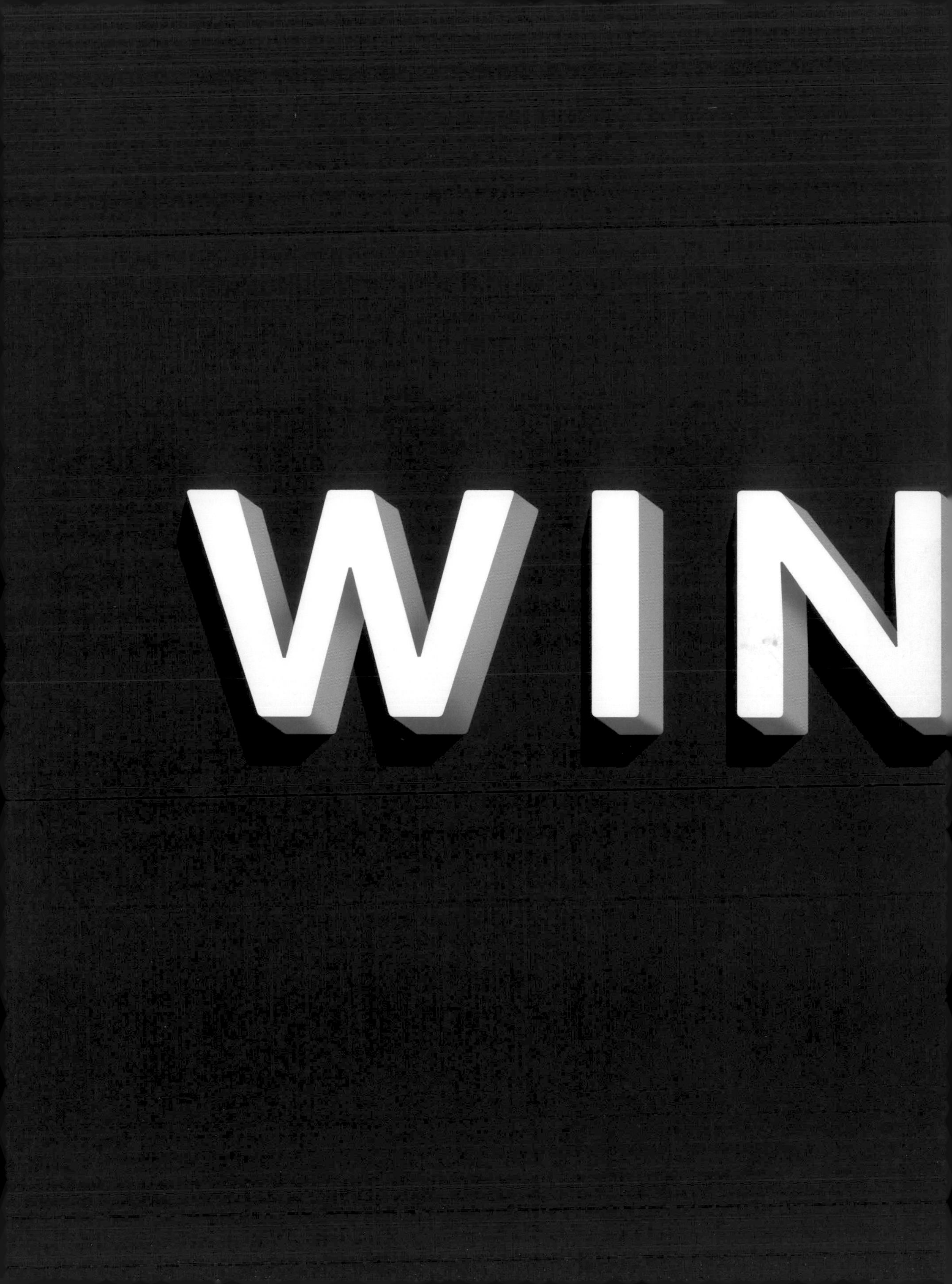
WIN

WINTER

The mere mention of winter brings to mind Norwegian firs, mistletoe, mulled wine and figgy pudding. Borough Market embraces that traditional vignette and then some: lights, fruits and foliage frame the old iron architecture; the Market's choir provides a tuneful backdrop of carols and hymns; traders sport festive woolly jumpers and Santa hats; while fairy lights add merriment and warmth, and there's a whiff of mulled wine and cider around each corner.

Small wonder, then, that many Londoners make a pilgrimage to the Market to pick up groceries and gifts for loved ones and themselves. Lines form at the butchers for family-sized turkeys, geese and ribs of beef, as well as smaller but similarly premium joints. With around twenty cheesemongers, there's no better place to pick up a platter to last the entire holiday season. December 'tis but one month, though. And while the frenetic pace of the festive period slows a little once the new year begins, other edible treats continue to arrive through January and February.

Citrus fruits truly come to the fore as the year turns: bergamots, clementines, tangerines and mandarins are joined by oranges from Seville which beg to be boiled for marmalade, and blood oranges with their crowd-pleasing sharpness and shocking red centres. Their vivid colour and flavour are matched, exceeded even, by eye-catching sticks of pink rhubarb from Yorkshire. Many autumnal vegetables continue through these cold months, with parsnips, Jerusalem artichokes and swede arguably at their peak, the freezing nights and frosty mornings encouraging their sweeter notes. Sprouts, sprout tops and flower sprouts prove themselves to be for life, not just as a trimming for turkey. And winter squash (which confusingly arrived in autumn) is still going strong, now alongside red cabbage,

purple kale, and a full Pantone strip of pink and purple bitter leaves.

Winter is a time of stark contrasts: of generosity and celebration, but also resourcefulness; a desire to feast, but also to eat light, sprightly food too; and though much of nature's bounty is deeply savoury and muted, the sweet fruits of the season are sharp and feisty. Happily, the stalls and stands underneath the railway arches off London Bridge have all aspects covered.

SEASONAL HIGHLIGHTS

Beetroot
Brussels sprouts and tops
Cabbages
Celeriac
Chicories
Citrus fruits
Cranberries
Forced rhubarb
Jerusalem artichokes
Kales
Leeks
Parsnips
Pomegranates
Salsify
Swede
Turnips

Feathered game (see autumn, page 161)
Goose (until 31 January)
Guinea fowl
Turkey
Venison
Wild rabbit and hare

Clams
Halibut
Monkfish
Mussels
Scallops
Turbot

RHUBARB AND RICOTTA ON TOAST

Boxes of bright-pink forced rhubarb pierce the grey days of winter when they arrive from Holland in December and Yorkshire in January. The stems have the same, enlivening effect when eaten at the start of the day. For this savoury-sweet breakfast dish, which works equally well at brunch, the rhubarb is cooked to part compote, part tender baton and served with fresh, milky ricotta. You can and should cook the rhubarb well in advance of breakfast – it will keep for up to three days if covered and refrigerated.

The savoury elements are important – heavy sprinkles of salt and black pepper, fragrant thyme and a good glug of grassy extra-virgin olive oil – otherwise this would just be a dessert served on toast. Moreover, not all ricotta is created equal. Try, for example, **Kappacasein Dairy**'s Jersey cow ricotta to see how fresh cheese relies on the quality of the milk used to make it.

MAKES 6–8 SERVINGS

450g forced rhubarb, leaves and woody bases
   removed, stems cut into 4–5cm batons
50g golden caster sugar
3 tablespoons water

PER SERVING

1 slice of sourdough bread
60g ricotta
leaves picked from 2 sprigs of thyme
extra-virgin olive oil

Put the rhubarb pieces in a medium-large saucepan so that, ideally, they sit no more than 2 batons deep. Add the sugar and 3 tablespoons water, tumble the rhubarb around, then place the pan over a low-medium heat until the liquid is somewhere between a simmer and a boil. Reduce the heat to very low and place a lid on top. Cook for 5–10 minutes, checking once or twice to swap batons from the top to the bottom of the pile so they cook evenly, and to ensure the pan is never at much more than a simmer. When half the rhubarb has become quite soft, stringy and juicy, remove the pan from the heat and lid from the pan, and leave to cool, during which time the harder batons will soften in the residual heat.

Toast the bread until golden and fairly crisp. Spread it with plenty of ricotta (the exact quantity depends on the size of toast onto which you are spreading, but it should be a fairly generous wave of dairy). Sprinkle with a couple of pinches of flaky sea salt, a few grinds of pepper and some thyme leaves. Add a swirl of grassy, peppery extra-virgin olive oil, before finishing with a couple of spoonfuls of rhubarb, avoiding adding too much syrup (as you should save this for a cocktail later in the day (see page 124)).

KIPPERS AND LEMON BUTTER

There are two types of people in this world: those who see kippers on a breakfast menu and order them, without fail. And those that don't. We should all be in the first category, though there's no need to only order them off a menu, as they're very easy to prepare at home too.

At the Market, the likes of **Oak & Smoke** provide shoppers with the raw (smoked) ingredients to have kippers at home. They need just a few minutes under a hot grill. A puddle of lemon-heavy butter sauce might seem lavish, but does work very well.

SERVES *2*

60g butter
finely grated zest and juice of 1 lemon
2 kippers

TO SERVE

toast
poached eggs (optional)

Heat the grill and arrange the oven's shelves to that the highest is 8–10cm from the heat source.

Put the butter and lemon zest in a small saucepan and melt gently over a low heat – avoiding both browning at too high a temperature or the butter separating if it's too low. Take off the heat.

Put the kippers on a baking tray, skin side down. Use a pastry brush to paint a little melted butter on the flesh of the fish and grill it for 3–4 minutes. The temperature should be such that for much of that time the fish are simply warming, only catching and browning in the last minute.

Reheat the butter, adding the lemon juice and shaking the pan so the sauce comes together. Again, do this gently to avoid browning or splitting the butter.

Plate the kippers and spoon the lemon butter over the top. Serve with toast. A poached egg is a good partner as well.

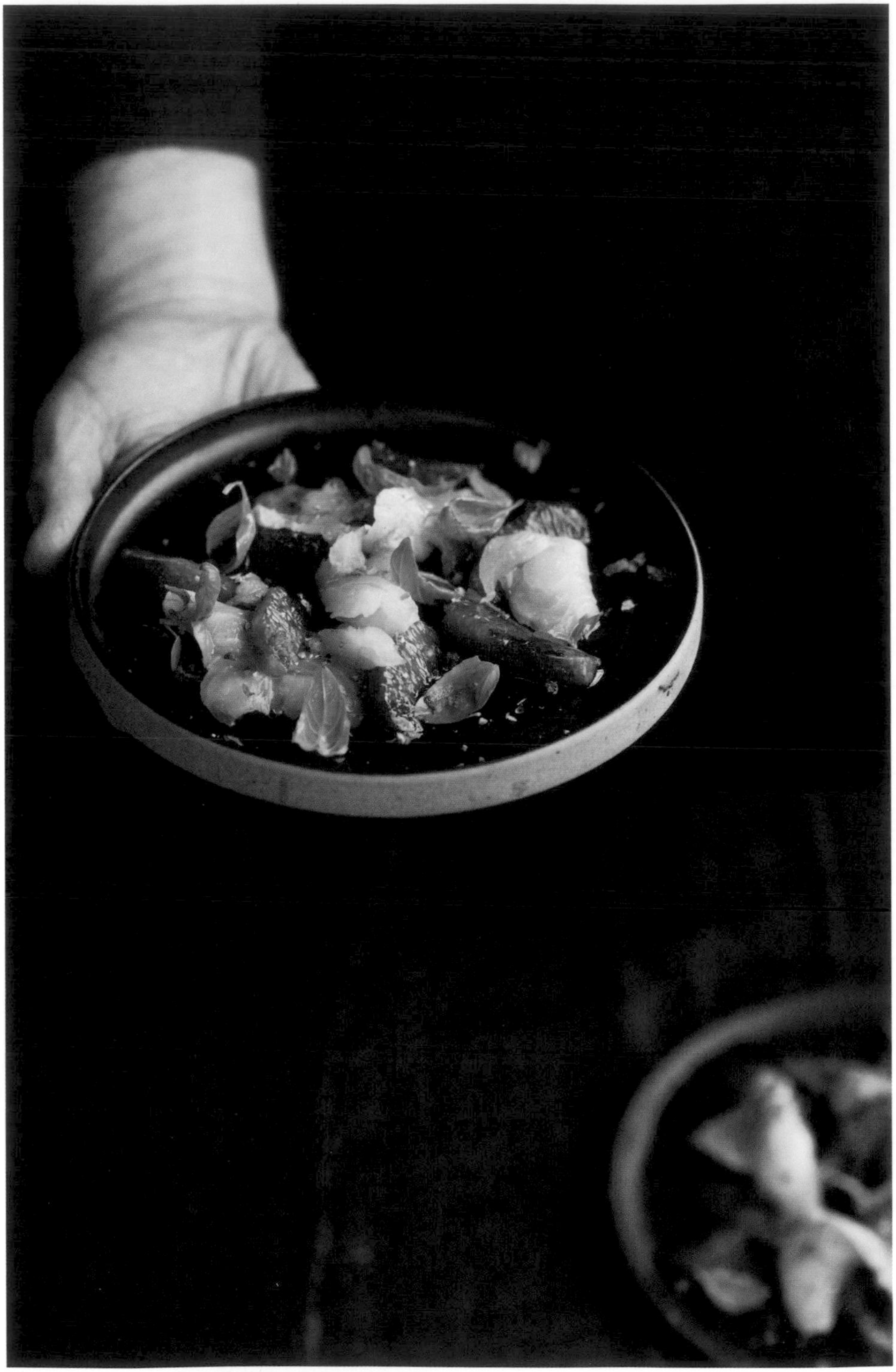

BREAM, BLOOD ORANGE AND BASIL CRUDO

The general rule with fish is that if it's fresh, you need to do very little to it to achieve a top-quality plate of food. Sometimes it's not even necessary to apply any heat; in a crudo the addition of a pinch of salt and a touch of acidity are more to season the fish than 'cook' it.

Blood oranges are a late winter and early spring highlight. The dark flesh is as sweet as it is striking, and while their flavour is still very distinctly orange, the redness provides raspberry notes, too. Alongside aromatic basil and a grassy, peppery extra-virgin olive oil, this is an easy but impressive dish. It's really good spread over a platter for lots of people to tuck into.

You could use sea bass or thinly sliced scallops instead of sea bream, if the fishmonger suggests they're a better option on the day.

SERVES 4–6 AS A STARTER

2 bream fillets, pin-boned
1 blood orange
16 small basil leaves
extra-virgin olive oil
fresh sourdough, to serve

Remove the skin from the fish fillets, then slice 5mm-thick slivers of flesh at a shallow angle. You should get 8–10 pieces per fillet.

Cut the top and bottom from the orange so it sits flat. Using a sharp knife, work around the orange cutting down to remove the skin and pith, then set the skin to one side. Cut the orange into segments, and each of those segments in half.

Arrange the pieces of fish over one platter or individual plates. Drop a pinch of flaky sea salt directly onto each of the pieces and leave for 5 minutes to lightly cure. Arrange the orange segments on the gaps between the fish.

Squeeze the juice from the bits of flesh still attached to the cuttings of skin directly onto each piece of fish. Add the basil leaves, plus a few glugs of a flavourful extra-virgin olive oil over and between the fish and oranges.

Eat immediately, with fresh sourdough to mop up the juice and oil.

RADICCHIO, POMEGRANATE AND GRACEBURN SALAD

From late autumn through to spring, space normally reserved for green lettuces is filled with burgundy and pink Italian radicchio. Their presence peaks in winter, in particular January and February, when relatively mild, speckled Castelfranco and pink radicchios sit flamboyantly next to the darker Trevisano, Chioggia and Tardivo, which have a bit more bite in both texture and taste.

Many of the radicchios can be cooked, but they're particularly enjoyable as a salad, provided their natural bitterness is complemented by a piquant dressing, and punctuated by other flavours and textures. As it happens, Italian pomegranates are on form at a similar time of year, and cheesemongers offer a wealth of sharp, acidic cheeses which work well crumbled among the leaves. One ideally suited cheese is Graceburn, which is made in Kent by **Blackwoods Cheese Company** and sold by them at the Market.

SERVES 4 AS A STARTER, 6–8 AS A SIDE DISH

FOR THE SALAD

1 head (200–300g) of Castelfranco
    or pink radicchio
1 head (150g) of Trevisano, Chioggia
    or Tardivo radicchio or 2 red chicory
leaves picked from 15 sprigs of parsley (20g)
200–250g Graceburn (or other feta cheese)
30g walnuts or skin-on whole almonds,
    very roughly chopped

FOR THE DRESSING

1 teaspoon honey
4 tablespoons extra-virgin olive oil
2 teaspoons pomegranate molasses
1 teaspoon tepid water
seeds from ½ pomegranate (80–100g seeds)

Refresh the bitter salad leaves in chilled water if they're looking limp, then drain and pat dry with kitchen paper.

Combine the honey, olive oil and pomegranate molasses in a large mixing bowl with a heavy pinch of flaky sea salt. Add a teaspoon of tepid water and whisk everything together. Add the pomegranate seeds to the dressing, discarding any white pith.

Chop the large radicchio leaves (the Castelfranco, pink radicchio, Chioggia radicchio) in half lengthways, then in half across their width. Ensure the red radicchio is cut to a similar size, or a touch smaller. Toss all the leaves, including the parsley, in the dressing. Crumble in the cheese, add the nuts and mix well.

This salad is best served immediately, though the leaves will last a reasonable amount of time before wilting, compared to regular lettuce, so it's is a good option for a buffet.

ROAST DELICA PUMPKIN WITH CRISP SAGE, SEEDS AND CURD

Delica pumpkin is a squat, green-grey pumpkin. Beneath the skin, though, is a dense and vivid orange flesh, which is intensely sweet, buttery, and reminiscent of cooked chestnuts. Some consider it the most prized of the winter squash, and it's particularly good when roasted with sage, sprinkled with its own roast seeds and slicked with a sheep or goat's curd. This treatment works well with sweet red kuri (onion), crown prince and butternut squash, too.

Cold-pressed rapeseed oil cooks to a higher temperature than olive oil, and also provides an extra nutty flavour. But use light olive oil if that's what you have, finishing the dish with your favourite extra-virgin variety.

SERVES 4 AS A STARTER, 6 AS A SIDE DISH

*1–1.2kg Delica pumpkin (or other winter
    squash or pumpkin)*
6 tablespoons cold-pressed rapeseed oil
*2–3 teaspoons Aleppo chilli pepper flakes
    (pul biber)*
20–24 sage leaves
*150g sheep's or goat's curd
    (or Greek-style yoghurt)*
extra-virgin olive oil, for drizzling

Preheat the oven to 200C fan/220C/425F/gas mark 7.

Clean the squash or pumpkin with a damp cloth to remove any dirt, then cut it in half from top to bottom with a large, sharp knife. Scoop out the seeds with a spoon and spread them out on a small baking tray. Drizzle a tablespoon of the rapeseed oil on top and mix with a fork, pulling away and discarding any fibres as you do so. Roast in the oven for 10–20 minutes, until golden and crisp. Remove from the oven, season generously with flaky sea salt and 1 teaspoon of the Aleppo pepper and set aside.

Cut the squash halves into 3–4cm-thick wedges, leaving the skin on. Place in a bowl with 4 tablespoons of the rapeseed oil and mix until glossy, then spread over a large baking tray or low-sided roasting tin, ideally in a single layer. Roast near the top of the oven for 20 minutes.

Mix the sage leaves with the final tablespoon of rapeseed oil, then once the squash has been cooking for 20 minutes, carefully flip the slices and scatter the sage under and around them. Roast for a further 10–15 minutes, or until the squash is tender and browning at the edges, and the sage leaves are crisp.

Spoon the curd (or yoghurt) onto plates or a serving platter. Drizzle a little extra-virgin olive oil onto this, then pile the squash pieces and crisp sage on top. Sprinkle with the roasted seeds, remaining Aleppo pepper, and perhaps one final glug of oil (extra-virgin, if you have used olive oil for the cooking).

AROMATIC HALIBUT PARCELS

Halibut is a pearlescent, firm white fish caught in deep and cold seas. It's technically flat, though they often grow very big, and as such their cross-sections are an impressive feature of any fishmonger's display. Wild stocks have been under pressure from overfishing in recent times, however a sustainable farm off Gigha in the Southern Hebrides provides an alternative source, and it is often available at **Furness Fish Markets**.

Wrapping the lean fish with Asian aromatics, such as kaffir lime leaves and lemongrass, and cooking it with a little liquid in self-steaming parcels, is a very effective way to present it. Cod, hake, haddock, pollack and salmon would all appreciate a similar treatment.

SERVES 2

10 dried kaffir lime leaves
1 stick of lemongrass, bashed and
    roughly chopped
1 teaspoon coriander seeds
2 halibut fillets or steaks (120–140g each)
sunflower oil, for brushing
30g piece of fresh ginger, peeled and
    finely shredded
1 medium-sized mild green chilli,
    deseeded and diced
finely grated zest and juice of 1 lime
50ml rice wine (e.g. Shaoxing, dry sake or
    dry sherry)
2 teaspoons toasted sesame oil

TO SERVE

steamed or stir-fried pak choi
rice
lime wedges

Preheat the oven to 180C fan/200C/400F/gas mark 6 and cut out 2 x 25cm circles of baking parchment or foil.

Fold each circle of foil or parchment in half to create a crease, then lay them flat again. You are going to place the dry ingredients in the centre of one half of each of those circles, before folding the circle over, crimping the edges, pouring in the liquid and finally sealing to form parcels (this is easier with foil, though the paper versions look prettier if serving at the table).

Make a little pile of kaffir lime leaves, lemongrass and coriander seeds in one half of each of the circles. Brush each piece of fish with a little sunflower oil, then place them on the aromatics. Sprinkle the ginger, chilli and lime zest on top of the fish, then crimp the edges of the circle together. Just before you finish sealing the parcels, mix together the rice wine or sherry, sesame oil and lime juice, and divide between the two parcels, before sealing tightly.

Place the parcels on a baking tray and bake for 15 minutes. The parcels can be undone at the table for effect – though take care as the fragrant steam will be very hot.

Serve with pak choi, rice and lime wedges.

VEAL CHOPS WITH ANCHOVY-DRESSED PUNTARELLE

This meal combines ingredients that you might walk by – the veal because of doubts about the ethics; the puntarelle as it looks untamable. Both concerns would be unfounded.

Contrary to memories of calves reared with little space and light, English rose veal is an extremely ethical meat, which makes use of a by-product of the dairy industry (male newborns) that would otherwise be wasted. **Wild Beef** sell veal from a well-looked-after herd of Jersey cows near to them in the West Country. The delicate, sweet meat is well worth trying. The rangy, crisp, fresh and slightly bitter leaves and bulb of the puntarelle (a variant of Italian chicory, which is in season and at **Elsey & Bent** in winter and early spring) are just as pleasing and make a great foil for the veal, particularly in this anchovy and parmesan dressing.

SERVES 2

½ head of punterelle, including outer leaves
2 veal t-bone chops (or rib-eyes), fridge cold
2 tablespoons cooking oil
25g butter

FOR THE DRESSING

8 salted anchovies in oil, roughly chopped
25g finely grated parmesan
1 teaspoon caster sugar
1 tablespoon red wine vinegar
75ml extra-virgin olive oil

Strip away the outer leaves of the puntarelle and pull the stiffer bulbs away from the core. Cut the leaves at the point they meet the thicker, white stems, then cut those stems and the bulbs into 4 or 5 long slices. Place all the bits in a bowl of iced water for an hour or more; this will ensure it's crisp and fresh and may also cause the puntarelle to curl. Leave in a colander or spread over a clean kitchen cloth or paper towel to drain and dry thoroughly just prior to cooking the veal.

Make the dressing in advance, too. Put the anchovies in a pestle and mortar and crush into a smooth paste. Add the parmesan, sugar and a few grinds of black pepper. Stir in the red wine vinegar, then gradually add the oil, a tablespoon at a time, stirring until the dressing is thick and glossy.

Liberally season both sides of each veal chop with flaky sea salt and black pepper. Set a heavy-based frying pan over a medium-high heat and add the cooking oil. Stand the chops in the pan on one of their fatty edges, using cooking tongs to balance them. Cook for 1–2 minutes on each edge, rendering and browning the fat, then lay each chop flat side down and add the butter to the pan. Fry for 2–3 minutes per side, spooning the foaming and browning butter over each chop as they cook. Veal is best cooked to medium or medium-rare, with blushing flesh and a slight spring to the meat. If you have a probe thermometer, stop cooking when the core reaches 50–52C. The core temperature will rise further as the meat rests. Alternatively, press your middle finger to your thumb and push the squidgy part underneath your thumb; look for a similar bounce in the meat. Leave the meat to rest for 5 minutes.

Serve the veal with a few spoons of butter and resting juices from the pan over the top of each chop, and a pile of dressed puntarelle on the side.

COD, SMOKED HADDOCK AND ROMANESCO BAKE

This is a quick and light riff on a classic, potato-topped fish pie. It's also a super way to use the less exotic offerings of a fishmonger's display – the likes of cod, pollack and haddock – with the pyramid-like light green romanesco florets and its leaves providing spikes of colour, texture and flavour. It's an excellent one-pot meal for a winter's evening (and the romanesco could be substituted for conventional broccoli at other times of the year).

It takes no time at all to make breadcrumbs from the end of a loaf if you have a food processor or blender. They store well in the freezer – you can continually top up the supply – and if very dry to begin with, can be used almost instantly with no need to defrost.

This is good on its own, though wilted spinach is a particularly strong accompaniment.

SERVES 4

*1 small romanesco broccoli (400–500g), outer
    leaves removed and florets cut from stem*
300g full-fat crème fraîche
50ml tepid water
70g finely grated parmesan
2 teaspoons Dijon mustard
25g brined capers, drained and roughly chopped
*leaves picked from 5 sprigs of tarragon,
    roughly chopped*
400g cod, skinned and pin-boned
*300g un-dyed smoked haddock, skinned and
    pin-boned*
80–100g dry breadcrumbs
3 tablespoons extra-virgin olive oil

Bring a saucepan of salted water to the boil and preheat the oven to 200C fan/220C/425F/gas mark 7.

Cut the romanesco stem into 2–3cm dice (you can use almost all of it) and halve any florets that are much bigger than the pieces of stem. Blanch the florets and diced stem in the boiling water. After 2 minutes add the outer leaves and cook for a further 1 minute. Drain through a sieve then leave under cold running water until cool.

Meanwhile, decant the crème fraîche into a large mixing bowl. Add 50ml tepid water and whip or whisk together with a spatula or balloon whisk. Add the parmesan, Dijon mustard, capers and tarragon. Stir well and set to one side.

Check the fish for bones then cut into 3–4cm chunks. Combine the fish chunks and the drained and cooled broccoli with the crème fraîche (it might not seem as though there's enough sauce, but it will thin out as it cooks). Transfer the fish and broccoli to an ovenproof dish, ideally snug enough for the fish and broccoli pieces to sit in two layers. Ensure the different components are evenly distributed (particularly the leaves).

Put the breadcrumbs in a bowl, add a heavy pinch of flaky sea salt and the olive oil and use a fork to combine. Spoon the breadcrumbs evenly over the fish mix then place towards the top of the oven and bake for 25 minutes, until the top is golden, the sauce is bubbling through, and the fish is just cooked and not yet dry.

Remove from the oven and serve straight away.

ONE-POT GOLDEN CHICKEN AND JUDIÓN BEANS

This is a low effort yet very effective and convivial meal. The cooking method – part frying, part poaching – ensures that the chicken is juicy but its skin golden and crisp, and the broth that's a natural result of the process is warming but still light. It's ideal at this time of year, and the comfort factor is heightened by **Brindisa Ltd**'s creamy, moreish Judión (butter) beans, which are a brilliant and quick way of adding both ballast and comfort. You could substitute other pre-cooked butter beans, though Brindisa Ltd's Judión are particularly plump and creamy.

Ask the butcher to joint a whole chicken for you, or use four legs. Either way, ensure you use meat on the bone as the dish is better for the flavour that provides.

SERVES 4

1.6–1.8kg chicken, jointed, or 4 legs,
*   split into thighs and drumsticks*
3 tablespoons vegetable oil or light olive oil
1 small onion, thinly sliced
6 garlic cloves, flattened (skin on)
300ml water
10 sprigs of thyme
grated zest and juice of 1 lemon
300g large leaf spinach, washed and stalks
*   finely chopped*
1 x 600g jar Judión beans (or 400g cooked
*   butter beans, plus 200ml cooking liquor)*
crusty bread, to serve

You will need a large (30cm diameter), heavy-based frying pan, skillet or flameproof casserole dish.

Lay the chicken pieces on a plate or tray, season liberally with flaky sea salt and leave for 5–10 minutes while you prepare the other ingredients.

Put your pan over a medium-high heat and add the vegetable or olive oil. Place the chicken pieces skin side down in the pan and leave to fry for 15 minutes without disturbing them. After 8 minutes slot the sliced onion and garlic in and around the chicken. (If using a whole bird, add only the thigh and leg pieces to begin with, adding the breast pieces at the same time as the onion and garlic.)

After 15 minutes the chicken skin should be golden and crisp. Turn the chicken pieces over and pour 300ml water into the pan. Crucially, this should come about halfway up the meat and not touch the skin. Add the thyme and lemon zest to the broth and simmer for 10 minutes.

Transfer the chicken to a warm plate and reduce the heat to low-medium. Put the spinach in the pan, decant the beans and the liquid from the jar on top, and leave to warm and wilt for 3–4 minutes. There should be 3–4cm of liquid in the pan as this should be a relatively brothy dish, so add extra water if you think it's necessary. Once the spinach has wilted, return the chicken to the pan (with skin still clear of the liquid). Warm through for 5 minutes more, before stirring the lemon juice through the broth.

Serve in wide bowls or deep plates, with some crusty bread to help mop up the juices.

BAVETTE STEAKS AND MUSHROOM KETCHUP

Bavette - also known as flank - is not quite the secret it once was, but it remains an economic way to enjoy premium aged beef (and something to enjoy with a warming glass of red wine on a cold day). It's best cooked in plenty of foaming butter to medium-rare and with a thick brown crust, and served with a punchy condiment, such as this mushroom ketchup. If the butcher has run out of bavette, ask for onglet, skirt or flat iron steak instead.

The ketchup will keep well in the fridge for up to five days - time enough to enjoy it with lamb chops, sausages or maybe another piece of beef, if you have some left over. Alternatively, stir it through a ragu or casserole for an extra layer of umami.

SERVES 2 (WITH KETCHUP LEFT OVER)

FOR THE MUSHROOM KETCHUP

20g butter
300g portobello mushrooms, roughly chopped
1 banana shallot, finely sliced
1 small garlic clove, crushed
2 tablespoons golden caster sugar
⅓ nutmeg, finely grated
4 teaspoons white wine vinegar
2 tablespoons tepid water

FOR THE STEAK

500–600g bavette
2 tablespoons cooking oil
25g butter

To make the ketchup, put the butter in heavy-based frying pan over a high heat. Once melted and frothing, add the mushrooms and cook them fiercely for 4–5 minutes until golden, much reduced in volume and the mushroom juices are leaching out. Add the shallot and a heavy pinch of flaky sea salt and reduce the temperature a little. Cook for 2–3 minutes, stirring occasionally, then add the garlic, sugar, lots of ground pepper and the grated nutmeg, and cook for a final 2 minutes, by which time the mushrooms should be dark and glossy. Add the vinegar, stir and remove from the heat. Put the contents of the pan in a blender (or a food processor) with 2 tablespoons tepid water and blitz until it forms a very smooth, silky purée that holds its form if spooned onto a plate. Add more water if necessary – conversely, don't panic if it's too loose, just heat it gently to evaporate the liquid until it's as thick as desired. Refrigerate until required.

Find a heavy-based frying pan which fits the steak snugly. Turn on the extractor fan. Put the pan over a high heat, add the oil and heat until near smoking point.

Season both sides of the bavette heavily with flaky sea salt and black pepper, then place it in the pan. Cook for 2 minutes without disturbance, then flip it over and cook for 2 minutes more. Add the butter and once it's frothing and browning, spoon it repeatedly over the meat as it cooks. Cook both sides for a further 1–3 minutes (the precise time will depend on the thickness of the steak and starting temperature of the meat). The bavette should plump up and its grain become obvious (most likely running lengthways). When it's ready it should have a similar spring to the squidgy part below your thumb, when you touch the thumb to middle finger. Alternatively, it's ready with the core reaches 50–52C on a probe thermometer. Transfer to a warm plate to rest for 5 minutes, then slice it across the grain, seasoning each piece with more salt.

TOAD IN THE HOLE WITH LARDON AND ONION GRAVY

The batter for a toad in the hole – that hearty and very English dish – is important: it should puff up like the grandest Yorkshire pudding, and be crisp and well seasoned, rather than doughy and bland. More crucial, though, is the calibre of sausage the batter surrounds, and the quality of the gravy that gets poured over the top. This is where good butchers come in, as only here can you get sausages that are both flavourful and fat (in all senses of the word) enough to last 40 minutes in the oven without drying out. While you're choosing your snags from the likes of **Ginger Pig** or **Northfield Farm**, pick up some lardons, too; it's these and a good glug of whichever fortified wine you have to hand that will help take your gravy to the next level.

Mashed potato and peas or broccoli are ideal alongside.

SERVES 4

FOR THE TOAD IN THE HOLE

3 medium eggs
250ml whole milk
50ml chilled water
150g plain flour
leaves picked from 3 sprigs of rosemary, chopped
4 tablespoons vegetable oil
8 fat sausages

FOR THE GRAVY

1 tablespoon vegetable oil
150g lardons (smoked, ideally)
300g onions, thinly sliced
1 garlic clove, thinly sliced
1 tablespoon plain flour
50ml port (or Madeira, Marsala or sherry,
*   depending what's in the cupboard)*
300ml water

Preheat the oven to 220C fan/240C/460F/gas mark 9. Ensure a shelf is positioned towards the top, with enough space to fit the depth of a roasting tin, plus a little extra room.

Make the batter in a blender if you have one. You can easily whisk it by hand, but a machine seems to help create a particularly airy finish. Crack the eggs into a blender and blitz for a minute until voluminous. Pour in the milk and 50ml chilled water and pulse again, before adding the flour, chopped rosemary and a heavy pinch of flaky sea salt and black pepper. Blitz for 1 minute more then leave to rest until required (some say it's best to leave the batter for an hour or longer, but the difference is not material – it can be used almost instantly).

Put the vegetable oil in a roasting tin, add the sausages and cook in the oven for 8 minutes, until they have a touch of colour and the fat is near-smoking hot. Remove the tin from the oven and place over a high heat on the hob. Arrange the sausages so they're evenly spaced and their brownest surfaces are facing down, then pour the batter into the tin and transfer immediately to the top of the oven for 35 minutes, by which time the batter should be well puffed, golden and crisp.

Meanwhile, heat the tablespoon of oil for the gravy with the lardons in a heavy-based saucepan over a medium-high heat. Cook for 5 minutes so the lardons release plenty of fat and turn golden. Add the onions, mix well and reduce the heat a little. Sweat them for 10 minutes, stirring occasionally, until the onions soften and become sweet. Turn the heat right down, add the garlic and cook for 5 minutes more. Stir the flour into the onions and cook for 1 minute. Increase the heat, add the port and allow to boil for 1 minute before pouring in 300ml water and letting the liquid reduce by about a third to intensify the flavours and thicken the gravy.

Serve immediately, with mash and greens, ensuring everyone has plenty of batter and gravy with their sausages.

SWEDE AND STILTON PIE

This is a cross between a cheese and potato pie and a root vegetable gratin, and is a particularly good way to use the less glamorous bits of stilton that might have been left on a cheeseboard. It takes a little effort (the pastry), a steady hand (to slice the swede thinly) and a fair amount of time (to cook), but the result is worth it – and indeed may surprise many. For though the stilton is the more heralded of the key ingredients here, it's arguably the swede that stars, and the combination of the two results in something that will please both vegetarian and committed carnivore alike. You could use it as a side dish, but it's better as the centrepiece, served warm with buttery sautéed spinach or kale, or a crisp and well-dressed salad.

*SERVES **6***

FOR THE PASTRY

230g plain flour
½ teaspoon flaky sea salt
125g cold butter, cubed
1 egg, lightly beaten
1 tablespoon apple cider vinegar
1–2 tablespoons chilled water

FOR THE FILLING

650g swede (about 1 small or ½ large)
2 medium onions
120g stilton, Stichelton or other creamy
*   hard blue*
50ml whole milk
300ml double cream
2 teaspoons Dijon mustard
whole nutmeg, for grating
70g rolled oats
4 tablespoons olive oil or cold-pressed
*   rapeseed oil*

You will need a 24cm diameter, deep, loose-bottomed tin or pie dish.

Combine the flour, salt and butter until the mixture resembles breadcrumbs – you can do this with your fingertips, but it is quicker in a food processor. Add half the beaten egg, the vinegar and 1 tablespoon of the chilled water and bring the mixture together to form a ball (use an extra tablespoon of water if needed). Flatten the dough into a disc about 2–3cm deep, wrap and refrigerate for at least 30 minutes. Unwrap the chilled pastry and roll it out between two sheets of greaseproof paper to a thickness of 3mm, then chill within the sheets for at least 30 minutes. Line the tart tin or pie dish with the pastry before chilling one more time in the fridge or freezer for 15–20 minutes.

Preheat the oven to 180C fan/200C/400F/gas mark 6.

Line the chilled pastry base with greaseproof paper and fill with baking beans or a dried pulse, then bake on the middle shelf of the oven for 10 minutes. Lift the greaseproof package from the tart, patch up any holes with pastry scraps, and bake for a further 5 minutes. Brush the pastry case with the remaining beaten egg and bake for 10 minutes more. Once out of the oven, trim the edges from the tart shell with a sharp knife.

Prepare the filling ingredients when the pastry is in the fridge: peel the swede, cut it in half lengthways, then slice very thinly (2mm) into half moons, ideally using a mandoline, food processor or, alternatively, a sharp knife; thinly slice the onions and crumble the stilton; warm the milk, cream, mustard and one third of the stilton in a small pan.

Arrange the swede slices in the baked pastry like the concentric petals of a flower, with the curved edges to the edge of the tart and each piece overlapping. Create one layer, sprinkle over half the onions, half the remaining cheese and grate over a generous amount of black pepper and nutmeg. Repeat (you'll probably use two-fifths or a third of the nutmeg), then finish with a third layer of swede, leaving a little gap between outer edge of swede and pastry sides. Pour the warm cream over the top, some of which should spill over into the gap between swede and pastry.

Place on a tray and bake in the top of the oven for 40 minutes. Mix the oats with the oil, spoon over the swede, and bake for 50 minutes more, by which time the cream will be bubbling, the swede tender and the oats golden. Remove from the oven and leave to cool for 10 minutes before attempting to remove it from the tin (alternatively, you could cook it in advance, cool completely before removing from the tin, then re-heat for 10–15 minutes in a warm oven to serve).

BRAISED WHOLE DUCK AND CHICORY

Geese and turkey get the headlines at Christmas. However, on other weekends during winter consider roasting an Aylesbury or Pekin duck, which can be found at butchers like **Wyndham House Ltd** and **Ginger Pig**. They braise and brown nicely, resulting quite effortlessly in juicy, flavourful breast and leg meat and crisp skin all over. If catering for more than six people, ask your butcher for an extra leg or two and braise for the same amount of time in the same tin. And make sure you turn the carcass and any leftover meat into a broth or noodle soup on another day.

Chicory or Belgian endive is a bitter leaf that can be enjoyed both raw and cooked, and in this case sits happily underneath the duck, gradually softening in the braising juices.

Serve with a root vegetable gratin and redcurrant jelly on the side.

SERVES 4–6

2.5–3kg duck (Aylesbury or 100-day Pekin)
2 tablespoons cooking oil
3 garlic bulbs, halved through the middle
6 white chicory (about 150g each)
450ml dry white wine
12 sprigs of thyme
juice of ½ lemon
leaves from 6 sprigs of parsley, chopped
redcurrant jelly, to serve

Preheat the oven to 150C fan/170C/325F/ gas mark 3, remove any giblets within the duck (use these later on when making a stock) and season it generously with flaky sea salt and black pepper, both inside the carcass and over the skin.

Put a large flameproof casserole dish or frying pan over a medium-high heat. Add the cooking oil and brown the duck all over for 15–20 minutes, methodically moving the large carcass around and cooking each part of the skin for 2–3 minutes at a time. You will need to have the extractor fan on full blast.

Find a high-sided roasting tin that fits the duck snugly. Place the halved garlic bulbs in the base, cut side up, and the chicory on and around them, ideally in a single layer. Add the wine, then sit the browned duck on top, breast side facing up. Pour any hot fat from the pan over the duck's skin, stuff half the thyme in the cavity of the bird, and dot the remaining sprigs in the wine. Cover the tin tightly with foil and cook in the oven for 2 hours. Remove from the oven and take off the foil, increase the temperature to 220C fan/240C/460F/gas mark 9, and when the oven is up to temperature cook for 15 minutes more, so that the skin is crisp and golden, and the flesh yielding and juicy. Strain off and reserve the cooking juices, and leave the duck to rest for 20 minutes.

Near the end of the resting period, remove the chicory from the roasting tin and cut them in half lengthways. Lay them on a warmed platter, cut side up. Spoon some cooking juices over the top, then season with salt, black pepper, a good squeeze of lemon juice and the chopped parsley.

To carve, cut the legs from the duck and remove the breasts, and slice them across the width of the breast. Serve with a root vegetable gratin and redcurrant jelly on the side to cut through the richness, with the fragrant cooking juices as a luscious gravy.

SALT-BAKED SEA BASS

This is an impressive way to cook and serve fish; the moment you break through the hard casing is as striking and memorable as any first slice into a prime roast joint, and in that sense alone it's a suitable centrepiece for the festive season. More importantly, though, it's also extremely tasty. The lemon and herb-flavoured salt crust creates a self-seasoning oven, which when cracked into and opened at the table presents steaming, tender and flavourful sea bass – which are best, in every sense, when line-caught, not netted or farmed.

Serve with boiled or gratin potatoes, seasonal greens and wedges of lemon. Use the leftover egg yolks to make a custard, ice cream or other eggy dessert (a Christmas trifle, perhaps?).

SERVES 4–6

5 sprigs of rosemary
finely grated zest of 1 lemon
4 large egg whites
1kg fine salt
1.5–2kg line-caught sea bass, gutted and scaled

TO SERVE

lemon wedges
boiled or gratin potatoes
seasonal greens

Preheat the oven to 180C fan/200C/400F/gas mark 6.

Strip the leaves from 3 of the rosemary sprigs, chop them roughly and set aside, then slice the lemon. Whisk the egg whites in a large mixing bowl until they're loose and beginning to foam. Add the salt, lemon zest and chopped rosemary, and mix thoroughly. Pack the cavity of the fish with the lemon slices and remaining rosemary sprigs.

Put a quarter of the salt mix on a baking or roasting tray big enough to fit the fish. Spread it out to mirror the footprint of the fish, then lay the fish on top. Spoon the remaining salt over the top, plastering it tightly around the fish. If you run out of mix, it's fine if the head and tail stick out from the igloo.

Bake on the middle shelf of the oven for 30 minutes, then remove and leave to rest for a further 10 minutes.

Carefully open the salt casing with a heavy knife, brush away any excess salt, and peel back the skin as you serve. The fragrant flesh should come away in fairly meaty chunks from the central bone.

PHEASANT, LEEK AND CHESTNUT PIE

By December we're already a few months into the pheasant season, and the birds shot from now on (and available, plucked and prepared at the Market and good butchers across the country) are both larger and a little tougher than in autumn. Rather than roast them, use them to fill a suet pastry-topped pie. There are a few stages to this, but it is a dish that can be prepared in advance, then just placed in the oven with its pastry top when you return from a bracing winter walk.

Serve with mashed root vegetable and piles of a brassica such as sautéed kale, buttered green cabbage or braised red cabbage.

SERVES 8

3 plump pheasants, plucked
2 tablespoons cooking oil
2 celery sticks, roughly chopped
1 onion, roughly chopped
1 small carrot, roughly chopped
8 garlic cloves, 4 thinly sliced
500ml dry cider
12 sprigs of thyme
30g butter
350g leeks, trimmed, sliced into 1cm-thick
*   rounds and washed*
250g chestnut mushrooms, halved
50g plain flour, plus extra for dusting
200g full-fat crème fraîche
200g cooked chestnuts, halved

FOR THE PASTRY

300g self-raising flour
150g shredded beef suet
180ml chilled water
1 egg, beaten with 1 tablespoon milk

Preheat the oven to 120C fan/140C/275F/gas mark 1.

It is necessary to braise the leg meat well in advance of making and eating the rest of the pie. Sometime the day before is ideal. Remove the legs and breasts from the pheasants. Chill the breasts for later on, and don't discard the carcasses.

Heat the cooking oil in a large ovenproof stock pot or flameproof casserole dish over a medium-high heat. Add the celery, onion, carrot and the unsliced garlic cloves. Soften gently for 3 minutes, then increase the heat and add the pheasant legs, skin side down. Cook for 5 minutes, to colour the pheasant skin. Pour in the cider, add 5 of the thyme sprigs and the carcasses and cover with cold water. Bring to the boil, then reduce the heat to a gentle simmer and cover with a lid. Cook in the oven for 2 hours, then remove from the oven and leave to cool. Pick the meat from the cooled pheasant legs and carcasses. Strain and discard the soft vegetables and bones, and boil and reduce the stock to approximately 600ml of liquid.

To make the pastry, sift the self-raising flour into a mixing bowl and add the suet. Mix, then add the fridge-cold water. Combine and press together into a ball, adding a splash more water if necessary. Wrap and place in the fridge for 1 hour.

Put a large saucepan over a medium-high heat, add the butter, leeks, mushrooms and a pinch of flaky sea salt and cook for 2–3 minutes until the leeks begin to soften. Add the thinly sliced garlic, pick the remaining thyme leaves and add them to the pan, then add the plain flour and stir for 3 minutes before adding the pheasant stock and crème fraîche. Strain the mixture through a sieve, reserving the liquid.

Cut the pheasant breasts into 3cm chunks. Then, in an ovenproof dish about 6cm deep, combine the breast and leg meat, the leek and mushroom mix, the chestnuts, and plenty of salt and black pepper. Dampen the mix with 200ml of the reserved liquid, and transfer the remaining liquid to a saucepan to bubble down for use as gravy.

Preheat the oven to 180C fan/200C/400F/gas mark 6.

Dust a surface with a little flour. Unwrap the pastry and roll it out to a thickness of 1cm, and in a shape to fit your dish. Lay the pastry over the dish, overlapping the sides by 1–2cm. Brush half the egg wash over the pastry and bake the pie in the oven for 25 minutes. Brush the remaining egg wash over the top and return to the oven for a further 25–30 minutes, until the top is golden brown and crisp.

Remove from the oven and serve with vegetables of your choice.

GALETTE DES ROIS

Over the Christmas period, many of the bakeries sell their versions of Britain's traditional puddings and treats. It's no surprise to see fantastic examples of figgy pudding, iced fruit cake and, of course, mince pies! There are sweet things from other cultures as well, for example, **Olivier's Bakery** mark Epiphany on 6 January with galette des rois, an almond paste-filled puff pastry dessert. It is a delicious way to mark the end of the festive season. If you are unable to make it to the Market, try this method at home.

SERVES 8–10

100g salted butter at room temperature
80g golden caster sugar
150g ground almonds
1 tablespoon cornflour
2 eggs, beaten
dash of milk
2 tablespoons dark rum
plain flour, for dusting
375g block all-butter puff pastry
4 tablespoons greengage or apricot conserve

Cream the butter and sugar together until light and a little fluffy. You could do this by hand, though it is easiest using a stand mixer fitted with the paddle attachment. Keep the mixer beating and tip in the ground almonds and cornflour, then half the beaten egg. Once incorporated, add half the remaining egg (add a dash of milk to the rest, for brushing over the pastry later), then the rum, beating until smooth and all the ingredients are fully combined. Scoop the paste into a container and put it in the fridge.

Dust a surface with flour. Cut the pastry block in half. Wrap one half and return it to the fridge. Roll the other half to a thickness of 4mm, then cut a 23–25cm circle from the pastry using a plate as a guide. Lift the pastry circle on to a baking sheet and spread the jam from the middle outwards, leaving a 3cm border. Spread the almond paste evenly on top of the jam, leaving the same 3cm border. Now roll out the fridge-cold pastry half in the same way. Brush the uncovered edge of the pastry base with beaten egg wash, then lay the second circle on top, pushing the pastry edges together with the back of a fork. Refrigerate for 1 hour or more to firm up (this is an important step as it allows the pastry layers to bond, and makes it much easier to cut and decorate).

Preheat the oven to 200C fan/220C/425F/gas mark 7.

Pierce the centre of the chilled pastry with the tip of a knife to allow air to escape. Score 5 evenly spaced lines across the top, and diagonal chevron-style lines between them, creating a wide herringbone pattern (a pithivier-style spiral from the centre of the pastry is also common, as shown opposite). Brush liberally with the egg wash and bake at the top of the oven for 30–35 minutes. If you have any leftover egg wash, brush the pastry again after 20 minutes and rotate the baking sheet to ensure the galette cooks and colours evenly. Remove from the oven and leave to cool for at least 15 minutes before serving. The galette is also enjoyable at room temperature.

CLEMENTINE SPONGES WITH CRANBERRY SAUCE

The appearance at the greengrocers of stacks of pale wooden boxes containing clementines is a sure sign that it's winter and Christmas is coming (if the decorations around the Market haven't already given it away).

You can serve these little clementine puddings as an alternative to figgy pudding and brandy butter, though really they're too good to confine to just one day; the citrus sponge and syrupy, tart, cranberry-studded sauce (served loose, not stiff like the condiment that goes with turkey) fit the comforting pud category throughout the colder months.

Both the sponges and sauce can be cooked in advance of eating.

SERVES **8**

FOR THE SPONGES

60g light muscovado sugar
5 medium clementines
4 large eggs
about 220g salted butter at room temperature
*   (see method)*
about 220g golden caster sugar (see method)
about 220g self-raising flour (see method)
½ teaspoon baking powder

FOR THE SAUCE

80g fresh cranberries
juice of 4 medium clementines
60g light muscovado sugar
2 cloves

double cream, to serve

You will need 8 x 150ml dariole moulds or ramekins. Preheat the oven to 160C fan/180C/350F/gas mark 4 and grease the base and sides of your moulds with butter. Divide the light muscovado sugar between each greased mould, rolling the sugar around so that it covers and sticks to the base and sides, and leaves about 1 teaspoon of the sugar in each base. Finely grate the zest from the clementines and set aside. Peel the fruit and use a sharp knife to cut each into four 1–2cm-thick rounds. Place the biggest eight slices in the base of the moulds on top of the sugar, and put the rest in a small saucepan (to be used in the sauce).

Weigh the eggs, then measure the same quantity of butter, caster sugar and self-raising flour (about 220g of each) into separate bowls. Combine the sugar and butter and cream together until light and fluffy (by hand with a wooden spoon and plenty of elbow grease, or in a stand mixer fitted with the paddle attachment). Crack in the eggs one at a time, incorporating each egg fully before adding the next, then mix in the flour, baking powder and clementine zest. Divide the batter evenly among the moulds so they are three-quarters full. Place the moulds on a baking tray and bake in the oven for 25 minutes until risen and golden. A metal skewer inserted into the middle of one of the sponges should come out clean.

Add the sauce ingredients to the clementine segments in the saucepan. Heat gently for 5–10 minutes, until half of the cranberries have popped, a few have split and the rest remain intact. Avoid bursting too many as the sauce will become mushy and thick.

If you've made the sponges and sauce in advance, warm the sponges in a 120C fan/140C/275F/gas mark 1 oven for 10 minutes, and reheat the sauce gently for 3–5 minutes, again avoiding popping too many cranberries. Use a small palette knife to loosen the warm sponges from their moulds and invert them onto plates or bowls. Spoon the sauce over the top, and serve with double cream.

RHUBARB, ORANGE AND GINGER FREE-FORM TART

Bright, forced pink rhubarb is a highlight of winter - the stems really stand out in a greengrocer's display - while citrus fruits, including oranges, are also at their striking peak right now. This free-form tart brings the two together and uses ground and stem ginger to tie and mellow the sour and the sweet fruits. Serve with ice cream, double cream, custard, or all three.

SERVES 6–8

FOR THE PASTRY

250g spelt flour, plus extra for dusting
130g cold salted butter, cubed
1 heaped teaspoon ground ginger
70g icing sugar
½ teaspoon flaky sea salt
grated zest of 1 orange
2–4 tablespoons cold milk

FOR THE FILLING

500g forced rhubarb, cut into 3–4cm batons
2 pieces of stem ginger, cut into thin matchsticks,
*   plus 3 tablespoons of syrup from the jar*
flesh of 1 orange, cut into 2–3cm chunks
50g golden caster sugar
50g ground almonds

ice cream, double cream or custard, to serve

To make the pastry, combine the flour, butter, ground ginger, icing sugar and salt until the mixture resembles breadcrumbs – you can do this with your fingertips or in a food processor with the pulse setting. Add the orange zest and 2 tablespoons of the cold milk and press together to form a ball of dough. Use an extra 1–2 tablespoons of milk if necessary. Push the pastry into a disc 2–3cm thick, wrap completely and refrigerate for at least 1 hour, ideally more.

When the pastry has been in the fridge for 1 hour, put the rhubarb batons, stem ginger (not the syrup) and orange into a bowl, scraping any juice from the orange on top. Add the caster sugar, mix and leave to macerate for 10 minutes or so.

Preheat the oven to 180C fan/200C/400F/ gas mark 6 and line a large baking sheet with greaseproof paper, using a smudge of butter to secure it in place.

Unwrap the pastry and roll it out on a lightly floured surface into a rough 2–3mm-thick circle. Trim the rough edges with a knife, then lift the pastry onto the lined baking sheet by rolling it onto a floured rolling pin, and flopping it flat onto the sheet. Spoon the ground almonds into a circle in the middle of the pastry, leaving a 4–5cm border between the almonds and the edge of the pastry. Arrange the fruit on top of the almonds (but none of the residual liquid), then create sides for the tart by turning the pastry up, towards and a little over the fruit in 6 or 7 moves. Bake the tart towards the top of the oven for 50 minutes, until the pastry is golden and firm, and the rhubarb pink and soft.

While the tart is baking, mix the stem ginger syrup with any residual macerating juices.

Remove the tart from the oven and brush the syrup over the pastry and the fruit to give it a pleasingly sweet and spicy sheen before slicing and serving with ice cream, double cream or custard.

SPICED APPLE SOUR

Walking around the Market over the festive period, there's an unmistakable smell of mulling spices – warm, spiced wine, cider and apple juice are all on offer from steaming casks outside **The Cider House**, **Borough Wines**, **Cartwright Brothers Vintners Ltd** and elsewhere.

This cocktail invokes the spirit of those drinks, and is also a particularly enjoyable way to use up any egg whites left over from a day's cooking.

FOR THE CINNAMON SUGAR SYRUP (ENOUGH FOR 8 COCKTAILS)

100g caster sugar
1 cinnamon stick
5 cloves
1 thick slice of fresh ginger
120ml water

FOR 1 SPICED APPLE SOUR

50ml calvados
25ml lemon juice
25ml cinnamon sugar syrup
20g egg white (½ large egg white)
ice cubes
nutmeg, to garnish

Make the cinnamon sugar syrup in advance. Warm the sugar and spices in a small saucepan with 120ml water over a low heat for 10 minutes, stirring halfway through to encourage the sugar to dissolve (avoid boiling the syrup). Remove from the heat and leave to infuse and cool to room temperature for 30 minutes, then strain into a jar, seal and store in the fridge until required. It will keep for at least 2 weeks if refrigerated.

When cocktail hour is up, measure the calvados, lemon juice, sugar syrup and egg white into a cocktail shaker. Shake with all your might for 20–30 seconds to get the egg whites frothing. Add a handful of ice cubes and shake some more, until the liquids are thoroughly chilled.

Strain the cocktail into a coupe or low ball glass and grate a little nutmeg over the top.

A DAY IN THE LIFE OF BOROUGH'S TRADERS

It's a lively scene, the set-up. An assault on the senses. And is in stark contrast to the silence of commuters walking from London Bridge station to the City, or the gentle quiet of an office. It's physical and bracing; there's banter and the occasional muffled obscenity. Yet the practicalities and effort belie the fact that all stalls require a creative, artistic touch, and there's much talent on display in that regard.

The first hour or two of trading is relatively quiet. Shoppers in the know take advantage of this, and for many traders it's a convivial warm-up. Sam of From Field and Flower finds it's the time to chat to her regulars: 'We take the opportunity to swap recipe ideas, or just have a catch-up with what we've been up to.'

The Market bell rings at 10am from Monday to Friday, and at 8am on Saturdays. Though it signals the start of trading, for most of Borough's traders this is long since the beginning of their day.

From 6:30am onwards there's activity under the railway arches. You'll find greengrocers, like Kath of Ted's Veg and Frederica of Turnips, sorting through new stock and re-installing their impressive displays. Furness Fish Markets' seafood spectacle takes at least two hours to get ready, and they'll have been in early anyway in order to receive the day's haul.

The clattering sound of stalls being wheeled from storage areas to the Green Market drowns out even the trains going overhead; an area that's empty overnight is suddenly transformed into a bustling marketplace, full of red and yellow umbrellas, colleagues catching up and unloading, and crucially getting their coffee and tea from fellow traders.

Packing down begins late afternoon. Again, it's physical, not least for the Market operations team in their green jackets, who you'll see moving waste and directing traffic as tables fold, produce is stowed away and stalls are rolled back across the cobbles to their parking spots.

By 6:30pm it's strangely quiet compared to the bustle of a few hours before. A wind-down with colleagues is appealing, and many, like Marianna, enjoy the community feel: 'There's always an interesting story, and I love hearing about culinary traditions from traders from all over the world.' But you can understand, too, those like Kath, who might prefer a break following 12 hours or more on their feet. 'I enjoy the new challenges and new people you get every day. Sometimes we'll go for a beer afterwards, but I'm usually too shattered!'

Soon enough, though, the scattering of shoppers becomes a swarm, and on most days lunchtime until 2pm or 3pm is busy. Really busy. There's less chance to chat now, beyond the swapping of banknotes for change, and maybe a bit of produce for lunch when there's a moment to take a bite.

Ask any stall worker and they'll tell you they prefer it this way. Time flies when there's a buzz. That skill of catching eyes without being pushy, of managing multiple customers at once and always smiling takes time and a particular personality. So many of the traders who've been working at Borough for years speak of how they enjoy the opportunity to interact, to tempt through tastings, to chat and explain, and ultimately to sell. For Marianna of Oliveology, it's a thrill when customers 'leave with a smile, and thank you saying "I have learnt something today".'

THE BUTCHERS

Shoppers in search of fresh meat are spoilt for choice in this triangle of land just off London Bridge – Market butchers, such as Northfield Farm, Rhug Estate and Ginger Pig offer sustainably reared, rare breed beef, pork, lamb and more in classic and contemporary cuts. There's wild venison, rabbit, hare and feathered game too, at the likes of Wyndham House Ltd, Furness Fish Markets and Shellseekers Fish & Game Ltd.

Indeed, the ability to source responsibly farmed, dry-aged meats from the whole carcass – the kind you just can't find at supermarkets – has provided the impetus for many to visit Borough Market since the retail trade was ushered in twenty years ago. One of the original butchers, Wild Beef, continue to trade today, every week bringing their cuts of rare breed meat up from Dartmoor in the West Country for the benefit of Londoners in the know.

LIZZIE VINES, WILD BEEF

My husband Richard and I are Dartmoor farmers, first and foremost. We are a tiny family business with around 30 hardy Welsh Black and North Devon cows. They like the outdoors, the rain and are what we call 'good grass converters' – they don't need a lot to get fat! They're beautiful, wonderful, friendly creatures. We like to say that they're beyond organic as they're wild, always out, even in the depths of winter only coming in if it's very, very wet.

We slaughter the bullocks at around two-and-a-half years old, hang them for four weeks for taste and to tenderise, then bring a whole carcass here each week, already portioned up. Proper nose-to-tail stuff. What you see is what you get, and when it's gone, it's gone. And Borough is our main outlet, our market.

We were one of the first four traders to set up here in 1998 when this area began morphing from its wholesale existence to what it is now. Neal's Yard Dairy and Brindisa were open at that time, though at weekends it was quiet, completely dead really. So they used to have an open day once every three months to draw people in. In the middle of November, the food writer Henrietta Green put on a Food Lovers' Fair to showcase the fifty 'finest' British producers, and a week later the butcher and farmer Peter Gott organised four of us to come back and join up with one of the open days, to see what might happen. We were all farmers specialising in meat; us with beef, Peter wild boar and pork, Denhay bacon and another who sold chicken and foie gras.

For that weekend we said to our butcher that we wanted a whole bullock, butchered and jointed from the tongue to the tail, and he looked at us and said: 'You must be joking,

and other barbecue cuts. Still, people clearly love the idea of red meat, slow-cooked meals and comfort food in the darker months.

I think our way of trading, the flavour of our meat, and the ethos of what people call 'whole carcass' or 'nose-to-tail' butchery helps to highlight the fact that meat comes from an animal, and the best animals are from small farms where they're allowed to roam free. It sounds obvious, but people forget there are only ever two fillets, one tongue, once the sirloin is sold there's no more… that sort of thing. The cheeks always go the first day. Rib-eye too. Onglet is popular as well. Most of our customers understand, and it's a good opportunity to explain how things work if not.

Each of the butchers at Borough Market offers something different. Rhug Farm do Aberdeen Angus but also their super salt-marsh lamb. Northfield Farm have a completely different breed of beef to us, plus rare breed pork and sheep too, and Ginger Pig are different again. Wild beef is our thing.

We have moved to a bigger stall in recent years and extended our range, promoting food from friends nearby in north Devon and Cornwall – happy chickens, hens' eggs, Cornish sea salt and dried seaweed. Ultimately, though, we try not to sell anything that isn't as good as the beef – only things that we're proud of, and that we would eat ourselves.

you'll never sell that much!' But we did. We sold out in four hours, give or take a bag or two of stewing meat. It was quite incredible. By February 1999 there were eight traders; by March, sixteen. Bread came, the grocers, Monmouth Coffee Company set up a stall – which was a real blessing as there was nowhere else to get a coffee after our drive up – and by the end of that year we were trading twice a week. We brought two bullocks a week and took over an old friend's farm and herd so that we could grow with demand.

We always sell about two thirds of our beef between October and March. People don't seem to want nearly so much during hot-weather periods, though we change how things are portioned to try to help: topsides are cut into frying steaks, we make mince for burgers

SWEETBREAD NUGGETS AND CARROT HUMMUS

Sweetbreads are just one example of the lesser-known cuts of meat you can buy from butchers who make the most of an entire animal, as the Market's butchers do. Though some will wince when told that sweetbreads are a gland, they're actually one of the most approachable, and least 'offaly', of offal. It could be said they taste just like chicken. They will certainly be among the most tender and light nuggets that you've ever tried.

The carrot hummus is easy and delicious but also optional, as the nuggets would be perfectly good with ketchup, brown sauce, the mushroom ketchup on page 258, or a garlic mayonnaise, if you prefer a western, rather than Middle Eastern dipper.

Serve them, canapé or communal style with the hummus as a dip, or turn into wraps with flatbreads, fresh coriander, yoghurt and pickles.

SERVES *4*

FOR THE CARROT HUMMUS

2 teaspoons cumin seeds
1 teaspoon coriander seeds
500g carrots, peeled
2 tablespoons olive oil, plus extra if needed
4 garlic cloves, flattened (skin on)
2 tablespoons water
150g tahini
juice of ½ lemon

FOR THE SWEETBREAD NUGGETS

800g lamb sweetbreads
300ml buttermilk
100g plain flour
100g coarse polenta or cornmeal
1 teaspoon sweet smoked paprika
   (Pimentón de la Vera)
sunflower oil, for deep-frying

Preheat the oven to 200C fan/220C/425F/gas mark 7.

Separately dry-toast the cumin and coriander seeds in a frying pan until fragrant and grind in a pestle and mortar. Put the peeled carrots in a roasting tin and gloss with the olive oil. Add the ground cumin (saving ½ teaspoon for the sweetbread coating), coriander and garlic cloves, and roast in the oven for 45 minutes–1 hour, until caramelised and sweet. Remove from the oven, pick the skins from the garlic and blitz in a blender or food processor whilst the carrots are still warm, along with 2 tablespoons water, the tahini and lemon juice. Taste and season with flaky sea salt and add more oil if you like, blitzing for a little bit longer until silky smooth. Refrigerate until required.

Soak the sweetbreads in iced water for 1 hour then drain. Bring a saucepan of water to the boil and fill a bowl with fresh iced water. Blanch the sweetbreads for 3 minutes, then immediately drain and plunge them into the fresh iced water (or leave them under cold running water to cool). Peel away any membrane from the sweetbreads and trim off and discard knobbly bits of fat or unsightly tissue, then cut the large sweetbreads into nugget-sized pieces if necessary (roughly the size of a large thumb).

Coat the sweetbreads in the buttermilk. Mix the flour, polenta or cornmeal, paprika and reserved ground cumin in a bowl, then tip the mixture onto a baking tray or high-sided plate. Roll the buttermilk-coated sweetbreads in the dry coating, tap off any excess and line them up ready to fry.

Heat a deep-fat fryer filled with oil to 170C, or fill a wok 5–8cm deep with sunflower oil and use a thermometer to check the temperature. Fry the nuggets in batches for 3–4 minutes until golden. Lift them out with a slotted metal spoon and transfer to a tray lined with kitchen paper. Season with salt.

MOROCCAN-SPICED LAMB WITH SAFFRON COUSCOUS

The method of gentle roasting followed by searing, used for the forerib of beef on page 286, works well for lamb leg too. Unlike the forerib, though, this lamb seems to much prefer being fried in foaming butter at the end of the process, rather than in a hellishly hot oven, which would make the marinade burn and turn bitter.

The marinade brings a Moroccan twist to a British meat. Butchers like those at **Northfield Farm** will be happy to butterfly the lamb leg from the bone for you.

SERVES 4–6

FOR THE SPICED LAMB

800g butterflied lamb leg (off the bone weight)
1 garlic clove, crushed
1 tablespoon runny honey
3 tablespoons olive oil
1 tablespoon ras el hanout
leaves picked from 8 sprigs of thyme
30g butter

FOR THE SAFFRON COUSCOUS

10 saffron threads
2 tablespoons just-boiled water
150g couscous
240g drained tinned chickpeas
juice of ½ lemon
handful of chopped, fresh herbs (optional)

Remove the lamb from the fridge and pat it dry with kitchen paper if necessary. Mix the garlic, honey, olive oil, ras el hanout, thyme and plenty of flaky sea salt and black pepper in a bowl. Rub the spice mixture all over the lamb then place it in a roasting tin that fits the meat fairly snugly. Leave to marinate for at least 30 minutes, ideally more (overnight is fine – refrigerate if so).

A touch over 1 hour before you wish to eat, heat the oven to 100C fan/120C/250F/gas mark ½.

Place the lamb in its tin on the middle shelf of the oven and cook for 55 minutes (a probe thermometer, if you have one, should read 55C when inserted into the thickest part of the lamb). Remove from the oven and create a tent of foil over the tray, sealing it around the edges. Leave it to rest for 20 minutes (in this time the meat's internal temperature will rise to 56–58C). While it's resting, prepare the couscous.

Put the saffron threads in a heatproof mixing bowl and add 2 tablespoons just-boiled water. Leave the saffron to infuse for 5 minutes, then add the couscous and chickpeas. Pour freshly-boiled water until it sits 1cm above the level of the couscous. Cover the bowl with a clean tea towel and leave for 5 minutes, then remove the towel and fluff the cooked couscous with a fork. Season with the lemon juice, sea salt and black pepper, and chopped herbs if using (you can't really be too excessive if you do).

Heat a heavy-based frying pan big enough to hold the meat. Add the butter, and once it's foaming, add the meat. Sear for 2–3 minutes each side, until brown and crusted, then remove from the pan, carve and serve with the couscous.

ROAST FORERIB OF BEEF WITH YORKSHIRE PUDDINGS AND HORSERADISH CREAM

A forerib of beef is the joint for the big occasion – whether that's Christmas Day or otherwise. There's no hiding from the fact, though, that a well husbanded and aged piece of cow commands a lofty price, so some might be put off by the worry that they might not cook it to perfection. The following method, however, ensures a medium-rare pink from core to edge, as well as a moreish brown crust. You can use the method for any roasting joint of beef, though timings will vary, depending on size, and a probe thermometer will help avoid guesswork.

There's time to cook Yorkshire puddings, and though roast potatoes are slightly tricky logistically, they can still work if cut small and put in the oven from the moment the joint is first removed, and brought to the table once the beef has been carved.

A 2.5–3kg forerib serves around 8 people, with surplus for other meals - boil the bones to make a stock for soup or broth; fry any leftover meat for hot steak sandwiches.

SERVES 6–8

2.5–3kg forerib of beef (i.e. 2–3 ribs)
sunflower oil or beef dripping

FOR THE YORKSHIRE PUDDINGS

4 large eggs
250ml whole milk
270g plain flour
½ teaspoon flaky sea salt
80ml cold water

FOR THE HORSERADISH CREAM

juice of ¼ lemon
200ml double cream
70g fresh horseradish, grated

Ideally, unwrap the beef and keep it in the fridge at least overnight to dry, then remove it 4–5 hours before cooking to allow it to come closer to room temperature.

Season all sides of the meat generously with flaky sea salt and black pepper and preheat the oven to 100C fan/120C/250F/gas mark ½.

Place the beef in a suitably sized roasting tin, propped up on the ends of the bones, and cook in the oven for 1 hour 45 minutes– 2 hours 15 minutes, depending whether it's at the bottom or top of the 2.5–3kg weight bracket (2 hours is pretty dependable regardless). If you have a probe thermometer, remove the meat from the oven when most of the readings you take from the middle are 50–52C (the temperature will continue to rise as it rests). Increase the oven temperature to 230C fan/250C/480F/gas mark 10. Cover the beef with a tent of foil and leave to rest in a warm place for 30–40 minutes while you cook the Yorkshire puddings and get the rest of the meal together.

While the beef is cooking, whisk or blend together the Yorkshire pudding ingredients with 80ml cold water and refrigerate in a jug or other container from which it is easy to pour. Make the horseradish cream by adding the lemon juice to the cream in a bowl and very lightly whisking to ribbon stage (it won't take much effort). Stir in the grated horseradish and a pinch of salt and black pepper. Check for seasoning, tweak to taste and refrigerate until required.

Rearrange the oven shelves to ensure the Yorkshire puddings can sit near the top, with room to puff up. Put 2mm of sunflower oil (or 1–2 teaspoons of dripping) in the bottom of each hole in a deep 12-hole muffin tin. Place the tin in the oven and leave for 10 minutes to get very hot. Slide the shelf out and pour the batter into the holes to two-thirds full (with the tin still on the oven shelf), then quickly slide the shelf back into the oven and cook the puddings for 20–25 minutes, until crisp and much enlarged.

Increase the oven temperature to 240C fan/260C/500F/gas mark 10. Remove the foil and return the beef to the oven for 10 minutes, until an appetising crust forms. You can carve the beef almost immediately as it has already rested.

To serve the beef, first cut the meat away from the bones. You might then find it easier to remove the top cap, which will naturally be separating itself from the rib eye below. Carve both across the grain and ensure everyone gets a bit of each.

Enjoy with all the usual trimmings – not least the Yorkshire puddings and horseradish cream.

PORCINI-BRAISED BRISKET WITH DULSE

Brisket is from the breast of a cow. In Britain it tends to be rolled and pot-roasted until it falls apart, or perhaps diced and used in a stew. In Jewish cuisine it's braised or used to make salt beef. And in the Deep South of the United States, it is rubbed with spices and cooked low and slow on a barbecue, until wobbly and tender, but still ultimately sliceable. This method recreates the latter treatment without the input of charcoal or smoke, employing instead an umami-rich seasoning of dried mushrooms and dulse - a seaweed you can buy from **Wild Beef**.

You will probably need to request this particular cut from the butcher in advance. Ask for the point end, trimmed of much but not all of its surface fat, and not rolled. This is not as uniform as the flat end, which is typically used for salt beef (and could be used here), but the point has more marbling and will be juicier once cooked.

The first, long, cooking stage could be done overnight or the day before eating if you prefer.

Serve with mashed root vegetables and market brassicas.

SERVES *10–12*

20g dried porcini
1 teaspoon black peppercorns
1 teaspoon flaky sea salt
20g dried dulse seaweed
2–2.5kg brisket (point end)
200ml white wine, red wine or water
100ml just-boiled water

Preheat the oven to 100C fan/120C/250F/gas mark ½.

Use a spice grinder or other blender to grind the porcini, peppercorns, salt and 5g of the dulse seaweed to a powder. Lie the brisket in a roasting tin into which it fits fairly snugly and rub the spice blend all over it. Pour the wine or water into the tin, avoiding the meat so as not to wash the rub off. Cover the tin tightly with foil and place in the oven for 7–8 hours, until the brisket is tender. Remove from the oven and leave to rest, still covered, for 20 minutes, then transfer the meat to a carving board.

(If you're cooking the brisket in advance, then separate the meat from the juices, and leave both to cool to room temperature before covering and chilling until required. Reheat the meat for 40 minutes at 150C fan/170C/325F/gas mark 3 before leaving it to rest on the carving board (covered with foil), as above. Remove the solidified fat from the cooking juices and add the latter to the meat when reheating.)

Increase the oven temperature to 150C fan/170C/325F/gas mark 3. Separate the top layer of fat from the juices in the tin if you can, replace it with 100ml just-boiled water and add the rest of the dulse to the cooking juices (break it into pieces if the seaweed you have is in one clump).

Cut the beef into 1cm-thick slices across the width of the brisket (across the grain of the meat) and lay the slices flat in the liquid. Return to the oven, covered, for 20 minutes while you prepare the rest of your meal, basting the meat from time to time.

Serve the brisket on a platter with the cooking juices and re-hydrated seaweed spooned over the top, with mashed root vegetables and market brassicas alongside.

BEEF CHEEK AND LAMB HEART PUDDING

The classic steak and kidney combination is actually fairly unsuitable as a filling for a suet pastry 'pudding', as both cuts toughen when cooked for a long time. Beef cheek and lamb heart, on the other hand, only get better with time, turning rich and unctuous, and so are ideal for this old English dish.

This requires a little bit of effort and long cooking times, but it is an impressive and warming centrepiece. Think of it as a slow-cooked casserole served in a pastry-lined pudding bowl (the filling can be made in advance). Serve with braised red cabbage or a steaming mound of seasonal brassicas, perhaps a mashed root vegetable, and definitely lots of gravy.

SERVES 6

cooking oil, for frying
150g smoked lardons
2 beef or ox cheeks (about 1kg), trimmed
*   of sinew*
10 small round shallots, peeled
2 celery sticks, cut into 1–2cm dice
2 carrots, cut into 1–2cm dice
2 garlic cloves, flattened (skin on)
leaves picked from 3 sprigs of rosemary,
*   finely chopped*
2 tablespoons tomato purée
1 x 750ml bottle of red wine
3 lamb hearts, trimmed of hard fat
2 teaspoons Worcestershire sauce

FOR THE PASTRY

350g self-raising flour
150g shredded beef suet
1 teaspoon baking powder
1 teaspoon ground turmeric
1 teaspoon English mustard powder
½ teaspoon flaky sea salt
½ teaspoon ground black pepper
200ml chilled water
butter, for greasing
plain flour, for dusting

You will need a 1.5-litre pudding bowl.

Preheat the oven to 150C fan/170C/325F/gas mark 3.

Heat a little cooking oil in a heavy-based, ovenproof saucepan (for which you have a lid) or a flameproof casserole dish over a medium-high heat, add the lardons and fry until the fat renders, then add the beef or ox cheeks and brown them on both sides, in batches if necessary. Remove the cheeks, set them to one side, then add the shallots, celery and carrots and fry for 3 minutes. Add the garlic, rosemary and tomato purée, stir them into the vegetables and return the cheeks to the pan. Pour in the red wine and Worcestershire sauce, and add a heavy pinch of flaky sea salt and grind of black pepper. Cover and place in the oven for 1 hour 10 minutes.

Cut the lamb hearts open so that they lie flat, then cut them into 2–3cm squares. Add them to the casserole, then cook in the oven for a further 1 hour–1 hour 20 minutes, until you can just pull the beef apart with a fork or spoon. Remove from the oven and use a couple of forks to tear the meat into bite-sized chunks. Decant three quarters of the cooking liquid and reserve this for making gravy. Season the meats and remaining sauce in the casserole to taste with salt and black pepper and leave to cool.

Make the pastry while the filling is cooling (or 30 minutes to 3 hours before lining the pudding bowl). Mix the dry ingredients in a large bowl. Add the water and stir with a knife until the mix comes together as a dough. Pat the dough into a ball, wrap and refrigerate.

Smear the sides and base of the pudding bowl with butter. Create a foil lid 4–5cm bigger than the top of the pudding bowl, with a pleat in the middle (to allow for the pudding to expand) and grease one side of it with butter, too. Trim off a quarter of the chilled pastry dough, wrap it and put it back in the fridge. Dust a work surface or board with flour. Shape the larger piece of dough into a ball then roll it out to a 0.5–1cm-thick circle large enough to line the bottom and sides of the pudding bowl plus a 2–3cm overhang. Line the pudding bowl with it, cutting a line from one edge to the middle to help you fit it in. Trim any excess and push the pastry together, then cut away the overhanging pastry to leave just 2–3cm.

Using a slotted spoon, fill the pastry bowl with the meat, vegetables and the liquid in the pan (not the liquid reserved for gravy). Roll out the remaining quarter of pastry to the same thickness as before to create a lid, and use the overhang to tuck this in and close

the pudding. Seal with the pleated foil lid and tie a string handle around the bowl. Place in a large saucepan with water halfway up the bowl, cover with a lid, bring to rapid simmer and steam for 2 hours. You may need to top up the water. In the meantime, boil the remaining meat juices to reduce and thicken them for the gravy.

Unwrap the pudding then invert it onto a lipped platter with a rim (it's likely there'll be lots of gravy once the pastry is pierced). Cut the pastry away in segments, spooning out the meat as you go and encouraging people to slosh plenty more gravy over the top.

MARKET EVENTS

CHRISTMAS
AT BOROUGH MARKET

There are few places more likely to hurry Christmas cheer than Borough Market.

During December the dark-green arches, corrugated ceilings, glass-roofed halls and umbrella-topped stalls are adorned with fir and foliage, decorations made from Market-sourced fruits, herbs and spices, paper-chains carrying wishes and tidings of joy, and a good number of baubles, ribbons and twinkling fairy lights. A whiff of mulled wine, cider, warm-spiced apple juice – or all three – greets shoppers as they round each bend, the bakery stalls are laden with mince pies, and there's even a specialist Christmas pudding vendor on hand for those who've not got round to stirring their own. Even the most Scrooge-like of characters would agree that the sights, sounds and smells make a visit at this time of year a necessary ritual.

Of course a festive scene is nothing without its players, and it's no disservice to the decor to suggest that it's the electric atmosphere created by the interaction of traders and shoppers that makes the market particularly appealing. The area is a hive of activity from the moment the Christmas lights are switched on at the beginning of Advent, until the last shopper rushes to pick up their turkey by 4pm on Christmas Eve. Chefs in Market Hall embark on a schedule of recipe demonstrations on the likes of edible gifts, feasting menus, canapés and typical trimmings; the Borough Market choir adds tuneful carols to the persistent beat of the trains overhead; while traders, working non-stop throughout the month, continue to run the conversation, cajoling wanderers and offering catering and food-matching advice to those who want it. There's banter, and laughter, and some urgency too – this is the most important time of year for Market businesses – but all is undertaken in remarkably good cheer, given the rush and often inclement weather. The mood is infectious.

Of course the main reason for a visit remains the need to fill a shopping basket, which is where this gathering of minds and produce comes into its own. With over twenty cheesemongers and even a dedicated Evening of Cheese, there's no better place to pick up that most important of platters. Customers stock their fridges, cupboards and pantries with heritage breed meats, the best and freshest haul from the ocean, and with smoked and cured fish; they add seasonal fruit and vegetables, charcuterie, preserves, spiced biscuits and cakes, confectionery and sweetmeats, wines, spirits, craft beers and cider, speciality teas and coffee… basically, everything to ensure that Christmas is a time of plenty. That said, should something have been forgotten, the traders return every day after Boxing Day until the turn of the year.

GIVING TO OTHERS

Borough Market and its traders support a number of charities over the Christmas period, including local organisation Better Bankside's 'Together at Christmas' appeal, which collates and wraps gifts for distribution to local community groups that support homeless, vulnerably housed and elderly people estranged from family and friends. And though it's a project that runs twice weekly throughout the year, yielding tens of thousands of meals since the partnership began in 2014, Plan Zheroes' redistribution of surplus food from the likes of Ted's Veg, Turnips, Chegworth Valley and Olivier's Bakery to local charities and shelters is particularly fitting at a time of year when companionship, inclusion and generosity are at the forefront of people's minds.

THE BAKERS AND CONFECTIONERY MAKERS

The bakers and confectionery makers' tables are packed high every morning with fresh produce, although those stacks diminish rapidly through the course of the day.

Each trader has a niche: there are reams of different sourdoughs, baguettes and brioche at The Flour Station; Karaway Bakery's Baltic and Russian breads are rye-based; all of the cakes and pastries at The Free From Bakehouse are gluten-, and often dairy-, sugar- and egg-free too; The Cinnamon Tree Bakery's biscuits are spiced; and Luminary Bakery's cookies and cakes are made by an all-female team of apprentices and trainees from disadvantaged backgrounds. There are French and German bakers, including Olivier's Bakery, Artisan Foods and Comptoir Gourmand, fudge and chocolate makers, such as Whirld, So Chocolicious and Artisan du Chocolat, and even goat's milk ice cream via Greedy Goat.

Some of the bread only travels a few metres from where it's made to the stall it's sold at, as the Bread Ahead Bakery & School is now an integral part of the Borough Market furniture.

MATT JONES, BREAD AHEAD BAKERY & SCHOOL

I have sold bread here since 1999 – the first stall I had was with my previous bakery, set up on a table. Borough Market was unrecognisable back then, just empty warehouses and railway arches, completely deserted for much of the week. It was a very different time in terms of the food, restaurant and indeed bread scene too. The dark ages, compared to now.

In 2013 an opportunity came about to make use of some space on Cathedral Street backing on to the old wholesale units, and I jumped at the chance of being able to produce bread on-site. Very quickly we've established ourselves as a bakery with three key elements: retail via the market stalls, wholesale to restaurants and delis, and a really popular baking school. As a result we're here in the centre of the Market twenty-four hours a day – we use around 10 tonnes of flour a week, supply over 100 restaurants, and the lights and ovens are never off.

There's been a bread revolution over the last ten to fifteen years and I'm pleased we're major players. We specialise in sourdough bread, which thanks to its long fermentation period has proper depth of flavour, an open crumb and a good chewy crust. It's a totally different product from sliced white. Our customers know that real bread contains only flour, salt, yeast and water, but that when you combine those humble ingredients with experience and patience, the results can be remarkable. Once it's part of someone's diet, they're not going to give it up easily. It's a staple, but if you're used to having really nice bread, you look forward to it. I reckon about half our sales are to regular customers.

We've a nice range of breads and sweeter baked goods. From sourdough loaves, ciabatta

of questions. What's spelt? What's rye? What's gluten? What's sourdough? And so on. So I wanted to create an environment where we could answer those properly. It's ideal that we can do that within the context of a working bakery, where our professionals can pass on pockets of knowledge and thoughtful tips based on their experience, that also really work at home. We offer everything from 30-minute demos, through seasonal workshops covering a variety of different styles, to three-day sourdough courses. They all help to build an appreciation of bread and baking, and people really do get it. It's brilliant. You see the lightbulbs flash on, and know they'll never go back. I can't say I imagined we'd teach 300 people a week, but now we do.

I'm really proud that I get to employ, train and grow bakers here in Borough. It's a nice thing to do, especially as I live locally. There'll be between eight and thirty bakers on site, depending on the time of day people walk past, and I think it's so positive that Market shoppers can see in and watch things being made – we don't have enough visibility or connection with artisan food production in the UK compared to the Continent. We have ambitions to take our educative role further, and will soon open a Bread Ahead Baking Academy, which is aimed at training the bakers of the future. If real bread is going to take a slice of the supermarket loaf, we'll need more bakers to help do that.

To have the bakery, a working environment, in the middle of Borough Market is vital, I think. It's great for our customers too: you can't get fresher. We're part of a community, and it feels good and healthy to be able to simply walk our bread from the bakery to the stalls just a few metres away.

and loaded focaccia, to things like brownies, viennoiserie, mince pies at Christmas and hot cross buns for Easter, and of course our famous doughnuts. Aside from the seasonal specials, everything sells well throughout the year. Again, I think it's because good bread becomes part of a diet. You buy a loaf and it lasts you a few days, but you'll need to get another loaf later on in the week too, and any surplus bits that start to dry out make great breadcrumbs, croutons for panzanella and so on – we use our surplus in bread pudding. The sweet products are more of an indulgence, but we all want them. And it's a great tradition of markets, isn't it, for the bakeries to sell sweet products, and for there to be tables of confectionery as well as all the savoury treats?

Right from the start, education has been a really important focus of Bread Ahead. I knew from previous experience that when you're working on a market stall you get lots

A BOROUGH MARKET TOASTIE

One of the most satisfying ways to celebrate freshly baked bread is to sandwich it around world-class ingredients. And then to toast it.

Cheese is obligatory; ideally a combination of one that melts well and another that packs a powerful punch. But that dairy needs another savoury item to provide interest beyond the first bite. This could be a cured or cooked meat, or a thinly sliced but still punchy vegetable, like onions, leeks or fennel. Condiments are essential, be it a piquant or sweet pickle or conserve, or something hot and spicy from **Pimento Hill**. Finally, the toastie must be cooked with care - compressed from time to time, and fried at a pace that ensures the outside is crisp and golden, and the centre molten.

To prescribe just one combination of ingredients would not do justice to the possibilities, so following the main recipe are a few ideas to inspire when out shopping or raiding the fridge.

SERVES 1

2 x 1–2cm-thick slices of sourdough
butter
60g cheese, ideally a 50/50 combination of
    melting and strong, both coarsely grated
20g sliced cured meat or 40g sliced cooked meat
    (optional)
15g onions, spring onions or leeks, finely sliced
    (optional)
condiment of choice

Butter what will become the external sides of each piece of bread. Build the sandwich, with a sprinkle of cheese on the base first, then the meat or alliums, followed by the remaining cheese, then add pickles or spread the condiment onto the inside of the top slice, finally pressing that on top.

Place a heavy-based frying pan over a low-medium heat and allow it to warm up for a minute.

Transfer the sandwich to the frying pan and cook very gently, regularly pushing down on the sandwich with a fish slice or palette knife. After 2 minutes, some but not all of the cheese will have melted and the base of the bread will be browning. Carefully flip the toastie over and repeat the gentle frying and pressing for 2 minutes more. Repeat, frying both sides for another 2 minutes each, so that the cheese and fats are oozing out of the sandwich and the bread is golden and crisp.

Remove from the heat and leave to cool for 1–2 minutes before eating – the centre will be hotter than the sun.

POSSIBLE COMBINATIONS

- stilton (or other strong blue), Fontina and kimchi
- 'Nduja, honey and mozzarella
- cooked ham, raclette, Comté and mustard
- cheddar, Ogleshield, leeks and chutney
- soft-rind white cheese, turkey and cranberry sauce
- bresaola, tapenade and emmental on rye bread
- fennel salami, Umbrico (drunken cheese) and dill pickles
- tallegio, roast peppers, spring onions and chives

KALE MIGAS WITH PORK AND CLAM STEW

If your bread dries out before you reach the end of it, buy a fresh loaf for your sandwiches and turn the rest into a new ingredient.

There are many ways to use up stale bread, not least in the form of breadcrumbs and croutons, as on pages 255, 147 and 175. The Iberian approach is slightly different, as it treats the leftover bread as the base of a savoury dish, rather than a garnish or topping. Migas (crumbs) are partially rehydrated in milk, fried in oil and garlic and bolstered, in this case, by kale and white beans. They are a hugely satisfying accompaniment to a Portuguese-style pork and clam stew.

SERVES 4

2 tablespoons cooking oil
800g pork shoulder, cut into bite-sized pieces
40g parsley
1 medium onion, finely diced
3 garlic cloves, thinly sliced
500ml dry and floral white wine, such as
    vinho verde or white Douro
2 teaspoons sweet smoked paprika
    (Pimentón de la Vera)
2 romano peppers, deseeded and finely sliced
200g clams, purged in cold water
    (see page 228), and any broken or open
    clams discarded

FOR THE MIGAS

⅓ large, old sourdough loaf (around 300g)
200ml whole milk
4–5 tablespoons olive oil
3 garlic cloves, thinly sliced
200–250g kale, leaves stripped from the ribs
    and chopped

Tear the bread into 3cm chunks and spread out in a single layer on a baking tray. Pour over the milk and leave to soak, turning the bread from time to time so the dry sides become wet.

Place a heavy-based saucepan or flameproof casserole dish over a medium-high heat. Add the cooking oil and, when hot, the diced pork. Let the pork colour for 5 minutes, stirring occasionally. Finely chop the parsley stalks to the point they thin and become leaf bearing. Add the chopped stalks, onion and a heavy pinch of sea salt to the pork and cook for a further 3 minutes, then add the garlic, and pour in the white wine (leaving a large glass for the chef). Add the paprika, reduce the heat and cook very gently for 25 minutes with the lid ajar. Add the peppers, then simmer for 15–20 minutes until the pork is tender.

Once the peppers have been added to the stew, measure 4 tablespoons of the olive oil into a large heavy-based frying pan or sauté pan over a medium-high heat. When hot, add the milk-soaked bread and cook until it colours and begins to crisp, squashing the bread down with an implement from time to time. After 10 minutes the bread will be golden and crisp but still squidgy. Add the garlic and chopped kale and cook for 3–5 minutes until the kale has wilted, turning the ingredients frequently and adding an extra glug of olive oil if it seems necessary.

Add the cleaned clams to the stew and place the lid on top. Simmer for 3 minutes until the clams are fully open, then stir the remaining parsley through the stew – leaves still attached to the thin stalks – and serve immediately, accompanied by the migas.

SALTED CHOCOLATE FUDGE BROWNIES

Two sweet things at the Market that are a constant source of attention and salivation are the Jenga-type stacks of chocolate brownies on most bakers' tables, and the piles of crumbly, melt-in-the-mouth fudge at **Whirld**.

Sea salt caramel, spicy chocolate chilli, liquorice, and more conventional vanilla and clotted cream flavours of fudge are all on offer (among others), and any of them can be dropped into this bitter chocolate brownie – something that's good to have a recipe for, given any you buy from a Market baker probably won't survive your journey home uneaten.

MAKES 8–10

200g salted butter
80g unsweetened cocoa powder
100g dark chocolate (85% cocoa solids),
  broken into pieces
4 large eggs
200g light muscovado sugar
125g dark muscovado sugar
3 teaspoons flaky sea salt
100g self-raising flour
150g fudge of choice, roughly chopped

Preheat the oven to 150C fan/170C/325F/gas mark 3 and line a 27 x 20cm (or similar area) baking tray with baking parchment.

Put the butter in a saucepan over a low heat. Once melted, stir in the cocoa powder then add the chocolate. Stir until fully melted and incorporated, then remove from the heat.

Break the eggs into a large bowl. Add both the sugars and 1 teaspoon of the salt and beat thoroughly until light and frothy, by hand with a balloon whisk, electric whisk (or in a stand mixer). Mix in the butter and chocolate until smooth and glossy. Sift the flour into the mixture and fold it in with a large metal spoon or spatula. Pour the batter into the prepared tray and level it out.

Scatter the fudge pieces on top, pushing each piece down into the mixture a little, then sprinkle the remaining 2 teaspoons of salt over the top. Bake in the centre of the oven for 20 minutes, or until a light crust has formed and the edges are firm but there's still a slight wobble below the surface in the middle.

Remove from the oven and leave to cool, then refrigerate for at least 2 hours (this helps ensure a pleasing fudginess) before portioning.

Serve the brownies at room temperature, or reheat for 15 minutes in a low oven if you fancy them as a pudding with ice cream (see page 137). Theoretically, these brownies could be stored in the fridge for up to 3 days, but it's unlikely they'll last so long.

LIQUORICE ROOT PANNA COTTA

Another stall at Borough Market dedicated to just one ingredient is **Sweet Roots**, which only sells items involving liquorice – liquorice marinades, liquorice jams, liquorice candies and liquorice root ready to be used in a herbal infusion.

It is the gentle aniseed flavour of the root that this panna cotta makes use of, resulting in a dessert that's subtly spiced, clean and smooth rather than outlandishly flavoured, so even those who think they dislike liquorice will enjoy it. You can either use whole root, or root that has been ground to a powder in this recipe, whichever is easier to find.

The panna cotta can (and should) be made well in advance of when you're planning to eat it as it needs at least eight hours to set. Serve it with a quickly roasted or gently stewed sharp fruit (which can be cooked and chilled in advance, too). In winter, rhubarb, blood orange or apples are perfect; in warmer seasons, greengages and plums match the spice very well.

SERVES 4

1 heaped teaspoon liquorice root powder or
   3 liquorice root sticks (25g)
300ml double cream
200ml whole milk
60g golden caster sugar
2 gelatine sheets (3.5g)

You will need four 150ml dariole moulds, ramekins or tea cups. If using the whole liquorice root sticks, snap each stick into 3 or 4 pieces (or use a heavy knife to chop them).

Place the pieces of liquorice stick or the liquorice root powder into a small, heavy-based pan with half the cream and all the milk and sugar and gradually heat to almost boiling point, stirring to dissolve the sugar. Reduce the heat and let it simmer very gently for 5 minutes, then remove from the heat, leaving the liquorice root to infuse for 1 hour.

After that time gently reheat the infused cream. Put the gelatine sheets in a bowl of cold water and leave to 'bloom' for 3 minutes, then squeeze out the water and dissolve them in the warm cream. Remove the saucepan from the heat and strain its contents through a fine sieve into a heatproof jug. Leave to cool to room temperature, with a little cling film or baking parchment pressed to the surface to prevent a skin forming.

Put the remaining cream in a mixing bowl and beat it with a balloon whisk until it just begins to ribbon and thicken (this will take only a few seconds because the volume is small). Pour the infused cream mix into the whipped cream, mix, then transfer back to the jug, using a silicone spatula to scrape out every last drop. Pour the mixture directly from the jug into the moulds, ramekins or tea cups. Cover with cling film or baking parchment and leave to chill and set in the fridge for at least 8 hours.

If you've used dariole moulds and you want to turn the panna cotta out onto a plate, you may need to briefly dip the moulds in hot water (or use a blowtorch!) to help release the panna cotta.

DULCE DE LECHE TRUFFLES

Facing out onto Stoney Street, **Porteña** sell freshly baked meat- and cheese-filled empanadas, small 2–3-bite pasties that are as commonplace in Argentina as steak and malbec. Also synonymous with that country, and on offer at this stall, is dulce de leche – a creamy, caramel paste (essentially the same as caramel made by boiling tins of condensed milk) that's used in desserts and sweet snacks.

This fiendishly moreish treat makes a pretty remarkable store cupboard ingredient, and is increasingly available in the UK. If not simply eaten with your fingers straight from the jar, it can be spread on pancakes and waffles, used as a filling for sponge cakes, or the base for a banoffee pie. Here, it's used to brighten a classic chocolate ganache truffle. These could be simply rolled in cocoa, but the crack of bitter chocolate shell around the soft, sweet middle is worth the extra effort. They would be a particularly welcome gift or after-dinner treat at Christmas time.

MAKES *24–30*

130ml double cream
120g dulce de leche
100g milk chocolate (40–60% cocoa solids),
    broken into small pieces
unsweetened cocoa powder, for dusting
100g dark chocolate (70–85% cocoa solids),
    broken into small pieces

Put the cream in a small, heavy-based pan and bring to the boil. Measure the dulce de leche into a heatproof mixing bowl and add the milk chocolate pieces. When the cream begins to boil, pour it into the bowl of dulce de leche and chocolate and whisk energetically until the mixture is smooth and silky. If the liquid and solids 'split', add a little more cream and whisk again. Chill this ganache for 2 hours or until firm.

Use a teaspoon or melon baller to scoop out marble-sized amounts of chilled ganache (if you have an electronic scale, 10–12g of ganache per truffle is ideal). Do this methodically until you have 24–30 portions of ganache, place on a tray then chill the ganache again (as they will be soft – you can speed the process by using your freezer). Dust your hands with a cocoa powder and roll each ganache portion into balls, then place in the freezer again.

Place a heatproof bowl over a saucepan of simmering water, making sure the base of the bowl isn't touching the water. Add two thirds of the dark chocolate to the bowl and leave it to melt without stirring. Remove the pan from the heat and set aside (leaving the bowl over the warm water). Use a cocktail stick to pick up each chilled ganache ball and dip it into the melted chocolate. Place on a wire rack or silicone mat to set.

There are more professional ways to ensure a shiny, snappy and perfectly spherical coating, but this method is perfectly good among friends.

A MARKETPLACE OF IDEAS

DONALD HYSLOP AND KATE HOWELL

The notion that a city's food market might provide a platform for the sharing of ideas is hardly a new one. The Agora of classical Athens – an open square, located beneath the Acropolis, where bakers, fishmongers, vintners and craftspeople gathered to sell their wares – provided a public forum where the philosophical and political ideas that would shape the ancient world were given voice. It was at this marketplace that Socrates began questioning the city's leaders and inspiring his young followers, Plato among them. It was also here that Diogenes lived in a barrel, emerging during the day to wander round with his lamp, searching for the souls of honest men. The Agora was somewhere you'd go to buy some baklava, but it was also a crucible of radical ideas, intrigue and gossip.

There is something of the Agora about Borough Market – including the intrigue and gossip. None among us is a modern-day Socrates, and no one here is living in a barrel – although, in the very early days of the retail market, some of the traders who travelled long distances did keep sleeping bags behind their stalls – but ours is a public space that brings people together, embraces change and facilitates debate, just like that ancient marketplace.

It was at Borough Market in the late-1990s that arguments about the inadequacies and injustices of industrialised food production gathered powerful new voices, when a pioneering group of traders came together to create a new sort of market. The traders at Borough are not just producers and merchants, they are also articulate advocates of sustainable production techniques that elsewhere are threatened by volume and convenience. Many of them seek to preserve traditional methods and foodstuffs, and the Market itself is also unafraid to learn lessons from the past – a case in point being its drive to reduce plastic waste through the installation of public water fountains, which harked back to the campaigning work of Victorian progressives. But the instinct to look backwards comes not from blinkered nostalgia but the belief that ideas from other eras might help us mould a more sustainable and equitable future. Historic though it may be, Borough Market

is not a museum, so lively discussion and the practical application of alternative thinking will continue to find fuel here.

This openness, this commitment to ideas and progress, is visible throughout the Market. The estate has been steadily evolving since 1756, and it continues to do so, combining new architecture with old to improve the accessibility and functionality of the spaces. There is a vibrant sense of creativity and diversity: the urban art interventions, the pop-ups for bright young (and not so young) chefs and restaurateurs, plus the use of our historic Cathedral Street building as the venue for Bompas & Parr's boundary-pushing, head-spinning Museum of Food.

Borough's charitable status means that the pursuit of profit is not what drives us. Instead, we can invest in and work closely with innovators whose ambitions chime with our vision and values. Borough Market is large enough and visible enough to act as both test-bed and display window. This allows small businesses with big ideas to show off their ground-breaking products and services: it's the laboratory that used a biodegradable casing to create edible spheres of drinking water; the sustainable packaging developer that pioneered a fully recyclable coffee cup; the clean energy company that takes waste coffee grounds from Borough's traders and uses them to make bio-fuels. During London Food Tech Week we created an entire Food Tech Village at the Market, where innovators could demonstrate their use of technological wizardry in the pursuit of improvements in food safety, waste reduction and urban growing.

The most important idea to flourish here is the belief that food businesses can have a societal impact that extends far beyond their stalls. It is in this spirit that we have consistently sought to provide support for social enterprises that use food and drink as a vehicle for change. Change Please provides opportunities for homeless people to train as baristas, earn a living wage and

receive help with housing, banking and mental health. Luminary Bakery, a London-based enterprise, provides training and employment opportunities for disadvantaged women. The Colombian Coffee Company sources coffee from small farms in Colombia, pays above market prices and uses its profits to support social-development projects in rural areas.

As well as a place to trade, Borough Market provides businesses like these with a platform to promote their ideas. For Eduardo Florez, the director of The Colombian Coffee Company, having the opportunity to educate coffee-loving Londoners about his war-torn homeland and the problems of the globalised coffee trade is as much a part of his mission as providing income to farmers. These messages are propagated by the conversations that take place every day between traders and customers in this most interactive of spaces, but also through more structured channels: the annual Borough Talks series, which brings expert panels to debate in public; the Market's own magazine and website; the broadcasters and journalists drawn here by our international reputation and readiness to engage.

We see the Market as a constantly evolving ecosystem (it takes a thousand brushstrokes to make a painting), so we take every opportunity we can to stimulate discussion about what happens here. Through the words and actions of our diverse, active and often noisy community, we hope to influence and inspire the people who visit Borough Market and contribute to discussion and change far beyond this estate. Many of the millions of people who visit Borough Market each year are content to shop, browse, eat and experience the sights, sounds and smells of market life. But they can also experience debates, cookery demonstrations, public art and London's diversity in all its forms.

This may be a market for the 21st century, but much of what happens here would be recognisable to Diogenes – and given the chance, he would no doubt be quickly using Twitter in his daily quests. The ideas shared here now may not change the world in quite the way that Socrates and Plato did. But if Borough Market can inspire people to think and talk as well as eat, then a little bit of the Athens Agora will continue to live on.

DONALD HYSLOP is head of regeneration and community partnerships at TATE and became a trustee of Borough Market in 2007, serving as chair from 2011 to 2018.

KATE HOWELL joined Borough Market in 2011 and is Director of Development and Communications.

INDEX

DIRECTORY OF TRADERS

BAKERS AND CONFECTIONERS
Artisan du Chocolat
Artisan Foods
Bread Ahead Bakery & School
Comptoir Gourmand
Gelateria 3BIS
Ion Patisserie
Karaway Bakery
Konditor & Cook
Luminary Bakery
Olivier's Bakery
Rabot 1745
So Chocolicious
Sweet Roots
The Cinnamon Tree Bakery
The Flour Station
The Free From Bakehouse
The Turkish Deli
Whirld

BOROUGH LIFE
Borough Kitchen
Bread Ahead Bakery & School
Hobbs Barbers
Neal's Yard Remedies
Richard Bramble

BUTCHERS AND GAME DEALERS
Exotic Meat Co
Furness Fish Markets
Ginger Pig
Northfield Farm
Rhug Estate
Shellseekers Fish & Game Ltd
Wild Beef
Wyndham House Ltd

CAFES, RESTAURANTS AND PUBS
Applebee's Fish
Arabica Bar & Kitchen
Bedales of Borough
Brindisa Kitchens Ltd, Restaurants
Elliot's
Feng Sushi
Fish! Restaurant

Maria's Market Café
Monmouth Coffee Company
Padella
Rabot 1745
Roast Restaurant
Silka
The Globe Tavern
The Rake
WOKIT
Wright Brothers Borough

CHARCUTIERS
Alpine Deli
Bianca Mora
Brindisa Ltd, Wholesale & Retail
Cannon & Cannon
De Calabria
Gastronomica
Taste Croatia
The French Comté
The Ham & Cheese Company
The Parma Ham and Mozzarella Stand
Une Normande à Londres

DAIRY AND CHEESEMONGERS
Alsop & Walker
Bianca Mora
Blackwoods Cheese Company
Borough Cheese Company
De Luca London Mozzarella & Co.
Heritage Cheese
Hook & Son
Jumi Cheese
Kappacasein Dairy
Le Marché du Quartier
L'Ubriaco Drunk Cheese
Mons Cheesemongers
Neal's Yard Dairy
The Bath Soft Cheese Co.
The French Comté
The Ham & Cheese Company
The Parma Ham and Mozzarella Stand
Trethowan's Dairy
Une Normande à Londres

DRINKS
Borough Wines
Cartwright Brothers Vintners Ltd
Change Please
East London Liquor Company
Flat Cap Coffee Co
Organic Life
Tea2You
The Cider House
The Colombian Coffee Company
The Natural Smoothie Co
Total Organics
Utobeer

FISHMONGERS
Furness Fish Markets
Oak & Smoke
Richard Haward's Oysters
Shellseekers Fish & Game Ltd
Sussex Fish

GREENGROCERS AND FLORISTS
Chegworth Valley
Chez Michèle
Elsey & Bent
Fitz Fine Foods
Grovers
Jock Stark & Son
Mini Crops
Paul Crane
Paul Wheeler Fresh Supplies
Tartufaia
Ted's Veg
The Gated Garden
The Tomato Stall
Turnips

MARKET LARDER
Arabica
Borough Olives
Butter Nut of London
Cool Chile Co
De Calabria
De la Grenade
Fitz Fine Foods
Food & Forest
From Field and Flower
Gastronomica

La Tua Pasta
Le Marché du Quartier
Local Honey Man
Mini Magoos
nibs etc.
Oliveology
Pâté Moi
Pimento Hill
Porteña
Rosebud Preserves
Spice Mountain
Tartufaia
Taste Croatia
Temptings
The Olive Oil Co.
Wiltshire Chilli Farm

PREPARED FOR YOU
Balkan Bites
Big V London
Cumbrian Speciality Meats
Ethiopian Flavours
Gourmet Goat
Gujarati Rasoi
Hobbs Roast
Horn Ok Please
Kappacasein Dairy
Khanom Krok
La Tua Pasta
L'ailolive
Mountain's Boston Sausage
Mrs King's Pork Pies
Nana Fanny's
Pieminister
Porteña
Richard Haward's Oysters
Roast Hog
Scotch Tails
Soul Food
The Turkish Deli
Turnips

SEASONAL
Crouch Cobs
Greedy Goat
McLaren's Christmas Pudding
Nut Farms
The Christmas Cake

ED SMITH

Ed Smith is an award-winning food writer and regular contributor to Borough Market's online magazine and Market Life, its print magazine. Ed is the author of the celebrated food blog RocketandSquash.com and *On the Side: a sourcebook of inspiring side dishes*, his debut cookbook published 2017. Ed's recipes and writing have appeared in the FT Weekend Magazine, the Guardian, Telegraph, Food52, Eater and multiple other publications and websites.

BOROUGH MARKET

Borough Market has existed in one form or another for over 1,000 years and has been trading from its current site – under the railway arches at the southern end of London Bridge, just off Borough High Street – since 1756. But despite its venerable status, it is as influential today as it has ever been. Run by a charitable trust, the Market's mission is to provide access to food of exceptional quality, made and sold in a way that places greater value on people and the planet than it does on purely profit. Many of its traders grow, rear or make the food they sell; others use their knowledge of specific regions or foodstuffs to source products directly from small-scale producers in Britain, Europe and further afield. With its colourful, dynamic community of traders, trustees, staff, customers, chefs, writers and supporters, the Market has done much to help shape the growing public interest in the quality, provenance and sustainability of the food we eat.

Stay in touch
Sign up to our weekly newsletter with recipes, features, news and events.
www.boroughmarket.org.uk
@boroughmarket
🐦 f 📷

ACKNOWLEDGEMENTS

BOROUGH MARKET AND ED SMITH WOULD JOINTLY LIKE TO THANK:

The Hodder & Stoughton editorial and design team – Tamsin English, Liz Gough, Laura Herring, Natalie Bradley, Laura Nickoll and Alice Laurent – for making the book happen.

Issy Croker, Emily Ezekiel, Steph McLeod and Kitty Coles for bringing the food to life on the page; always with such skill and humour too.

FOR THEIR PART IN THE MAKING OF THIS BOOK, BOROUGH MARKET WOULD LIKE TO THANK:

All the Market traders, past and present, without whom there simply wouldn't be a book or indeed a Market. Their exceptional produce not only fills these pages but provides endless inspiration to millions of shoppers every year. We are also indebted to those shoppers for their ongoing custom and enthusiasm for world-class produce.

The Borough Market trustees, who volunteer their time and expertise in guiding the Market, particularly Drew Cullen, who has provided support and encouragement throughout the creation of this book.

The Borough Market staff, led by Darren Henaghan, who make this extraordinary place thrive daily.

Kate Howell, whose ambition it had long been to create a beautiful, timeless Borough Market book and whose leadership and drive ensured that it happened.

Claire Ford, whose guidance, culinary expertise and expert project management have been instrumental in turning an idea into a reality.

Mark Riddaway, who, alongside his talented team at LSC Publishing, has helped tell the story of the Market and whose lightness of touch and intelligence has helped shape the Market's narrative.

Justin Kowbel of Borough Kitchen, whose generous loan of beautiful homewares helped bring many of these recipe images to life.

Jon Elek of United Agents, who introduced us to the wonderful team at Hodder & Stoughton and whose counsel and support has been invaluable.

Our recipe testers, drawn from staff and friends of Borough Market, who cooked, ate and cogitated.

And last but by no means least, Ed Smith, who has been a dream collaborator throughout the complex process of conceiving and producing this wonderful book. He was set the daunting task of capturing the essence of Borough Market through his distinctive recipes and sparkling prose, and he rose to the challenge magnificently.

ED WOULD ALSO LIKE TO THANK:

Claire, Kate and the trustees for the opportunity to collaborate and work on this project. It's a privilege and pleasure to have been entrusted with the task. Thanks, in particular, to Claire for having both a creative mind, and meticulous attention to detail.

Laura for your never-ending support, super tasting and thoughtful feedback. You gave up lots and put your own work on pause so that I could concentrate on the task of testing and writing. Thank you xx.

Diana for all your help with Barney, particularly during the busier moments of cooking and writing – we really appreciate it.

Barney you have been literally no help at all. The opposite, in fact. But I really look forward to years of shopping at Borough Market, and cooking delicious things with you.

Most importantly, to all the Borough Market traders who work relentlessly through wind, snow and rain (and occasional sunny patches too), to bring brilliant, stimulating and world-class produce to market. It's a real treat and inspiration to find so much quality and variety in one buzzing and vibrant space. A cookbook like this can be only a snapshot of the community, and barely hints at the innumerable culinary possibilities, but I hope this captures this special place in its current form, and entices people to explore, shop and ultimately cook and enjoy your produce.